A SHORT HISTORY OF PARLIAMENT, 1295–1642

A SHORT HISTORY OF
PARLIAMENT

1295-1642

❁❁

FAITH THOMPSON

UNIVERSITY OF MINNESOTA PRESS, Minneapolis

PRINTED AT THE NORTH CENTRAL PUBLISHING COMPANY, ST. PAUL

Library of Congress Catalog Card Number: 53-10471

PUBLISHED IN GREAT BRITAIN, INDIA, AND PAKISTAN BY
GEOFFREY CUMBERLEGE: OXFORD UNIVERSITY PRESS, LONDON, BOMBAY, AND KARACHI

Preface

THIS little book is not a history of parliament in the usual sense. No attempt is made to discuss obscure points of origins nor to do justice to certain thorny questions upon which reputable historians still disagree. It does include the main facts to be found in standard constitutional texts, and some of the more technical data, figures, and dates are supplied in notes and appendices for those who want them. It is addressed to students of college age, and may serve as collateral reading for college courses in English history or literature. It is hoped that it may also have some value for a wider reading public, including those interested in parliamentary government wherever it may be found in the world today.

The purpose is fivefold: (1) to make available the valuable results of recent research scattered through learned monographs, essays, and review articles; (2) to give something of the flavor and points of view of the eras concerned by some quotation from the contemporary sources; (3) to bridge the division, usually too sharply made, between "medieval" and "modern"; (4) to bring the "men of law" into the picture — the legal historian who illuminates the subject by a special approach and the man of law in parliament who made many a practical as well as theoretical contribution; (5) last but not least, to bring parliaments — even those of "medieval" times — and their members to life, to dramatize, as it were, their personnel and activities.

The period covered is roughly that of the late Middle Ages and early modern period: i.e., from the reign of Edward I and his so-called

"Model Parliament" of 1295 through the first two years of the "Long Parliament" to the outbreak of the Civil War in August of 1642. Except for occasional allusions by way of comparison or anticipation, the account obviously stops short of such modern developments as the growth of the cabinet system, the democratization of the Commons through successive franchise acts, the curbing of the veto power of the Lords, and certain changes in procedure. Nevertheless, the period covered is rewarding in itself, whether one is concerned with constitutional progress or with attractive parliamentary personalities.

Obviously I have borrowed freely from many authors, and have followed somewhat the line of the medieval story-tellers: "For as a man goeth to and fro he heareth many a thing that is good to tell again; and those who know and may venture the emprise, should give to it all care and heed and study, even as did those who came before us the good masters of old time." The works of modern authors are listed in the bibliography and, where the use is extensive, also accorded recognition in text or notes. Monographs and essays on special topics used in just one connection are cited in footnotes only. Where possible, sources are quoted not from the massive volumes of *Parliament Rolls, Statutes of the Realm,* and the like, but from such source books as those of Tanner and of Stephenson and Marcham, which are more likely to be available to the student. If I have been tempted many times to quote from brilliant literary historians like Pollard and Trevelyan, perhaps this may be justified if it leads the reader to turn directly to their volumes or, if these are not available, enables him at least to have enjoyed a sample.

Hearty thanks are due to Professor D. H. Willson for reading much of the manuscript and making helpful corrections and suggestions. To the late Professor A. B. White and to other colleagues and students I am indebted for their interest and encouragement. It is a pleasure to add a word of appreciation to the staff of the University of Minnesota Press.

F. T.

Minneapolis
August 1953

Table of Contents

Part III. Parliament in the Early Stuart Period

List of Illustrations

✿✿

ix

by A. F. Pollard, *The Evolution of Parliament*, pp. 383–384. (From Robert Glover, *Nobilitas politica vel civilis*, 1608; reproduced by permission of the Trustees of the British Museum.)

The House of Commons in the reign of James I (1624)

This is believed to be the earliest picture of the Commons, in their "House," St. Stephen's Chapel, their customary meeting place since 1547. (Reproduced from Arnold Wright and Philip Smith, *Parliament Past and Present*.)

A SHORT HISTORY OF PARLIAMENT, 1295–1642

Introduction

WITH *justice is the phrase "mother of Parliaments" applied to the British Parliament at Westminster. . . .*

The British House of Commons, its origin and development, and the system according to which the representatives sitting in the Commons were elected, deserve, perhaps, more detailed discussion than that devoted to the medieval electoral systems of the other countries on the Continent of Europe. Not only on the Continent in the nineteenth century, but in America, Australia, South Africa, and the Far East, elective institutions of modern times owe their character in large measure to their British prototypes.

SOME years ago there appeared an attractive popular book entitled *How the World Votes*. In the words quoted above, the authors, Seymour and Frary, emphasize the British parliament. Quite naturally their stress is on the popular elective element, the House of Commons. Yet in its origin parliament was aristocratic, *feudal* — an assembly of the king's tenants-in-chief, meeting at intervals, perhaps two or three times a year, to advise, sometimes indeed to control or coerce, their lord the king in great matters. Its work was not primarily legislative, although sometimes an ordinance or statute did result. Business might include matters of state — war and peace, administration, the assessment and fulfillment of feudal obligations, disputes over fiefs, nice points of feudal law, and the trial of one of its own members accused of treason or felony. In contrast to such a "great council," there was the "small council" (*curia regis*), a group of household servants and public officials, ever present with the king to assist in the actual day-to-day business of government.

3

The evolution of parliament involved two great processes, both of which have their beginnings in the thirteenth century but belong more particularly to the fourteenth. There was a gradual but fundamental change in the personnel of the great council from that of feudal tenants-in-chief to a select group of hereditary peers, but always with some spiritual lords — bishops and abbots — in attendance. When the change was completed, that body had become the House of Lords. At the same time there were being added certain new representative elements which were finally to constitute the House of Commons.

In modern times it is hard to realize that the term *parliament* did not always denote the august assembly at Westminster or other assemblies later devised in its image. The word, derived from the French *parler* (to speak or parley) and the more impressive Latin *parliamentum,* was used loosely to denote a conversation, a parley, or an interview. The thirteenth-century French writer, de Joinville (the knight who wrote a chronicle of his king, Louis IX), uses it in three ways: of an informal gathering of the barons; of a judicial session of the king's court; and, quaintly, even of a tryst between the young king and his Queen Marguerite, which took place on a secluded stairway in the palace at Pontoise to escape the dominating presence of the Queen Mother Blanche!

In England *parliamentum* creeps into official records as a vulgar substitute for *colloquium* (colloquy), appearing on the *Close Roll* in 1242 and on the *Memoranda Rolls of the Exchequer* in 1248. Quite naturally it was used of diplomatic parleys, such as that between Alexander II of Scotland and Richard, Earl of Cornwall, in 1244, and the meeting of the kings of France and Castile. Thus a parliament, to quote Maitland, "is rather an act than a body of persons. One cannot present a petition to a colloquy, to a debate. It is only slowly that this word is appropriated to colloquies of a particular kind, namely those which the king has with the estates of his realm, and still more slowly that it is transferred from the colloquy to the body of men whom the king has summoned. . . . The personification of 'parliament,' which enables us to say that laws are made by, and not merely in, parliament, is a slow and subtle process."

It was the noted English chronicler Matthew Paris of St. Albans who first applied the term to a great council of prelates, earls, and barons, in 1239 and again in 1246. From this time on it was used increasingly, though not exclusively, for such an assembly. Not only chroniclers but government clerks were inconsistent in their usage. The term did not necessarily connote the presence of the Commons.

Some historians have tended to take these clerks too seriously — to insist that "only those assemblies are to be accounted parliaments which have been summoned by writs in which the word 'parliament' appears." Thus we are led to believe that some great councils without the Commons are parliaments and some assemblies with the Commons are councils. Professor Plucknett has convincingly demonstrated that this theory is untenable: it "asserts that there was a verbal distinction, but no actual difference; and this objection seems fatal." In these studies we shall adopt his cue: "In writing the history of parliament as an institution all the assemblies which contained the later parliamentary elements must evidently be considered." [1]

At the close of the thirteenth century these elements were the Lords and Commons — the "community of the realm" — but how different in numbers, status, and relative importance from the two Houses and their members which those terms call to mind in modern times! It is helpful to be reminded that the "number of people interested in politics, the size of the 'political nation,' has varied from age to age, increasing with the growth of population, the advance of education, and in general with what may be called the expansion of democratic sentiment." [2]

Historians have elected to call Edward I's assembly of 1295 the Model Parliament because of its complete embodiment of all the elements of parliament. There were bishops and abbots, earls and barons, invited individually; elected representatives, the knights and burgesses, summoned through the sheriff; and even representatives of the lower clergy, a temporary feature.

To account for the presence of these elements, we may look back briefly over the preceding century. The attendance of the nobles at a great council was originally a feudal obligation. The duty of *suit of court,* as it was called, as well as military service, was required of each vassal in return for his fief (land).

The class of king's vassals was large and diverse. In the twelfth century it numbered perhaps five hundred. Naturally most of the great

[1] Plucknett, "Parliament," in *The English Government at Work,* pp. 82–84, 87. A helpful survey of the variety of approaches to this subject and of the contributions of recent historians to early parliamentary history is the essay by G. Templeton, "The History of Parliament to 1400 in the Light of Modern Research."

[2] R. B. Mowat, *England in the Eighteenth Century* (London, 1932), pp. 33–34.

landholders were Crown tenants, but there were also many little men, the knight with a small fief — a single *knight's fee* — who also held directly of the king. The king did not insist on the presence of these lesser tenants, and they in turn were glad to escape the burden of attendance. Thus arose the distinction between *major* and *minor barons*. This is recognized in Magna Carta, which prescribes that an individual summons be sent to the greater barons, while to all the lesser tenants-in-chief merely a general summons through the sheriff.

As time went on the process tended to become even more selective. Not all the great men received a personal summons. There was a capriciousness due at times to politics, at times to personalities, but some men were inclined to expect a summons year after year. Bishops and abbots, no doubt, had the interests of the Church at heart, but they too were present on a feudal basis — they *held by barony* like the lay lords.

The presence of the Commons, which seems so natural today, was novel indeed in that age. The whys of their introduction have fascinated historians. Some questions may be asked and at least partially answered here.

First, why did England have a House of Commons? Why did the Commons in parliament become a permanent and successful feature of the English government in contrast to that of continental countries, where representative institutions were either nonexistent or transient, such as the French Estates General and the Cortes of Aragon and Castile? One reason certainly was that England had the elements out of which such a representative body could be formed — a middle class. It was a complex and rather artificial middle class, containing elements we should not expect to find. There was the vigorous and growing urban class of citizens and burgesses (the true *bourgeoisie* of the French third estate) and the non-noble freehold farmers, but there were also persons of "gentle birth" — the knights. These were small tenants-in-chief (the minor barons of early days) and also the tenants of mesne lords, such as might have only a single knight's fee, or not even the land requisite to a knight and be reckoned as esquires. Even the younger sons of the barons may be included, for because of the emphasis on primogeniture they were technically commoners. In the narrow English sense the term *noble* applies only to the small select group of the peerage whose evolution we shall trace.

Although it takes us a little ahead of our story, it would not be too far-fetched to borrow for our question the answer which an English judge, Fortescue, made to the young Prince Edward, whom he was instructing. Fortescue was writing in the fifteenth century. He was from Devonshire, one of the rich and lovely southwestern counties, land of rolling green hills and clotted cream. An exile in France, he looked back on England with something of nostalgia and longing. Yet, other travelers were impressed with the same contrasts in the status and well-being of the population, if not in the gifts of nature. This is what Fortescue says:

"You were a youth when you left England, prince, so that the nature and quality of that land are unknown to you; if you had known them, and had compared the products and character of other countries with them, you would not wonder at those things which puzzle you now. England is indeed so fertile that, compared area to area, it surpasses almost all other lands in the abundance of its produce; it is productive of its own accord, scarcely aided by man's labour. For its fields, plains, glades and groves abound in vegetation with such richness that they often yield more fruits to their owners uncultivated than ploughed lands, though those are very fertile in crops and corn. . . . Hence the men of that land are not very much burdened with the sweat of labour, so that they live with more spirit, as the ancient fathers did who preferred to tend flocks rather than to distract their peace of mind with the cares of agriculture. For this reason the men of that land are made more apt and disposed to investigate causes which require searching examination than men who, immersed in agricultural work, have contracted a rusticity of mind from familiarity with the soil. Again that land is so well stocked and replete with possessors of land and fields that in it no hamlet, however small, can be found in which there is no knight, esquire, or householder of the sort commonly called a franklin, well off in possessions; nor numerous other free tenants, and many yeomen, sufficient in patrimony to make a jury in the form described above. Furthermore, there are various yeomen in that country who can spend more than £100 a year, so that juries in that country are often made up, especially in important causes, of knights, esquires and others, whose possessions exceed £333 6s. 8d. a year in total. Hence it is unthinkable that such men could be suborned or be willing to perjure themselves, not only because of their fear of God, but also because of their honour, and the scandal which would ensue, and because of the harm they would do to their heirs through their infamy."

In other words, position and property mean responsibility and honor — *noblesse oblige*.

Members of this middle class had long been active in useful capacities in local government. They served on the medieval equivalents of our grand and petty juries and in the amateur police duties of the tithing and the hue and cry, as coroners, and eventually as justices of the peace. Duties not connected with the courts included the sworn inquest to furnish information useful to the government, the assessment of taxes, and the assize of arms — an assessment of their neighbors' wealth with a view to determining their proper military equipment. Some posts called for knights, others for "lawful knights or other free men"; again, "good and lawful men" sufficed.[3] Some tasks were survivals of the local self-government of Anglo-Saxon days, but many had been imposed from above since the Conquest — "self-government at the King's command," in the apt phrase of A. B. White. "One of the notable things in English constitutional history from the twelfth century to the end of the middle ages," he says, "was that the king was getting his work done largely by the people, and that with little or no compensation." At least in local life there was no hierarchy of officials, no bureaucracy. His thesis is "that English kings, working in what they believed to be their personal interest, so used the English people in government, laid upon them for centuries such burdens and responsibilities, that they went far toward creating the Englishman's governmental sense and competence. . . ."[4]

What was the source of the representative idea in England? Historians are not agreed on this point. Perhaps a happier conclusion than some is that of Professor Adams: "It seems altogether likely that the final decision will be that the idea was derived from one source and the institutional forms, through which it was given expression in the constitution of the state, from another." We need not discount entirely influences coming from medieval Church polity. The Dominican Friars had their representative assemblies; the bishops, in theory at least, were elected by their cathedral chapters, and the abbots of some orders by the older brothers. Still a more direct source would seem to be the ideas and practices of election and representation, separately or in combination, to be found in local government — in fact, in connection with some of the very jobs just described. Every kind of jury represented its

---

[3] "Lawful" or "law-worthy" men (*legales homines* in the Latin of the day) meant those whose oath would be accepted, who had never been guilty of perjury.

[4] *Self-Government at the King's Command* (University of Minnesota Press, 1933), a small, scholarly book making an intensive study of a short period.

neighborhood; it was the voice of the countryside. The county court was the legal embodiment of the shire. It represented its whole community, acted and spoke for it.

Representation does not necessarily involve election, but in some instances election was used, partly as a means of checking undue influence by the sheriff. For instance, in the choice of the important jury which determined the best right to land, four knights chosen by the sheriff chose twelve, usually including themselves. By the thirteenth century coroners were regularly elected in the county courts, as were knights for various occasional purposes.

As to the urban or bourgeois element, small groups of burgesses had been consulted locally or summoned to a central point from time to time when the king and his officials wanted to utilize their practical knowledge and ability in the fields of finance and trade or, in one instance, in founding a new town. Even in the regular parliamentary summons of later days, the government occasionally specified the type of advisers it wanted, as on one occasion when the emphasis was on persons sufficient in knowledge of navigation and merchandising. Citizens and burgesses had another asset: their wealth was not in lands and crops but in "moveables"; that is, in merchandise and ready money.

The House of Commons was "the child of authority and not of rebellion." The king and his officials found it good business to call together at some central point the same men or type of men who had been employed and consulted locally. A "concentration of juries," White calls it. The records afford us several instances, probably not a complete list, of this practice in the reign of Henry III.[5]

We have to wait for Simon de Montfort, leader of the barons in the civil wars, for the summons of knights to meet with a great council. In 1261 de Montfort summoned three knights from each county to St. Albans, whereupon the king issued a countersummons to Windsor. Again after his victory at Lewes in 1264 de Montfort summoned four knights per county to meet with the magnates at London. It was de Montfort again, on December 14, 1264, who issued, in the name of the captive king, writs summoning his famous parliament to meet at London, thus instituting the happy innovation of including not only two knights from each county but two citizens and burgesses each from a number of cities and boroughs.

As to Edward I, a recent writer, William Seagle, who has honored

[5] See Note A at the end of the Introduction.

this king with a chapter in his *Men of Law,* believes that as a young prince he was influenced by de Montfort, but used his ideas in the "triumph of the royal cause." Although after de Montfort's victory at Lewes the prince was taken captive, de Montfort's parliament with its knights and burgesses was not lost upon the prisoner at Kenilworth. In the first twenty years of Edward's reign great councils attended only by prelates and magnates outnumbered assemblies with representative elements. The king's policy in summoning knights and burgesses was opportunist and variable, but it was a policy which was tending to become a custom.[6]

The Model Parliament was summoned under pressure of wars and rumors of wars. Edward needed the financial help and the backing of all classes. Novelty lay in its completeness, and its legality in contrast to de Montfort's revolutionary and factional meeting of 1265. The remaining twelve years of the reign saw frequent parliaments. Three, at least, those of November 1296, Lent 1300, and March 1305, were replicas of the Model in the elements included, though not in exact numbers.

Better than generalizations and statistics, as a point of departure for the evolution of Parliament, let us imagine that we could visit such an assembly — that which met in 1305, since for it we have unusually complete descriptive records.[7]

THE PARLIAMENT OF 1305

THE *king has his court in his council, in his parliaments, in the presence of the prelates, earls, barons, lords and others learned in the law, where doubts about sentences are determined, where new remedies are provided for new injuries that have happened, and where justice is meted out to each according to his deserts.*

This statement occurs in a little treatise (*Fleta*) of Edward I's reign. Naturally perhaps, the author, a man of law, emphasizes the role of parliament as a court and also the more important elements in its personnel. A description of an actual parliament late in the same reign indicates that his definition is rather good on the whole.

On November 12, 1304, writs were issued for a parliament to be held at Westminster on February 16, 1305. Edward, on his way south from the Scottish border, kept Christmas at Lincoln. Writs dated January 22, 1305, postponed the meeting to February 28. Meanwhile extensive prep-

---

[6] For Edward's parliaments 1273–1295, see Note B at the end of the Introduction.

[7] Maitland has given a full and attractive account of this parliament, together with the wealth of official records, including petitions.

arations were under way. Sheriffs of the nearby counties of Kent, Surrey, and Sussex were directed to send up to Westminster quantities of corn and ale and other supplies. That due publicity be given, proclamation was made in Westminster Hall, in the Chancery, before the justices of the Bench, at the Guildhall (which was the town hall of London), and in Westcheap, the city's market. The purpose of all this, of course, was to enable persons or groups seeking favors or the redress of grievances to present their petitions. Further, the judges of the three central courts were advised to refer to the parliament cases of novelty or difficulty pending before them. The king entered London on February 27, and the next day, as scheduled, parliament was opened in Westminster Hall.

Prelates and magnates, of course, received individual writs of summons. From these we can ascertain that those invited included 9 earls (if we include the Prince of Wales and the Earl of Angus), the rather large number of 94 barons, and 95 prelates. The representative element included about 145 of the lower clergy, 74 knights (2 from each of the 37 shires), and about 200 citizens and burgesses. There were also present such great officers of state as Philip Willoughby, Chancellor of the Exchequer, the barons of the Exchequer, and justices of the two Benches, as well as men employed as itinerant justices. Since barons and bishops also served as officials, some were present in a twofold capacity: Walter Langton, the treasurer, for instance, was Bishop of Lichfield, while the bishops of Durham and Carlisle were really governors of key areas in the north. Clifford and Despenser were forest justices, Valence and Brittanny the king's best generals. The men who had done the most to prepare for the session and make it a going concern were the members of a virtual civil service staff, masters of Chancery, clerks of the Council and the Household. Chancery, of course, was not yet the great court of equity it would become late in the century. At this time the chancellor was the "principal secretary of state for all departments," the Chancery a great secretarial bureau. "If for a moment we may use such modern terms," says Maitland, "we may say that the chancery is Home Office, Foreign Office, Board of Trade, Local Government Board all in one." The masters were clerks, virtually permanent undersecretaries of state. Though practice varied, it was increasingly the chancellor himself who formally opened a parliament in the king's name.

The duration of the session for all elements was three weeks (February 28 to March 21). A proclamation then dismissed the estates. King and Council continued to work into April with those who still had business to transact. It was typical of Edward I's parliaments that, although the barons were not a negligible factor, the leadership and initiative came from the king and his official staff. Such an assembly, as Maitland reminds us, really included all that England had to show in the way of "legal learning, official experience, and administrative ability," and, we may add, in view of the presence of the king, the prerogative powers of the crown. The work of this parliament included (1) discussion of affairs of state, (2) pleas (cases), (3) legislation, (4) supply (taxation), and (5) audience of petitions. The following will give some idea of each type of business, beginning with the matters in which Lords and Council were most concerned.

Affairs of state at this time centered on Gascony and Scotland. For the first, recently retrieved from the threat of direct control by the king of France, new officials were to be appointed and sent out. The northern kingdom was temporarily a conquered land, though soon to regain its independence under the leadership of Robert Bruce. It was a premature optimism that had summoned the estates to treat of matters touching "our realm of England and the establishment of *our land of Scotland*." As a settled form of government was to be provided, a committee was asked to suggest how Scotland be represented at another parliament to be held later in the year.

Most typical of the pleas, since trial by peers was involved, was the case of Nicholas Seagrave, a baron accused of treason. His trial properly took place before his fellow earls and barons "in full parliament." Some of the other cases, involving various rival interests — communities, cities, prelates, and royal officials — may have been handled by the King in Council in the narrow sense. These included, for instance, a quarrel between the Governor of Oxford Castle and the University students; the refusal of the cathedral city of Salisbury to pay a tallage (tax) set by their bishop; and the case of the Crown against the City of Winchester, which had been unlucky enough to incur the royal displeasure by allowing the escape of a citizen of Bayonne, "a hostage in the king's hand," committed to their care. No great civil plea is recorded, though appropriate for handling by this full court of magnates was some complicated point of feudal land law. On the whole it was typical of the parliaments of Edward I that judicial work was important. Contemporary records indicate that judges and other officials rather expected a parliament twice a year, usually at Easter and Michaelmas, and looked forward to it for its usefulness in administrative business. Numerous writs and instructions set some unusual problem or suit, or adjourn some unfinished business, "to the next Parliament."

No notable statute was enacted. The great legislation of this reign had been accomplished in earlier and more peaceful years, in the Statutes of Westminster I and II and others. There were a few minor measures, but of the character and procedure of law-making we shall hear more below.

What were the knights and burgesses doing during their three weeks at Westminster? Here "we shall hardly get beyond guesswork." They had probably been present at the formal opening session, standing at the end of the Hall ("as many as could get in," as the Clerk tells us on later occasions), to hear the opening speech and receive directions. At this time the knights may have met with the barons, for some purposes at least, and the burgesses by themselves. As to supply, to those who have been wont to see the presence of the Commons as due mainly to their tax-granting function, it may come as a surprise to learn that no money grant was made. Normally, however, all the estates would have been invited to approve a grant of nonfeudal taxation, the customary percentage of moveables, still variable, but presently to be established as the *tenth and fifteenth.* We do know that the Commons joined in a petition with the magnates about the exportation of the wealth of the monasteries and in a few other petitions of common interest. Although they were not asked to vote a subsidy, some account of the financial situation of the government may have been presented to them.

Though largely unrecorded, it may be assumed that the Council learned much of value in the way of unofficial testimony about local conditions and points of view. As Maitland puts it, the Council "desires to know what men are saying in remote parts of England about the doings of sheriffs, escheators, and their like, and the possibilities of future taxation have to be considered." There is a good opportunity to size up some of the knights as likely candidates for local official posts. Probably the Council "gives audience, advice, instructions to particular knights and burgesses."

Equally important was the presenting of petitions of interest to themselves or their constituents. One of the benefits of parliament which probably loomed large in the minds of those who requested frequent meetings was its function in expediting petitions — speeding up the wheels of justice. Directions for the appointment of receivers of petitions had been issued as early as February 5. Four men — a judge of King's

Bench, an Exchequer clerk, and two Chancery clerks — were assigned the preliminary task of receiving and sorting petitions. A more responsible function was that of the auditors who must read and *answer* petitions. Actually the auditors did not necessarily answer in the sense of granting the petitioner's request or solving his problems, but indicated what remedy was appropriate and by what agency it should be handled. The petitioner did not get what he wanted; he was merely put in the way of getting it. Some petitions might be referred to the Lords, some to the Council. "Only those 'which are so great or so much of grace' that they cannot otherwise be dealt with, are to come before the king in order that his pleasure may be taken . . ."

It has been well said that an individual or private petition requires handling by a court, a common or Commons petition by a legislature. Of the vast number of petitions in 1305 collected by Maitland, the majority fall into the first class; that is, they come from individuals — an earl, a bishop, an heiress, the constable of a castle, or a sheriff — or from a group — a monastery, the two universities, merchants engaged in a particular line of trade.

There are several petitions from the two great universities, four from Cambridge and eleven from Oxford. The chancellor, masters, and clerks of Cambridge urge the king to found and endow a college for poor students. The wool merchants protest having been "slandered and vexed" to their great damage for two years past at York and Westminster by the barons of the Exchequer. Merchants of St. Omer complain that their ship is detained, although they have paid the proper customs.

Officials are petitioners as well as petitioned against. The sheriff of Cumberland asks lenience as to his account, which is in arrears. He cannot collect because of the "destruction, impoverishment and arson" made in his county by the Scots. The justices of both Benches and the barons of the Exchequer and their clerks complain that they have not received what is due them. The treasurer and barons are instructed to pay "when they can."

Significant for the future of parliament are those petitions which come from the community (*communitas*) of a whole shire, or from a city or borough, our parliamentary constituencies. Further, as must have happened time and again in succeeding parliaments, the petition of an individual or group airs a grievance which proves to be of wide concern and calls for a remedy of general application.

As to the shires, the north seems to have been the scene of chronic troubles and disasters, whether from the elements, the Scots, or mere neglect due to remoteness. Cumberland details a foray by certain Scots, and also protests violation of established Forest boundaries by a justice of the Forest. The community of Northumberland complains that no justices have come to their shire to hold inquests and pleas, whence they have incurred injury and disinheritance; while Lancashire asks that certain justices be assigned to deal with disturbers of the peace.

Among the towns, little Cokermuth, up in Cumberland, calling itself "one of the king's boroughs," describes the damage done to that area by the great flood before Christmas, including the washing away of the town's three bridges. The king generously remits bridge tolls, thus enabling them to rebuild. The cities of Worcester and Norwich both ask and receive similar relief to build walls for the safety of the city.

There may have been some formal feasting at the close of the session, as was customary later. On March 21 a proclamation dismissed the *estates* — that is, the magnates and prelates who were not officials, the knights and burgesses, and lower clergy. King and Council continued to work into April with those who still had business to transact. One of the duties of the representative elements was to report back to their community. Publication by word of mouth, publicity if you like, was vital if taxes voted were to be readily paid, new or revised laws enforced, services rendered, liberties and concessions enjoyed. The value of parliaments consisted not only in what members brought with them but in what they took away.

The story that lies ahead of us from this point is a long one, but fascinating and not hard to comprehend if we realize that parliament was always the product of an era, typical of the times. As Professor Pollard puts it in his brilliant account of its evolution: "Parliament is not bound up with any political theory or any transient constitution; it has been the tool of monarchs, of oligarchs, and of democrats; it has been the means of opposition as well as the instrument of government, the preventer of revolution as well as the promoter of reform. It has been, and is still to some extent, a court of law, a council, and a legislature; and its forms, which were used by medieval kings, have been found still more effective by modern ministers. Its elasticity has known no bounds in the past, and we have yet to learn that it has no value for the forces of the future."

NOTE A. EARLY CONCENTRATIONS OF REPRESENTATIVES

In John's reign (1213) there were plans (which may not have been carried out) to summon to Oxford "four discreet knights to speak with us about the affairs of our kingdom." The earliest known concentration of popularly elected knights took place in 1226. Sheriffs of eight counties were instructed to send to the king at Lincoln four of "the more discreet and lawful" knights chosen in the county court, to voice complaints against the sheriffs for alleged violation of the Great Charter. Again in 1254, while Henry III was over in Gascony in need of men and supplies, officials summoned to Westminster two knights "whom the men of the county shall have chosen for this purpose in the place of all and each of them." They were delegates, empowered to report "definitely" what *aid* (tax) their communities were prepared to grant.

As to the burgesses, in 1207 there were summoned to Westminster all those having to do with the coinage in sixteen cities or boroughs; and in 1208 to Portsmouth the reeve and "two of the more discreet and wealthier men of each port." In 1296 writs went to twenty-four important towns ordering them each to elect and send up to Bury St. Edmunds the two citizens most capable in helping to organize a new town.

NOTE B. ASSEMBLIES OF EDWARD'S REIGN, 1273–1295

In the first parliament of the reign, 1273, and the first of 1275 there were present with the prelates and magnates representatives of the shires and of the cities and boroughs. The main purpose of the first was to swear allegiance to the new ruler, not yet returned from the Holy Land. The second came to be remembered for its approval of the customs on wool, woolfelts, and hides. At a meeting later in the same year knights were present to participate in the grant of a *fifteenth*. The Welsh wars occasioned odd variations. While the barons were busy in the campaign, knights and burgesses met in two groups, one at York and one at Northampton, apparently for financial business. Later in 1283 at Shrewsbury near the Welsh border, the barons, still in arms, met to judge Prince David of Wales, while at nearby Acton Burnell representative burgesses were consulted on a problem of interest to merchants.

In 1290 two meetings of the great council of barons dealt with purely feudal matters — in the first the granting of an *aid,* and in the second the enacting of the Statute of *Quia Emptores,* which concerned the king and other great landholders. A week later, representatives of the shires joined them to participate in a money grant, as they did in the grant of a *tenth* in 1294. On this occasion the towns paid a *sixth* but were dealt with separately by commissioners.

PART I. PARLIAMENT IN THE LATER MIDDLE AGES

I

England in the Later Middle Ages

＊＊

THE period to be covered by the first part of these studies has been commonly called by the nondescript name of the Later Middle Ages. It has not evoked the enthusiasm historians have accorded other centuries, the thirteenth or the sixteenth, for instance. One enthusiast, writing on western European culture in the days of the Church at its height, has called the thirteenth "the greatest of centuries." [1] While English historians have not gone so far, they have made us feel its charm and its role as a heroic epoch. The fourteenth century can show no villain as black as John, no paragon of kingly virtues like Edward I, no prelate of the statesmanship of Stephen Langton or of the scholarship of Robert Grosseteste. A transitional age, neither quite "medieval" nor "modern," is harder to characterize. Furthermore, the fourteenth is best known for its calamities. We are prone to exclaim with Shakespeare's Richard II,

> For God's sake, let us sit upon the ground
> And tell sad stories of the death of kings,

as we reflect on two monarchs deposed. Then one recalls the Hundred Years War, the Black Death, and the Peasants' Revolt. The fifteenth, to the historians of the early modern era, is merely the "time of troubles" which those amazingly constructive Tudors were presently to set in order.

Yet no less an authority than Professor Tout, steeped as none other in the sources of the age, concludes: "I do not in the least believe that

[1] J. J. Walsh, *The Thirteenth, Greatest of Centuries* (New York, 1912).

19

the fourteenth century was any worse than the thirteenth. On the contrary, it was on the whole a better, and certainly a more pleasant, time to live in." In the opinion of a predecessor of Chaucer,[2] "England is a strong land and a sturdy, and the plenteousest corner of the world, so rich a land that unneth it needeth help of any land, and every other land needeth help of England. England is full of mirth and of game, and men oft times able to mirth and game, free men of heart and with tongue, but the hand is more better and more free than the tongue."

To be sure, nobles and gentry had the land, the wealth, and the political power. Some were eager for the adventure and, still more, the plunder in horses and arms and rich ransoms afforded by the wars with France. Others were content to stay at home and develop their estates. They were becoming less the armored knights and more the country gentlemen and squires so typical of later English rural life. As we shall see, the gentry served in many capacities in local government as well as "knights of the shire" in parliament. Not far behind was the non-noble freeholder, unique in England, on his way to becoming the sturdy yeoman of Tudor days. These were the men who wielded the famous longbow and took pride in its feats of speed, aim, and penetration. On many manors even the villein (serf) was emerging into the more desirable status of freed man and copyholder. As travelers testified, in comparison with the French peasantry these small farmers lived in "peace and rude plenty." Again, in contrast with the French *Jacqueries,* the Peasants' Revolt revealed the participants to be men with leaders and a program. Its events, says Trevelyan, "give a human and spiritual interest to the economic facts of the period, showing the peasant as a man, half beast and half angel, not a mere item in the bailiffs' books."

Chaucer was born into an age in which he could witness the increase in size and importance of urban communities, including his own London. Only in his day could the city boast of crafts involving skill and artistry such as that of the cofferers and painters, pewterers, glass-makers, and even tapicers (tapestry-weavers), though the latter could not yet compete with those of Arras. As Clerk of the Works he must have been acquainted with the new and peculiarly English perpendicular style in churches and chantries, and very likely knew of William of Wykham's famous foundations of Winchester and New College, Oxford. Castles had not yet given place to the unfortified mansions of the

---

[2] Bartholomaeus Anglicus, quoted by Coulton, p. 11.

Tudors, but checks were imposed on building them. One had to have a royal "license to crennelate."

The fourteenth and early fifteenth centuries witnessed a growing spirit of nationalism engendered partly by the French wars. Chaucer may not have been aware of measures such as that of 1356 providing that cases in the sheriff's courts of London be pleaded in English, or of an act of parliament (1362) to the same effect for the royal courts. But he himself was to accomplish much more than these by abandoning the French tongue for the English of the midlands in the famous *Canterbury Tales*. To be sure, the tales were imported, but the tellers, the pilgrims, were typically English. In 1404 two ambassadors to France, a knight and a doctor of laws, are quoted as admitting, "We are as ignorant of French as of Hebrew." William Nassynton, writing in Chaucer's day, says:

> Some can French and no Latin
> That have used courts and dwelled therein:
> And some can of Latin a party
> That can French full febelly.
> And some understandeth English
> That neither can Latin nor French:
> But lerid and lewid,[3] old and young,
> All understanden English tongue.[4]

At that time the galley quay almost touched that of the Customs House. So broad is the Thames estuary that even at the present day London is a port. Great ocean liners and innumerable cargo vessels from all over the world come up to unload in the elaborate system of docks below Tower Bridge. In the fourteenth century the set-up was relatively simple. Wharves along Thames-side below London Bridge were assigned to certain classes of merchandise. Most important for foreign trade were Billingsgate and Queenhithe. Billingsgate, which by association has come to denote the vigorous invective of the fishwives, was the place where fish was landed, not in wooden trucks as today, but in baskets called dorsers, adapted to be carried on the back. A custom of one fish for every dorser was exacted for the use of the sheriffs. Although writers of historical novels have accustomed us to the picture of the Englishman sitting down to a platter of roast beef, next to bread fish was the main article of food in the city. It was not only required

[3] "Lerid and lewid," learned and ignorant.
[4] Quoted by Trevelyan, *English Social History*.

for the many fast days, but it was cheap and plentiful. Even after the Reformation had reduced fast days, people were directed to eat fish on Wednesdays and Fridays, for the fisheries furnished likely recruits for the navy!

To Queenhithe came wines, of all imports from abroad "one of the largest and perhaps the largest." In 1242 Henry III bought 360,000 gallons of wine for the royal cellars, and the country as a whole imported over 2,500,000 gallons yearly. On arrival at Queenhithe the wine was stored in the nearby Vintry Ward, where foreign wine merchants lodged and had their cellars. As the wine ships passed under London Bridge a toll of 2d. was levied on every cask for the repair of the bridge. This trade gave us our word *tonnage* in respect of the capacity of ships; not a measure of weight, it designated (spelt *tunnage*) the number of *tuns* or casks of wine a ship would hold. Though wine was the greatest in bulk, there were many other imports. A list compiled in 1315 names some forty items, including sugar, rice, figs and raisins, pepper and other spices, alum and dyes, wax, glass, furs and fine textiles, including cloth of gold.

In the fourteenth century, however, English merchants had little share in the carrying trade. The luxury products of the East were brought in Venetian galleys which came regularly to Southampton, Sandwich, or London. The Hanse towns were the link between England and northern Europe. Their walled headquarters in London included a wharf on the Thames River bank, a hall, armory, houses, warehouses, and a *staalhof* or sample yard, in which they displayed their wares, whence the English *steelyard*. They brought amber, wood, timber, horses, herrings, and cheese. At times they carried three fourths of the exports of British wool, and nearly all of the cloth. Still, prophetic for the future, comes in Richard II's reign the first navigation act. There were not enough English ships to make it enforceable, but it was a sign that at last the English government was taking some interest in protecting native merchants and shippers.

In an age in which it is the "King in his Parliament" with which we are concerned, the personality of the ruler is a factor to be reckoned with. Three long reigns (two with minorities), covering four generations, virtually span the fourteenth century — the last of the Angevin or Plantagenet line.

Turning to the first, Edward II: it is revealing at the outset to note the charges framed on his deposition. It is not too much ruling —

tyranny — of which he is accused, but too little — neglect. He has proved "utterly insufficient." A medieval king was the real executive, whether in peace or war. There was no place for a monarch who would not take the trouble to work at his job! Edward was strong and handsome, brave enough (as he proved at Bannockburn, in spite of rumors to the contrary), but idle and wayward. He liked the wrong things and the wrong people. One almost gets the impression that the barons might have borne with him had he indulged in the same interests and pursuits as they. While he did not entirely disdain hunting and tournaments, he preferred the humbler tasks of farmer or craftsman. Once his courtiers found him helping some workmen thatch a roof. Like a more famous monarch of equally tragic end, Louis XVI, he was "a man of his hands, not of his head." Louis played at being a blacksmith. Edward, we are told, in the evenings "worked at his own anvil, learning the techniques of metal." Professor Tout has cleverly imagined the role such a youth as Prince Edward might have played in an English university:

"Had the medieval point of view allowed a lay prince to study at Oxford, and had fourteenth century Oxford known the meaning of sports and past-times, Edward would likely have distinguished himself as a driver of fours-in-hand and as an athlete. He would have shown his skill in 'mechanic arts' by his knowledge of motor cars and perhaps even have rowed in the University eight. Unluckily his ignorance of Latin would have made it impossible for him ever to have passed Responsions."

Opposition to the royal favorites and criticism of misgovernment came mainly from the barons, yet it was natural to attempt to enlist the Commons on one side or the other. They were summoned to twenty-five parliaments in the twenty years of the reign. Their presence was becoming a habit, and their position improving.

In Edward III the barons found a king exactly to their liking. He possessed ambition, energy, and *joie de vivre*, was fairly able as both soldier and ruler, yet with a kind of graciousness and affability which won all classes. He took keen delight in the ceremonial aspects of kingship and the cult of chivalry. "During the early years of his minority," Miss Evans says, "French romanticism invaded the tiltyard and gave to the tourney the further glamour of dramatic make-believe." By 1330 the king was old enough to joust himself. In one tournament held in Cheapside, "between the Eleanor cross and the Great Conduit, he and his friends paraded the city dressed as Tartars on the Sunday before the lists were opened. Each knight had a lady on his right hand, robed in ruby velvet and led by a silver chain. The great tournament of the Round Table in 1344 was marked by the making of a huge round table for the knights to sit at, by the beginning of a great round tower to hold it, and by the taking of a vow by the king to restore the Round Table in all its glory. A certain number of barons and knights were sworn in as companions of the Round Table, and regulations for the observances of the brotherhood drawn up, providing for an annual feast at Whitsuntide. The successful phase of the French War was followed by an infinity of tournaments in 1347 and 1348, in some of which the Scottish prisoner knights took part." [5]

In this phase of the war castles and manor houses were enriched with the spoils brought home by the victors. Prisoners held for ransom were guests rather than captives, and shared with their captors in knightly sports and splendor. Among them were King John himself, four royal dukes, and thirty-six substantial citizens sent over by the greater towns as pledges for the indemnity (though this was never fully paid).[6] As we shall see, throughout this long reign there was never a feudal revolt nor an attempt to put the government completely in the tutelage of the nobles. With few exceptions harmony prevailed. But the pressure of the French wars meant frequent parliaments (forty-eight in fifty years), the chance to bargain, and consequent royal concessions to both Lords and Commons, with notable gains for the latter.

Richard II had the misfortune to become king at the tender age of ten years. Some months before the death of his grandfather, but only a few days after that of his famous father, the Black Prince, the Commons insisted that some recognition be accorded the heir to the throne. The little prince was brought into the Good Parliament by Archbishop Sudbury, who told Lords and Commons that "the dead prince was still present with them, having left behind him a fair son, his very image, as the true heir apparent to the throne." But alas, Richard did not prove to be the image of his father, "that young Mars of men" described by the Duke of York:

> In war was never lion raged more fierce,
> In peace was never gentle lamb more mild,
> Than was that young and princely gentleman.

[5] Joan Evans, *English Art, 1307–1461* (Oxford at the Clarendon Press, 1949), pp. 56–57.

[6] "One of the royal princes had sixteen servants with him in his captivity; all

About the only praise accorded Richard comes from historians of the arts, like Miss Evans, who rates him as "a dilettante of taste, with a passion for the pageantry of kingship," under whose leadership "all the arts of England entered upon a phase of fruition." Yet the older historians were perhaps too much impressed with Richard's last years of virtual tyranny to evaluate the reign correctly. Recent studies mark it as a complex but not a barren or retrograde period for parliament.

The fifteenth century is hard to picture fairly. It was an age of transition, sometimes retrogression, again real progress. Even its rulers (the three Lancastrians and three Yorkists), four of them immortalized for good or ill by Shakespeare, present striking contrasts, and the king was still an important factor in government.

The conception of a "Lancastrian constitution" — premature parliamentary government — in the early decades of the century, attractively portrayed by Bishop Stubbs, is rejected by modern historians. Yet scholars who have delved deeply into the sources of the era insist that it was a significant period in parliamentary history: ". . . habits of parliamentary initiative — especially that of the Commons — and a great deal of compliance on the part of Henry IV and Henry V, do give the appearance of a new character to the period" (Joliffe).

Henry IV was enthusiastically received by most of the population, lay and ecclesiastical, and especially by the citizens of London, whose liberties had suffered at Richard's hands. Henry was, of course, already well known as Bolingbroke, heir of the great Duke of Lancaster, and had distinguished himself as a crusader in the armies of the Teutonic Knights. He proved to be a careful administrator, some would even say a wise statesman, but his position was a difficult one. It is summed up in the plaint which Shakespeare puts into the king's apostrophe to sleep — "Uneasy lies the head that wears a crown." Uneasy, yes, when that crown is not based on the best hereditary claim. The playwright has well dramatized the problem of those who helped Henry to the throne — the Percies and others who felt themselves the king's peers:

> For bear ourselves as even as we can,
> The king will always think him in our debt,
> And think we think ourselves unsatisfied,
> Till he hath found a time to pay us home.

moved freely about the country on parole, hawking and hunting, dancing and flouting, rather like guests than prisoners . . . a natural freemasonry between the French nobility and the French-speaking courtiers of England." Coulton, p. 33.

Concessions to the parliament which had confirmed his title were inevitable.

"Prince Hal," as Henry V, was not only the hero of Agincourt, but was accorded unstinted praise by the clerical chroniclers because of his orthodoxy and measures against the Lollards. Yet his revival of the French war in 1415 had created a situation much like that of the early decades of Edward III's reign. King, Lords, and Commons again worked harmoniously together. The Commons were able to repeat and define earlier powers and practices. As Professor Plucknett puts it, there was "a hint of modern political self-consciousness." All this was too good to last, but these two reigns and their records served as a golden treasury for later generations of precedent-seekers.

The mid-decades of the fifteenth century witnessed strangely troublous times. Henry VI's minority, incompetence, and lapses into virtual insanity, and the rise of the ambitious and capable House of York led to factional strife and ultimately to the dynastic Wars of the Roses. The most famous picture of the age is that furnished by a composite of the *Paston Letters* and, in more critical vein, Sir John Fortescue's *The Governance of England*. Some modern historians have characterized the age as one of "bastard feudalism." The new chivalry included bannerets who had served in France with at least ten lances. Retainers were engaged by the new salaried indenture. Another historian demonstrates rather convincingly that late medieval lordship "has not much in common with feudal *dominium*. When a man asked another to be his 'good lord,' he was not commending himself and his land; nor did he become anything remotely like a vassal. Rather he was acquiring a temporary patron." Such lordship "lasted only so long as it was found to be *good* lordship or until it was ousted by a better." Hence the "right deduction seems to be that the opinion of the gentlemen of the shire counted for much. These men would take, as they would give, advice; they appreciated the value of 'good lordship'; and they were willing to be guided by those who had claims on their support; but it was foolish to attempt to drive them with too tight a rein. 'Management' was already a necessary art for those who wished to influence elections." [7]

The typically English agencies of government which had functioned well under able kings and ministers did not disappear but were made tools, not of use, but of abuse. "Justices of the Peace might be ap-

[7] K. B. McFarlane, "Parliament and 'Bastard Feudalism'," *Transactions of the Royal Historical Society*, 4th Ser., XXVI (1944), 53–73.

pointed, who would maintain the quarrels of the party to which they owed their appointments; sheriffs might be nominated, who could be trusted to impanel a jury favorable to their patron's views, sometimes consisting of his servants or liveried retainers. Should the sheriff prove less pliable than usual, the lord or his friends at court for him might obtain royal letters directing the sheriff to impanel such a jury. . . ."

A transaction "might be veiled under the name of a horse for my lord, or a kerchief for my lady, or a book for a prince of a literary turn like Gloucester. But in reality, if not in name, money was given for money's worth; for, as Sir John Paston cynically remarked, 'men do not lure hawks with empty hands.' . . . nothing can be more naive than the complaints as to the difficulty of being sure of jurymen, because either they are 'ambidexter,' i.e., take bribes from both sides, or they fear 'a turning world,' i.e., some sudden change in the relations of parties. Very quaint too is the astonishment expressed by John Paston *not* at being attacked in an unprovoked manner at the door of Norwich Cathedral, so much as at being attacked by a dependent of the Duke of Norfolk who was his 'good lord'; for it is evidently regarded as a great scandal to a lord, that two of his dependents should be at feud." [8]

Yet we must remember that not all Englishmen had as many difficulties as the Pastons. Further, it has been suggested that the Tudors found it good policy to play up the evils they had so adroitly remedied.

The age was not without some cultural interest. The Italian humanist Poggio was in England from 1418 to 1422. The very persons who figure as leaders of factions were notable as patrons. Humphrey, Duke of Gloucester, interested himself in the classics, corresponded with scholars abroad, and even invited Italian humanists to England, one of whom, Titus Livius of Forli, at the duke's request wrote a life of Henry V in Latin. Humphrey was also interested in collecting a library, part of which he presented to Oxford. John, Duke of Bedford, was not indifferent to the arts as encouraged at the court of his Burgundian ally. Cardinal Beaufort as Bishop of Winchester was "visitor" of Winchester College and New College. By 1440 Henry VI was planning Eton.

City governments, like their craft guilds, were tending to become more oligarchic, but industry and trade continued to flourish. A testimony to the wealth and importance of the wool merchants is reflected in "woolmen's brasses," a kind of monument which had earlier been

[8] Plummer, in Introduction to Fortescue's *The Governance of England*.

attainable only for nobles and ecclesiastics. The brass of one William Gravel (d. 1401) in the church which he built at Chipping Camden describes him as "flower of the merchants of all England" (*flos mercatorum tocius Angliae*). It is the first English brass to display a merchant's mark. The brass of another, John Fortey (d. 1458), shows him with one foot upon a sheep and the other upon a woolsack. Wool was no longer so much an export. The cloth trade was developing in towns like Norwich and, by the putting-out system, in the country villages.

Parliaments did not lapse into disuse, nor were they attacked with a conscious aim to abolish them. Shortcomings there were, yet there were compensating factors: increasing interest in elections and readiness to serve; progress in defining procedure and a parliamentary "vocabulary"; even some nice bits of constitutional theory. These will be described in a later chapter.

II

The Form and Composition of Parliament

❊❊❊

THE EVOLUTION OF THE LORDS

THE *British Government of our day is pivoted upon the House of Commons — more particularly, the relations between that branch of Parliament and the cabinet. This, however, was not always true; hardly two hundred years ago the House of Lords was, all things considered, the more conspicuous and powerful of the two bodies. Even now, although correctly termed a second, and even a secondary, chamber, that much discussed and oft maligned assemblage is a weighty part of the constitutional system, besides being the oldest, the largest, the most strictly hereditary, and in several respects the most interesting 'upper house' in the world. The Labor party would abolish it; men of other parties would reform it; and one can hardly doubt that it will see important changes in the coming, as it has seen them in the past generation. — OGG.*

OTHER states today have second-chamber problems: whether there should be a second chamber at all, and if so, what its powers should be, etc. But Britain, it should be remembered, has no written constitution, no judicial review. Parliamentary sovereignty in modern times extends even to the power to amend the frame of government. Thus the Lords may play a useful role in the use of the suspensory veto to check hasty or radical legislation.

As an assembly of the king's vassals in feudal days, the Lords, of course, have a much longer history than the Commons. Only gradually did that feudal Great Council evolve into a House of Lords composed of hereditary peers. It is possible to trace three successive types of

29

basis for membership: (1) the feudal principle of *suit of court* based on land tenure; (2) selection within the class of tenants-in-chief by the royal invitation or command — peerage by writ of summons; and (3) hereditary peerage, but always with the possibility of additions through new royal creations.

At the time of Edward I's parliament of 1305, as we have seen, there was still no clear-cut class of major barons who would always receive a summons. A certain capriciousness in the king's policy persisted well into the reign of Edward III. Some men were so great and powerful that they would always expect and demand a summons. There might be an abeyance due to natural causes, such as lack of a male heir or a minority. Again personal factors might operate — dislike, indifference, suspicion of disloyalty, factional strife. Yet always the special summons made the recipient a major baron if he had not been one before. The routine of the Chancery clerks probably tended to stereotype the list of barons to whom a writ was sent.

Originally *baron* was not a title of dignity but an old Norman French word simply meaning *man*. One can read in the early records such phrases as *baron et feme* (man and wife). In the fourteenth-century sense, a *baron* held a *barony*, a great landed estate variable in size. It was only the ingenuity of the lawyers later that equated a barony with thirteen and a half knight's fees! It was in the reign of Edward II that the whole body of magnates began loosely to call themselves, and to be called, peers. In some instances the peers are referred to in their capacity of counselors, again as judges. It was the factional strife of this reign that intensified and crystallized the right to trial of peers by peers — the *judicium parium* of Magna Carta. The "doctrine of peerage" was further emphasized in the parliament of 1341.

The third stage, the establishment of a select hereditary peerage, would come only when attendance as a lord of Parliament connoted political power and honor, advantage of some sort. This might lie in the opportunity of directing or checking the administrative policy of the king and his permanent staff, in securing fair trial by one's equals, in determining policy and participation in the French wars and the means to finance them. If a baron received a summons to one parliament, he was likely to expect one for the next. If he continued to receive summonses throughout his life, it was apt to be assumed that his heir would receive them, along with his inheritance of the title and estate. The older basis of attendance did not disappear at once, but we do have a small compact body of hereditary peers in the reign of Richard II. The hereditary principle was even carried to the point where if the land was alienated the peerage remained in the old family.

It had long been the practice for the king to create titles of dignity by letters patent, "open letters which differed from charters only in their less formal attestation." King Stephen first conferred the title of earl in this way. Richard II in 1385 conferred the title of marquis, borrowed from the continent. He was also the first to confer a dukedom outside the royal family (1397). The first dukedom was created by Edward III for his oldest son, the Prince of Wales; Lionel and John were made dukes in the parliament of 1362. *Viscount* appears only in the fifteenth century. The titles in order of importance were and are duke, marquess, earl, viscount. But such conferring of rank was not necessarily to create peers, for the recipients were probably already barons. The new title did not add to the numbers of the peerage. The novelty came in 1387, when the recipient, a simple knight, was created at once a baron and a hereditary lord of parliament. There were several such creations in the reign of Henry VI. By the end of the fifteenth century it was the normal method of creating peers.

Readers may recall the motives which in modern times have led to the creation of peers. Creations have sometimes been designed to change the political complexion of the House, as George III and the younger Pitt changed it for the Tories. Occasionally it served to reward a generous contributor to party coffers, a charge directed at one time against the Liberals. Most recently it has been designed to ensure cabinet representation and leadership in the upper House, as instanced by the creation of three Labour peers in 1924, MacDonald's first premiership. On the whole, however, in the nineteenth century the intent was to honor men of distinction in law, letters, science, art, statecraft, and business — Haldane, Tennyson, Macaulay, Lister, General Kitchener, Goschen, and notably Sir James Bryce, "a fitting reward for a long life of scholarly achievement and public service." "With some aptness," says Ogg, "the House of Lords has been called the Westminster Abbey of living celebrities."

In the fifteenth century — the troubled years of the Wars of the Roses — creations served to strengthen the political power of one or the other faction, virtually to pack parliaments. The two earliest instances, however, and most typical for the next two or three hundred years, indicate that a peerage was the reward of the man "whom the king delighteth to honor." Both recipients were knights, household officials, and quite possibly not only faithful "servants" but good friends and companions of their prince, witness the testimony of the letters patent.

The first, John Beauchamp of Holt, was knighted in 1386 and made steward early in 1387. Letters patent dated October 10 create him "peer and baron of our realm of England under the style of Lord of Beauchamp and Baron of Kidderminster," the same to descend to his heirs male. This was done "in consideration of his good and gratuitous services, his noble and trusty family and his great sense and circumspection." These "good services" included the upholding of the curialist party. Robert Botiller, knight and chamberlain, was created Baron of Sudeley by Henry VI in 1442. He is commended for his "talent, maturity in counsel, valor in arms, honesty, faithfulness and industry." In these letters patent, more complete and explicit than those of 1387, the king gives and concedes to him "the style, title and honor of Baron of Sudeley with the preeminences and dignities and all other things which belong to the status of baron of our realm of England *as well in sessions of parliament and in our councils as elsewhere . . .*," and "to the said Ralph and the heirs male of his body legitimately begotten forever (*imperpetuum*)."

Henry VI created duchies — Somerset for the Beauforts, Buckingham for the Staffords, Warwick for Henry Beauchamp. In most instances the title was that of the county or county town, and these were considered territorial lordships. Of course, in an age that loved ceremony and in which publicity meant permanence, the letters patent were followed by a formal presentation of the insignia, which varied in details with the title bestowed. For a duke there was the girding with the sword and the bestowal of a golden rod, cap of maintenance, and circlet of gold, with a pension of £40 a year on promotion, known as "creation money." [1]

As to individual earls and barons, it is unfortunate, perhaps that the best known are those who figured as leaders of opposition and revolt. In normal times most of them were loyal enough to their king, pillars of strength in time of war, companions of the chase and of the feast in time of peace. Similarly some of their wives and daughters were attendants and companions of the queen and princesses.

---

[1] For a marquess it was circlet, sword, and cap, creation money of £35; for an earl, the sword, creation money of £20 and, later, also the cap and coronet.

The number of lay lords summoned during the fourteenth and fifteenth centuries averaged from forty to fifty or a little over, the spiritual lords a few more. Prelates were more numerous during the Wars of the Roses. It was only when the dissolution of the monasteries removed the abbots that lay members became a permanent majority.

No peeress has ever been summoned to the House of Lords, even though attempts to secure the privilege have been made in fairly recent times.[2] Such was the claim of Viscountess Rhondda to a writ of summons in 1922, and the private bill introduced by Lord Astor in 1925. An heiress, of course, did and does transmit the right to her son, who, on coming of age, may claim the summons and seat. In the fifteenth century heiresses might also confer upon their husbands a presumptive right, although "some royal act of summons, or creation, or both was necessary to complete their status." Several reached the peerage in this way — for instance, Sir John Oldcastle, who, as husband of the heiress of Cobham, became Lord Cobham. A few years ago a London newspaper reported the almost unbelievable "find" of a precedent-seeker, the fact that in the reign of Henry VI five brothers sat together in the House of Lords! They were sons of Ralph Neville, Earl of Westmorland. Not one had had a peerage conferred on him. "Richard Earl of Salisbury, William Lord Fauconberg and Edward Lord Abergavenny had all married heiresses and sat in right of their wives. George was summoned in his father's title of Lord Latimer. The fifth brother, Robert, was Bishop of Durham." However, as the practice became established of creating peers with the title made to pass to male heirs only, and that by primogeniture, heiresses could no longer confer the dignity upon their husbands and thus carry it into new families.

It was inevitable that with the growth of the idea of a select peerage the Lords should look upon royal officials, councillors, as different from themselves, certainly not entitled to sit and vote with them. Still, the separation was not absolute. There were always a few peers who were councillors, or councillors rewarded with a peerage. The judges continued to be summoned and to act as advisers. Even today they and the law officers of the Crown are summoned by name to attend parliament. They do not vote and speak only when asked for their opinion. The House may compel their attendance when it is sitting as a court of law.

[2] In 1919 an amendment to the Sex Disqualification (Removal) Act was passed in the Commons but defeated in the Lords. This would have authorized English peeresses, of whom there were at that time twenty, to take seats in the Lords in their own right.

As to the "spiritual lords," in the fourteenth century the bishops were called and called themselves peers. It has been maintained that the original basis of their presence in the Great Council was feudal tenure; they too held baronies as did some of the abbots. The prelates themselves in the parliament of 1352 pleaded that archbishops and bishops "hold their temporalities of the king in chief and by the same are peers of the land as are other earls and barons." A few years later a letter of Bishop William of Wykeham refers to bishops, dukes, and earls as the "principal peers of the realm."

However, a difference in status was recognized in their writs of summons, which reminded them, not of their "faith and homage" to their king, the phrase used for the barons, but of their "faith and love." There were other respects in which the prelates differed from the magnates. Their offices were not hereditary. They did not share fully in the judicial work of the Lords, for the canon law forbade their presence or participation when judgment was passed involving loss of life or limb (i.e., trials for treason or felony). For themselves they preferred "benefit of clergy" to trial by peers. Hence the idea gradually arose that they could not be regarded as peers, though they were certainly lords of parliament, but formal declaration by the House to the effect that the bishops were "spiritual lords" came only in 1692. In the fourteenth and fifteenth centuries the two archbishops of Canterbury and York and nineteen bishops, as members of the secular clergy, attended rather regularly.

The abbots, as members of the regular clergy, were less inclined to take part in political affairs. Some disqualified themselves by proving that they did not hold a barony. As many as sixty-seven were summoned to the Model Parliament. The number fell to twenty-seven under Edward III, and so remained until the dissolution of the monasteries.

It is important to realize that the English Church also had its own ecclesiastical parliament. From the late thirteenth century on, the two convocations of Canterbury and York met separately but were thought of and spoken of as the Convocation of the whole Church. The prelates and others of official position constituted the upper house, representatives of the lesser clergy the lower house.[3] For the province of Canter-

[3] The upper house consisted of the following, attending in person: bishops, abbots, priors, the deans of cathedral and collegiate churches, archdeacons, and the heads of certain religious orders. The representative elements were the two proctors from each diocese (in York from each archdeaconry) representing the parish clergy, and one proctor for each cathedral and collegiate chapter. The bishops were commanded to

bury, which included most of the bishoprics, Convocation usually met about the same time as parliament and held its sessions conveniently at the Archbishop's Lambeth Palace across the Thames from Westminster or in nearby St. Paul's, London. Here in their own assembly the clergy granted subsidy for subsidy as granted by the Lords and Commons in parliament. Sometimes rather elaborate clerical petitions were framed in Convocation and then presented to King and Lords in parliament.

It cannot be denied that in practice the prelates were cast in a dual role, not an easy one in the England of the late Middle Ages. In this era of divided sovereignty they still owed loyalty to pope as well as to king. They had to defend the position of the English Church (*Ecclesia Anglicana*) against both at times. Naturally some of them opposed such antipapal statutes as Provisors and *Praemunire*.[4] The prelates did not join with the other estates in the parliament of 1366 in approving an end to the 1,000 marks tribute money due yearly to the papal treasury since King John's time. Wycliffe's theory of "disendowment" endangered Church property. One chronicler has left us a dramatic account of the Coventry Parliament of 1404, in which the bold Commons proposed to devote Church property to the use of the king for one year. They labored only to one end, he says, "to rob the patrimony of Christ, and take away the temporalities formerly granted by holy men and kings." Archbishop Arundel roundly censured them for their folly and greed and was supported by the Archbishop of York, but it was the shrewd Bishop of Rochester who effectually silenced the advocates of disendowment. He produced a book containing Magna Carta and read it to them. When he further showed that they were excommunicate, as indeed were all who subverted the liberty of the Church, many of them next day confessed their sin and begged absolution! With the extension of the theory of disendowment to lay holdings, however, landed classes in both Church and State tended to draw together on the defensive.

There were always among the bishops wise and learned counselors. As we have seen, some held important official posts as chancellor, treas-

cite beforehand (*praemunientes,* premonish) the deans or priors of their cathedral chapters, the archdeacons of their dioceses, one representative proctor from each chapter, and two representative proctors from the parish of each diocese. The representative clergy had been summoned to parliament from the time of the "Model," 1295, but accepted the royal summons with reluctance, and by about 1330 had made good their wish to appear in Convocation only.

[4] The first was aimed at checking papal appointments to English benefices; the second at preventing the carrying to the Papal Curia at Rome types of cases which were assumed to belong within the king's jurisdiction.

urer, etc. In constitutional crises they were usually ready to cooperate with parliament in reminding the king that he was "under the law." Archbishop Winchelsea, for instance, had been active in securing the Confirmation of the Charters in 1297, and was appointed one of the Lords Ordainers. The most scathing denunciation of the evils of purveyance is to be found in the treatise *Speculum,* penned probably by Archbishop Meopham in 1330. It abounds in good advice to the young Edward III. Archbishop Arundel, himself an exile, returned to England in time to officiate at the coronation of Henry IV, and supported the new Lancastrian regime.

THE EVOLUTION OF THE COMMONS

Early in the reign of Edward III the form of parliament was virtually settled, though it was still possible for a Great Council of magnates to meet occasionally, even into the age of the Stuarts. In the twenty years of Edward II's troubled reign there were twenty-five assemblies in which the Commons were represented, and in the fifty years of Edward III's reign, forty-eight such. This did not necessarily mean a parliament every calendar year; there were four in 1328 and three in 1340. A declaration that parliaments be held annually was made by the Lords Ordainers, and on two occasions by parliament itself. In 1330 it was prescribed simply that "Parliament shall be holden every year once, and more often if need be"; in 1362, that "for redress of divers mischiefs and grievances which daily happen a Parliament shall be holden every year, as another time was ordained by statute." Even in the reign of Richard II the average was good, though there were naturally more meetings during the minority than after the king assumed full power.[5] There were fewer parliaments in the fifteenth century, but no evidence of a design to abolish the institution which had become a customary and accepted feature of government. Various reasons have been suggested: less judicial work for parliaments; the convenience of voting taxes for more than a year; the disruptions of the civil wars; greater efficiency of the Council; the more aggressive leadership of the Yorkist kings.

The king's power to summon, prorogue, or dissolve parliament re-

[5] "The Nine years between 1380 and 1388 witnessed thirteen parliaments, whose duration varied from 16 to 99 days, giving an average of 41 days. In the 9 years between 1388 and 1397 there were only 7 parliaments whose average duration was only 21 days, the longest in 1390 lasting 44 days, and the 2 shortest, 20 days each." Tout, *Chapters in Administrative History,* III, 473–474.

mained unquestioned.[6] It was he who determined the length of a session, but short parliaments were popular. Sessions were normally two or three weeks. It was noted by contemporaries as very unusual that the Good Parliament of 1376 lasted six weeks. With parliament as with the courts at Westminster, it was realized that "agriculture was an exacting pursuit which made it impossible for a landowner to leave his estate at a moment's notice," and made him eager to return. "Relics of this still persist," says Plucknett, "for the long vacation of the courts and universities was once necessary to permit Bench, bar and litigants to reap and garner their crops and plow lands. Fixed terms, widely spaced, were designed to enable court work to fit in with agricultural work."

One question remains: Just when and why did the knights and burgesses unite as one estate, the Commons? This union was to be a vital factor in the permanence and vitality of the representative element.

The fusion was complete early in the reign of Edward III. In early parliaments, as we have seen, the knights sometimes sat and voted with the barons. Again they seem to have been regarded as a separate estate and deliberated apart. The evidence is meager, but the clerk who kept the parliament roll gives occasional hints as to the trend. For instance, for the parliament of 1330 it is recorded that there met for deliberation "the said prelates by themselves, the magnates by themselves, and the knights of the shire by themselves." In 1332 we read of the "knights of the shires, *and men of the commons*." But in the parliaments of 1339–1341 a change seems to be reflected in such statements as the following: "The reasons for the summons of this Parliament were set forth and explained to the lords and to the commons (*ceux de la commune*)." Again it is noted that a certain grant was made by the Lords, "and the commons gave their response in another schedule." "The men of the commons also presented two bills," etc. The real cue comes in the clerk's description of the opening of the spring parliament of 1343: "And the reasons for the summoning of Parliament were explained to them by the chancellor of our lord the king in the manner following . . . Whereupon the said prelates and lords were charged to meet by themselves in the White Chamber until Thursday May 1, in order to treat, consult and agree among themselves as to whether or not our lord the king should send messages to the court of Rome, setting forth and explaining

[6] When the king dissolved parliament, a new election to the Commons was necessary for the next meeting. If he prorogued (a device in use by the end of the fourteenth century, but not common until the reign of Edward IV) he set a date at which time the same members were to return.

his rights there before the said holy father the pope, as aforesaid. And in the same way the knights of the shires and the commons were charged to meet in the Painted Chamber in order to treat, consult, and agree among themselves on the same matter, and to report their answer and assent in parliament on the said Thursday." [7]

The reasons for the union are not far to seek. Knights and burgesses often wanted the same things. This is revealed in the common petitions they presented. It is evident in the agreement on subsidies: both groups represented constituents with small pocketbooks. Often those from the same part of the country must have had common local interests, perhaps have served together in local government jobs. Pronounced as were the distinctions between gentle and simple, interclass friendships and even marriages occurred. The wealthy merchant's daughter was a good match for the knight or squire of modest means. Yet the knights, as gentry, remained a vital link between the Commons and the Lords.

Historians from Macaulay to Plucknett have exulted over the result. Macaulay, himself a member of the Commons in Victoria's reign, emphasizes the role of the knight as the connecting link between the baron and the shopkeeper. "On the same benches on which sat the goldsmiths, drapers, and grocers, who had been returned to parliament by the commercial towns, sat also members who, in any other country, would have been called noblemen, hereditary lords of manors, entitled to hold courts and to bear coat armour, and able to trace back an honourable descent through many generations. Some of them were younger sons and brothers of lords. Others could boast of even royal blood. At length the eldest son of an Earl of Bedford, called in courtesy by the second title of his father, offered himself as candidate for a seat in the House of Commons, and his example was followed by others."

Professor Plucknett calls the fusion of the two elements "the result of one of those unions of happy accident and practical wisdom to which the English constitution owes so much. . . . The knights, who represented the landed property of the country, gave to the house of commons, from the first, stability, weight, and permanence, and obtained for it a respect which the citizens and burgesses alone could not have commanded, in a country so permeated with feudal ideas as England then was. . . . Without the knights of the shire the bur-

[7] Stephenson and Marcham, p. 217.

gesses would have been mere deputies to consent to taxation and advise on matters of trade; united with them on equal terms, they were enabled at once to claim a voice in the government of the nation, and to defend the liberties of the people against both king and nobles."

To contemporaries, at least in the fourteenth and early fifteenth centuries, however, there was no *House* of Commons, but still rather the Commons in and of parliament.

III

Elected, Electors, and Elections

✿✿

Knights of the Shire

"OUR modern suffrage," the authors of *How the World Votes* remind us, "is a composite of ideas and practices, which have their source in the most widely separated epochs of the world's history, from Pericles to Jeremy Bentham, and from the laws of Solon to the Declaration of the Rights of Man." They suggest four different ways in which man has regarded his right to participate in government by means of his vote: "He has, in distant times and comparatively simple conditions, considered it a natural accompaniment to his membership in the state, from which he could in no way divorce himself save by forsaking the state. Secondly, in the Middle Ages men voted only by virtue of the land or the title they held, not because of their manhood or their citizenship. This attitude was supplanted in the days of budding constitutionalism by the belief in the franchise as an abstract right, to which a man is entitled as he is thought to be entitled to the rights of life, liberty, and the pursuit of happiness. Finally, in the nineteenth century we have come to regard voting as we do office holding, a function of citizenship to be exercised for the service and at the will of the state." The second of these, the rule which formed the basis of elections in the medieval state, held that "voting was not a natural act of citizenship, but a privilege attached to a definite economic status, generally the ownership of land. This concept was a corollary of the general feudalization of society and government." [1]

[1] Seymour and Frary, I, 1–2, 7–8.

In England, of course, not only the electors but the elected, the "knights of the shire," were landed men. Such persons were thought to be a stable and responsible class. This attitude was reflected in the common law, essentially the law of land. Its procedure, designed to reach people who owned land, was generally, in Plucknett's words, "patient and long-suffering, for it well knew that the tenant's land at least could not be removed from its jurisdiction." As late as the famous case of *Ashby vs. White* (1704), Chief Justice Holt declared: "The election of knights belongs to freeholders of the counties, and it is an original right, vested in and inseparable from the freehold, and can no more be severed from the freehold than the freehold itself can be taken away." The same conception was carried to the colonies, although it had less weight in the new world with its vast areas of unclaimed land. "In passing an act discriminating against the landless freemen," Seymour and Frary tell us, "the Maryland Upper House justified itself thus: 'The freeholders are the strength of this province, not the freemen. It is their persons, purses, and stocks must bear the burden of the government, and not the freemen who can easily abandon us.'" Proprietors of the Jersey colonies wrote the Crown in similar vein.

The customs, and ultimately the statutes, governing the elected, electors, and elections may be briefly summarized before we turn to types and personalities among the members.

The elected were probably always knights in early parliaments, but some men, to avoid this and other governmental duties, paid the fine imposed by acts for "distraint of knighthood" rather than serve.[2] In the fourteenth and fifteenth centuries many below knightly rank were returned, including potential knights. Recent studies indicate that in instances in which the writs of summons demanded "belted knights" it was apt to be for a parliament whose main business was to provide for defense at home or campaigns abroad. Writs of 1371 and 1373, for instance, ask for the return of knights or, in the second, knights or squires "more approved by feats of arms." In any case the representatives must be county residents, men of ability, consideration, and property.

[2] "Beginning at least as early as 1224, there is a long series of enactments, known under the general term Distraint of Knighthood, whose object was, under penalty of fine, to make all who had the property qualifications for knighthood assume its name and insignia. Men were avoiding knighthood in order to escape the public duties which the king was crowding on the knights." "The belted knight, the knight girt with the sword, was of course the one who had assumed the knightly insignia and name." White, pp. 384n., 385n.

An ordinance of 1372 forbade the return of sheriffs and lawyers, and for a time the writs of summons included this prohibition. Complaints of the Commons protesting the election of sheriffs appeared as early as 1339. As many as seven, nine, ten, eleven, and in 1363, thirteen sheriffs have been spotted in various parliaments of Edward III. Sometimes apparently the sheriff returned himself! But it was felt that his presence and services were vital to his county, and after all, one function of the representatives was to report on their sheriff. The exclusion of lawyers was based on the charge that they advanced the interests of individual clients instead of the community as a whole, but this attitude was temporary, and we shall hear much of the lawyers in parliament.

An act of 1445 sums up the practice of previous years, with emphasis on the desirability of "belted knights," or at least men of "gentle birth." The elected must be "notable knights of the same counties from which they are elected, or else such notable squires of those counties, gentlemen by birth, as are able to be knights; and that no man who is of the rank of valet or lower is to be such knight [of the shire]."

Probably in early days representatives of the shires were elected, not merely by the small tenants-in-chief, but by all the freeholders of the county who were assembled in the county court. Who actually attended the ordinary monthly meeting of the court? Not all freeholders were required or desired to attend. Suit of court had become attached to certain holdings of land whose tenants were bound to this duty by the terms of their tenure. Others might be present merely as parties concerned in cases to be tried. Only as interest in elections increased do we hear of large numbers flocking to court on election days and of "undue elections," "swamping," etc. by unqualified voters.

In contrast to our popular elections in the modern democracies, with their secret ballot, ballot boxes, voting machines, election judges, counts, and recounts, these early elections would seem oddly casual and informal. Most commonly candidates were named by the sheriff and approved by acclamation without contest. Yet it was possible on occasion to object or propose other names. In case there were rival candidates there was a voice vote — not the familiar ayes and noes of today, but the names of the contestants shouted by their backers: "A Smith, a Smith"; "A Winslow, a Winslow." Then it was for the sheriff to determine which "had the greater number of voices." Rarely a close contest would require a *division*, the voters separating into groups to be counted.

Actual franchise acts come only in the late fourteenth and fifteenth centuries as popular interest increases. Edward III's answer to the petition of the Commons in the Good Parliament, 1376, seems to be reaffirming earlier practice in directing that election of knights of the shire be "by the better folks of the shire" and not merely by nomination of the sheriffs.

Rather surprising is an act of 1406 based on a complaint of the Commons of "improper election to parliament of knights of the shires, . . . made through the favouritism of the sheriffs or in other ways contrary to the writs directed to the sheriffs . . ." At first thought it is tempting to see a democratic gesture in the ruling that in the future "all who are there present, as well as suitors duly summoned for this purpose as others, shall attend to the election of their knights for the parliament, then freely and impartially proceeding with that election, any command or request to the contrary notwithstanding." Historians warn us against such an interpretation, suggesting quite the contrary: that the measure indicates that, owing to some temporary situation, the intent of the Lords was to swamp elections with their retainers, even to secure the election of some of them. If this is true, succeeding acts seem less reactionary and more justifiable. That of 1413 declared that electors in both counties and boroughs must be residents. Finally in 1430 was passed the famous "disfranchising statute," which was to govern the county electorate for four hundred years, down to the very year 1830, when Earl Gray introduced the Great Reform Bill.

The preamble of the act complains that elections of knights of the shires had of late been made "by too great and excessive a number of people dwelling within those same counties, of whom the larger part have been people of little substance or of no worth, each pretending to have the same voice in such elections as the most worthy knights or squires dwelling in the same counties, whereby homicides, riots, assaults, and feuds are very likely to arise among the gentlefolk and other people of the same counties unless a suitable remedy is provided in this connection . . ." It then restricts the county electorate to freeholders, "persons dwelling and resident therein each of whom shall have a freehold to the value of at least 40s. beyond the charges [on the estate]," with power to the sheriff to examine each elector on oath as to the annual value of his property. It concludes with a clause, a bit awkward, to be sure, but clearly a statement of the majority principle: "and such as have the greatest number [of votes] of them that may expend forty shillings by the year and above, as afore is said, shall be returned by the sheriffs of every county, knights of the parliament."

A *disfranchising* statute, yes, for forty shillings in those days had the purchasing power of over thirty pounds today. Furthermore, the key word, "freeholder," excluded the copyholder or leaseholder no matter how much income his land yielded.[3] Yet if our understanding of circumstances is correct, the statute was virtually a declaration of independence on the part of the gentry and freeholders, and an early recognition, perhaps the first in England, of the franchise as a political right. Perhaps we should not begrudge the gentry themselves a touch of pride in the very prestige and virtues which historians attribute to them.

The election over, the sheriff was expected to make a *return of writs* — that is, to write on the back of the writ authorizing the election the names of those chosen and to send it back to the Chancery at Westminster. Attendance was considered compulsory, as evidenced by the requirement of sureties or the pledging of property. The knight received as wages four shillings for each day of the session and the days spent in transit, depending on the distance he had to come. Judged by the purchasing power of the time, the compensation was liberal. At the end of the session each knight received from the government a *writ of expenses* to take back to the sheriff as authorization. Large numbers of these writs have been preserved in the official records to the present day, evidence enough to have enabled Professor Pollard to conclude that most parliaments had their full complement of seventy-four knights of the shires. Wages were not paid from funds in the sheriff's hands, but collected from those in the shire liable to contribute.[4]

Obviously the informality of elections and the control of the return of writs offered temptations to the sheriffs. Complaints of failure to make any return, and false returns, resulted in statutory regulation. The act of 1406 provided for a "true return" by requiring the names of the elected to be written in an indenture, authenticated by the seals

[3] "The qualification, however, was broader than might appear at first glance, since the term freehold was applicable to many kinds of property. Annuities and rent charges issuing from freehold lands were considered sufficient qualification, if they were of 40s. value; dowers of wives and even pews in churches might also be considered freeholds." There were other curious types. — Seymour and Frary, I, 68.

[4] This raised some problems. Exemption from liability claimed by all peers (including bishops) and their villein tenants was undisputed. Exemption of their free tenants, though disputed, was ultimately maintained. In early days there was the idea that a lord who attended parliament was representative of his tenants, and hence they need not contribute for expenses of knights of the shire.

of the electors. This practice was brought to the American colonies, where it was the custom, say Seymour and Frary, "to return the result of an election by an indenture signed between the sheriff and all the electors. But gradually three or four 'reputable men' came to stand for the whole body, and became the ancestors of the election officers." An act of 1410 gave justices of assize power to inquire into the legality of returns and to inflict the penalty of £100 on any sheriff returning a member not duly elected.

Not until the reign of Elizabeth did the Commons claim any jurisdiction in election disputes. An individual community, or more usually the Commons as a whole, prayed the king and Lords to take action. In 1404, for instance, the Commons prayed the king and Lords to act on an improper return by the sheriff of Rutland. "The lords thereupon sent for the sheriff and for William Ondeby, the knight returned, as well as for Thomas de Thorp, who had been duly elected, and having examined into the facts of the case, directed the return to be amended by the insertion of Thorp's name in lieu of Ondeby's, and committed the sheriff to the Fleet till he should pay a fine at the king's pleasure." [5] Even this procedure seems to have been considered unnecessary after the statute of 1445, which imposed an additional penalty against the sheriff — damages to the defrauded candidate secured by action of debt in the Court of Common Pleas.

> A Knight ther was, and that a worthy man
> That fro the tyme that he first bigan
> To ryden out, he loved chivalrye,
> Trouthe and honour, fredom and curteisye.
> Ful worthy was he in his lordes werre,
> And therto hadde he riden (no man ferre)
> As wel in Cristendom as hethenesse,
> And ever honoured for his worthinesse.
>
> . . . .
>
> And evermore he hadde a sovereyn prys.
> And though that he were worthy, he was wys,
> And of his port as meke as is a mayde.
> He never yet no vileinye ne sayde
> In al his lyf, un-to no maner wight.
> He was a verray parfit gentil knight.

[5] Instances of intervention by the Commons come first in the reign of Richard II, another sign of interest in elections. Before that "the cognisance of election disputes was originally vested in the king and his council, and where it was alleged that the sheriff was at fault, the matter might be remitted to the exchequer, which had special jurisdiction over sheriffs" (Plucknett's edition of Taswell-Langmead, pp. 223–224).

Chaucer found many a type or character in fourteenth-century England to serve as the butt of his kindly satire, but for the "gentle and perfect knight" he has only praise. Naturally we cannot expect any such abundant biographical material for the country gentleman of this age as we have for the vivid personalities of the Tudor period. Still we are not left completely in the dark. Recent English historians have compiled little thumbnail sketches and even longer biographies for some of the county representatives, reign by reign. These studies disprove the older views that the office was unwelcome, that re-election was uncommon, and that the knight was under the thumb of some peer. The members to be described here are not quite the ideal of Chaucer's epic, but they reward attention in their tremendous energy, ability, and in most cases, probity.

Attendance at parliament entailed, of course, a hazardous and, for some, long journey on horseback. Even the judges rode their circuits in this fashion, like those of pioneer days in the new world. But once arrived, a member might enjoy on a grander scale some of the advantages of attendance at local Quarter Sessions: a visit, not just to the county seat, but to the much more impressive London and Westminster; a chance to do some shopping or to pursue a private suit in Common Pleas or Chancery; to meet with friends and acquaintances of like interests, make useful contacts with central government officials, perhaps even receive favorable notice from the same; all this besides the real parliamentary business — in variable degree the opportunity to rate subsidies, voice complaints, and help to bring about useful legislation.

Professor Plucknett has summarized the careers of twelve men who represented Bedfordshire in the first decade of Edward III's reign (1327–1336). Of these the following may serve as typical:

John de Beauchamp. Of good family but unimportant; arrested for breach of the peace, but acquitted as it appears that he was in fact maintaining it. J.P.; twice M.P.

John Morteyn. Nine times M.P. 1307–1330; large landowner, several times summoned for military service; friend of Edward II and the Despensers; a strong partisan in politics with so many enemies that the king gave him permission to ride always armed; frequently on commissions of taxes and array.

Roger de Nowers. Seven times M.P. for Beds. or Oxon. Active partisan of Mortimer; "extremely turbulent"; imprisoned for killing a coroner. . . .

Richard de la Bere. Constantly on commissions of taxes and array; much land in several counties; sometime sheriff; five times M.P. . . .

Gerard de Braybrok. Great landowner; sixteen times M.P. in twenty-six years; apparently liked this service, for when sheriff he returned himself; his father had been seven times M.P. and his son became bishop of London and chancellor; frequently on judicial commissions.

John de Meperteshale. Ten times M.P.; many years coroner; charged with corruption while commissioner of array, but "rather more law-abiding than his fellows."

The study of other counties, we are told, produces similar results. Plucknett cautions us not to take too seriously the presence in the list of "seeming crooks and bandits," since these men lived in an era of fierce faction and sometimes civil war. "As for financial probity, it must likewise be remembered that the handling or collecting of public funds was a difficult task which often placed the official between the upper and nether millstone." Most noteworthy is the evidence that several had served in a number of parliaments as well as in various local government jobs. A few had seen military service, and one was to fight at Crécy. The assembly of "some seventy such men must have brought together a vast amount of local knowledge and experience in local administration." Repeated attendance meant parliamentary experience.

Similar evidence comes from a detailed study of all the men who sat in any of Edward II's parliaments for the five counties of Cambridgeshire, Huntingdonshire, Bedfordshire, Hertfordshire, and Essex.[6] Although the reign was one of factional strife, there seems to have been little attempt to pack parliament with either Crown tenants or retainers of Lancaster and the barons. One M.P. is characterized as "a follower's follower in the train of a public official who was himself a man of little political importance." Another is described as a strong partisan of John of Richmond, Earl of Brittany, and later of Queen Isabella's party. He was sheriff of Hertfordshire from 1314 to 1318 and again from 1324 to 1327, and either was returned or returned himself for the county four times (1316, 1318, 1321, 1322)!

Even more interesting are two of the knights who were tenants of the Crown. Benedict de Cokefield, who represented Essex in the Lincoln Parliament of 1316, illustrates the type of country gentleman "accustomed to the routine of local administration who came to parlia-

[6] G. Lapsley, "Knights of the Shire in the Parliaments of Edward II," *English Historical Review,* XXXIV (1919), 25–42, 152–171 (whence the quotations in this and the two following paragraphs).

ment with others of his kind to hear new administrative arrangements discussed, possibly to assent to them, and certainly to return home and help execute them." He was commissioned to raise troops provided by the parliament and to collect and assess the sixteenth granted by another parliament of the same year. He was one of the knights summoned to inform the Council on the Forests, and later took part in a survey.

John de Enfield (M.P., January 1315) was a country gentleman of importance in Essex and Middlesex, "with no trace of a political connection of any sort," engaged in activities of a wider range than most. "He had commanded a group of the King's ships on an expedition to Scotland and taken part in the defense of the coast. More than once he was employed as escort to foreigners who came to England, and acted in this capacity for the unlucky cardinals who were captured by Gilbert de Middleton, the Durham robber-baron. He was charged with special police duties, as when he was directed to search for and arrest people passing themselves off as members of the king's household or those resorting to illegal tournaments. At home he was employed on the more familiar and prosaic duties of levying troops, inspecting weights and measures, ditches and highways, and performing the many offices that fell to a conservator of the peace."

In the long reign of Edward III re-election was becoming even more common.[7] There is also an increase in attendance at consecutive parliaments: 124 had attended three in succession; 42, four; and 19, five such. Some knights served for more than one county and some for a borough as well as a county — the type of country gentleman who had land in several areas or had properties which gave him the status of knight and burgess. All this seems to indicate that parliamentary service, whether as a privilege or duty, was not undertaken altogether unwillingly. Applied to the next reign, this line of inquiry reveals that in spite of fluctuations under Richard II the practice of repeated elections persisted and even increased.[8]

Knights who were king's clerks and bore the curialist stamp included

[7] Using the writs of expenses as main evidence, Miss K. L. Wood-Legh compares some 29 parliaments of the two reigns of Edward II and I with those of Edward III. She finds a higher proportion of experienced men in the latter. In 32 parliaments experienced knights were in the majority, in 3 experienced and new men were equal in number, and in 18 men with previous experience were in the minority, though not inconsiderable at that. Five had served in 10 parliaments each, and one each in anywhere from 11 to 17. — "The Knights' Attendance in the Parliaments of Edward III," *English Historical Review*, XLVII (1932), 398–413.

[8] N. B. Lewis, "Re-election to Parliament in the Reign of Richard II," *English Historical Review*, XLVIII (1933), 364–394.

the Bushy of Shakespeare's *Richard II* and no less a person than the poet Geoffrey Chaucer. The latter, to be sure, served in only one parliament, that of 1386, which impeached Michael de la Pole and effected (through a baronial commission) dismissals including Chaucer and some of his fellow clerks.[9] Nevertheless, the career of this courtier, clerk, envoy, and man of business, to whom poetry was an avocation, affords a fascinating example of the rise of a household knight.[10]

Chaucer began as a page in the household of a princess, the wife of Lionel, Duke of Clarence, and in 1367 became a "yeoman" of Edward III's chamber. A few years later as squire "he might either have found himself still on duty in the King's chamber, or else an 'Esquire for the King's mouth,' to taste the food for fear of poison, to carve for the King, and to serve his wine on bended knee." From 1374 to 1386, "the most tranquilly prosperous period" of his life, as Comptroller of the Customs he lived over the Tower of Aldgate and worked at the Customs House. He served as justice of the peace in Kent in 1385, and was elected knight of the shire for the same in 1386. In 1389, when Richard assumed power, Chaucer's luck returned with the imposing assignment of the office of "clerk of our Works at our Palace of Westminster, our Tower of London, our Castle of Berkhampstead, our Manors of Kennington . . . [six others named], our Lodges at Hathebergh in our New Forest, and in our other parks, and our Mews for falcons at Charing Cross; likewise of our gardens, fishponds, mills and park enclosures, pertaining to the said Palace, Tower, Castles, Manors, Lodges, and Mews, with powers (by self or deputy) to choose and take masons, carpenters and all and sundry other workmen and labourers who are needed for our works, . . . and to set the same to labour at the said works, at our wages."

As to other distinctive personalities of the late fourteenth and fifteenth centuries, we shall meet them in special capacities: speakers, such as Peter de la Mare and Sir Arnold Savage; lawyers like the barrister Thomas Yonge and Judge Fortescue; Sir John Paston, of the famous *Paston Letters,* and his friends.

Citizens and Burgesses

In medieval England the distinction between a city and a borough was not one of size or type of government. A city was the center of a

---

[9] "It was doubtless the result of the commissioners' activity that in December 1386 Geoffrey Chaucer, king's esquire, who had sat for Kent in the recent parliament, was removed from his two posts in the customs." Tout, *Chapters in Administrative History,* III, 417.

[10] The following is based primarily on Coulton, pp. 31–32, 60–61, 76–77.

diocese with its cathedral and its bishop. Even "cities" were small compared with municipalities on the continent. England boasted none in the 100,000 class (such as Venice, Florence, and Paris). London alone, with 50,000, ranked with Milan, Genoa, Barcelona, and Cologne. No English town placed in the 20,000–40,000 class. In the rather vague 6,000–20,000 range came Bristol and York, on a par with Antwerp, Augsburg, and others.[11]

In England the status of urban communities and their degree of advancement also varied with their situation — whether on royal demesne or on the estates of a noble, or of an ecclesiastical lord, such as bishop or abbot. The king, perhaps because he had so many towns, was the most generous in granting charters of local liberties.[12] These varied greatly from town to town, with London always far in the lead. Rights were won slowly, one at a time, over many years; indeed, over many reigns.

As to representation in parliament, we find no such uniformity as with the counties, the evidence is less complete, and various questions arise. Why did some urban communities send representatives and others none? What proportion of those summoned actually attended? What can be ascertained about the elected, electors, and elections?

The parliamentary writ received by each sheriff required him to send, besides the two knights, "two citizens from each city and two burgesses from each borough" within his county. It has been suggested that in the days when communities were in transition from rural to urban economy the sheriff may have been in doubt as to which units in his bailiwick deserved to be termed boroughs. Again, it was possible for him to deal directly with boroughs on Crown lands, and it was tempting to ignore those in the liberties of the great lords. Still more vital was the fact that king and burgesses alike were content if the merchant *class* was represented.

Recent studies based on the civic records have thrown light on this

---

[11] Adequate statistics are lacking. These are estimates for about 1340.

[12] The most coveted of these were free personal status; burgage tenure, a kind of town freehold by which houses and lands were held subject only to a fixed rent, the right to pay to their lords in a lump sum all rents, tolls, and other dues (the *firma burgi*, or farm of the borough); the right to choose their own local officials and to have their own courts; a guild merchant or craft guilds, and freedom from tolls throughout England. Incorporation of the borough, which made it a fictitious person with a common seal and the power to sue and be sued and to possess and convey property, did not become common until the later Middle Ages.

and other problems and corrected earlier misconceptions.[13] These local archives supply the names of members of parliament missing from the official returns, information on methods of election and taxation, payment of parliamentary wages, and the uses made of their representatives by the urban communities.[14]

As to the question of attendance, some years ago when Professor Pollard's scholarly *Evolution of Parliament* appeared, fellow historians accepted as a clever and convincing piece of historical detective work his conclusions based on the official writs of expenses. These seemed to prove that there was virtually complete and regular attendance of the county representatives, the seventy-four knights, since practically all took out such writs, but that as for the burgesses, many were chosen but few served. Here he marks "a startling discrepancy" between the official election returns and the enrolled writs of expenses! A study of the civic records, however, reveals that the greater towns made their own arrangements for feeing their members. Others paid regularly with or without the writs, and still others "devised means of persuading certain persons to serve for little or no reward." Some of the odd bargains struck will be described below.

In the fourteenth century the number of cities and boroughs represented ranged from perhaps 75 to 85, producing over twice as many borough members as knights of the shire.[15] Returns seem to be made with increasing regularity as the century wears on. Boroughs which fail to respond are apt to have a good reason. For instance, in 1327 the sheriff of Northumberland endorsed his writ as follows: "The community of the county of Northumberland reply that they are so far destroyed by their Scottish enemies that they have not wherewith to pay the expenses of sending two knights to the council to be held at Lincoln; *and the bailiffs of the liberty of the town of Newcastle upon Tyne reply that they are so heavily burdened with the safe keeping of the town that they can spare no one from the said town.* So the execution of this writ is not possible at present." Some of the smaller boroughs did buy exemption or resent an unprecedented summons as evidence of the

[13] May McKisack, *The Parliamentary Representation of the English Boroughs*, is the most complete and effective treatment of the subject. Part of what follows here (pp. 51–54, 60–62), including data and quotations from civic records, is based on this study.

[14] Besides the records of London, most valuable for this purpose are those of King's Lynn, Norwich, Canterbury, Salisbury, Winchester, and Exeter.

[15] The average, reign by reign, as well as can be estimated, is, for Edward I, 86; Edward II, 70; Edward III, 75 (from 65 to 86); Richard II, 83 (from 78 to 88).

"malice of the sheriff." Average attendance for fifteenth century parliaments is not noticeably different.[16] A few new parliamentary boroughs were created by charter in the reigns of Henry VI and Edward IV, but the impetus is believed to have come from the squire and landlord class, not from the small boroughs themselves.

For the municipalities there is no franchise act like the famous statute of 1430 with its forty-shilling-freeholder clause, nothing at all of a general character, in fact, until the Great Reform Bill of 1832. On the whole, the sheriffs left elections to the borough governments, merely sending a copy of the king's writ to the bailiffs and accepting from them the names of the elected.[17] Such procedure is reflected in the return from Northumberland quoted above and in the following from the sheriff of Worcestershire: "As for the citizens of Worcester, this writ was returned to the bailiffs of the liberty of that city, who have full return of writs, who replied to me that two citizens have been elected in accordance with the tenor of the writ."

Elections usually took place in the borough court, the sheriff notified thereof by messengers. Each community followed its own custom, the electorate varying with the character of its government. The most common methods of choosing representatives were these: (1) the bailiffs themselves made the choice; (2) the bailiffs called a meeting of the most important burgesses and consulted them; (3) they called a general meeting of the burgesses. The tendency towards oligarchic forms of government meant a narrower franchise. The class of well-to-do merchants furnished both electors and elected. Re-election of burgesses was not uncommon, though less usual than for knights. Franchise rights might depend on having the "freedom of the city," guild membership, the performing of local civic duties and paying local rates, or on burgage tenure. In later times analogies with the shires were attempted. For instance, the statement from *Ashby vs. White* quoted above continues: "As for citizens and burgesses, they depend on the same right as the knights of the shires, and differ only as to the tenure; but the right and manner of their election is on the same foundation."

On the actual process of election there is little evidence. Probably as

---

[16] For Henry IV's reign, 75; Henry V, 80; and Henry VI, 87.

[17] The acts cited above correcting abuses in the return of writs for the counties applied to cities and boroughs too, as did the use of election indentures and the residence clause of 1413. Towns which were "shires incorporate" held their election in their own county court.

in the Italian communes rotation or lot was preferred as a fair and impartial assignment of what in early days was more of a duty than a privilege. At Rochester the citizens had an ingenious custom which may have been adopted by other small towns: ". . . from time immemorial, that if any stranger, not born in the city should take up his residence there, become a freeman of the city and enjoy its privileges and franchises, he should serve once in parliament, as a representative of the town, at his own expense. With this may be compared the arrangement made at Ipswich in 1469, whereby John Alfray of Hindley elected to the York parliament which was subsequently prorogued *sine die,* agreed to serve without payment 'in consideration of his admission to be free burgess of this town.' "

There is more evidence on the methods of choosing local borough officials, and it is possible some of these were adopted for parliamentary elections.[18] As early as 1362 at Lancaster, for instance, those taking part in the election of mayor were ordered to "give their voices privily and secretly everyone by himself." According to an ordinance made at Norwich in 1415, "each voter was to go to the polling officers and 'secretly' name the person whom he desired to be mayor." A similar practice is found at Lynn Regis, 1416.

Unlike the knights, burgesses received wages of not four but two shillings per day. Some of the wealthier towns paid a higher rate, though few were as lavish as London. Winchester supplemented wages when its representatives undertook special duties for their town. Some communities, on occasion at least, were able to substitute for shillings other acceptable rewards: the remission of a rent due, a certain lane and a "little corner place," an annuity in the form of a rent from two mills, and in 1465, for one of the Dunwich burgesses, a cade full of herring. Norwich accepted the offer of one of its representatives to the parliament of 1478 to forego the claim to £4 16s. in return for perpetual exemption from the offices of coroner, sheriff, and constable of the city. Some public-spirited citizens were prosperous or generous enough to forego wages. This happened more than once at Canterbury. In 1483, for instance, George Browne, " 'on account of the peculiar affection and love which he had and hopes to have for the city of Canterbury,

[18] Professor Charles Gross ("The Early History of the Ballot in England," *American Historical Review,* III (1898), 456–463) has found a variety of electoral methods, including vote by ballot, but for most of these the evidence comes from the sixteenth or seventeenth centuries.

and because of the many gracious words and deeds shown him by his
fellow-citizens on many occasions, freely and gratefully remitted his
wages in the aforesaid parliament.' "

> A Marchant was ther with a forked berd,
> In mottelee, and hye on horse he sat,
> Up-on his heed a Flaundrish bever hat;
> His botes clasped faire and fetisly.
> His resons he spak ful solempnely,
> Souninge alway th'encrees of his winning.
> He wolde the see were kept for any thing
> Bitwixe Middelburgh and Orewelle.
> Wel coude he in eschaunge sheeldes selle.
> This worthy man ful wel his wit bisette;
> Ther wiste no wight that he was in dette,
> So estatly was he of his governaunce,
> With his bargaynes, and with his chevisaunce.
> For sothe he was a worthy man with-alle,
> But sooth to seyn, I noot how men him calle.

In their choice of representatives the smaller towns were more
limited. Their candidates were usually persons who had held office
in the borough council or merchant guild, but who were not capitalists
or merchants on the grand scale. On the other hand, cities like London,
York, and Bristol were able to send persons of wealth and experience,
notable not only in their own community but in the growing national
economy of trade and finance.

Some of London's representatives combined city offices with posts
under the Crown, as did Richard de la Pole (M.P. 1332), alderman of
Bishopsgate and King's Butler. A citizen of York with the picturesque
name of Henry Goldbeter (M.P. 1336, 1340, 1341) was a member of
the wool syndicate of 1337 and undertook much government business.
Thomas Graa, Mayor of York, who represented the city in twelve of
Richard II's parliaments, was appointed by that king as ambassador
to Prussia. Hull returned its mayor, William de la Pole, head of the
great merchant family of de la Pole, ancestors of the earls of Suffolk. He
served as King's Butler, Baron of the Exchequer, and on more than
one occasion advanced money to the crown. Such men must have
furnished an effective link between Crown and Commons, civic and
national economy. These two groups, whether great capitalists or small
traders and craftsmen, were those whom the king had in mind in issuing

summons, the men who ought to be there. Only after the middle of the fifteenth century and more particularly in the reign of Edward IV, "the estate of knights begins to overflow into the estate of burgesses," as the smaller boroughs begin to return country gentlemen, knights and esquires.

In making the acquaintance of individual cities and boroughs and their members, we must read out of the picture the great modern manufacturing towns like Manchester and Birmingham, products of the industrial revolution, mere straggling villages in the period with which we are concerned. Even by the end of Elizabeth's reign about three fourths of the population was still rural. Towns were larger and more numerous in the south and east, toward the Continent.

Along this coast were the Cinque Ports — Dover, Hastings, Hythe, Romney, and Sandwich. The term *cinque* (five), typical of the survival of Norman-French words in England, persisted even after the addition of Rye and Winchelsey raised the number to seven! To understand the importance of the Cinque Ports it must be remembered that there was no royal navy. Until the reign of Henry VII it was their duty to furnish nearly all the ships and men needed for the king's service, whether in peace or in war. Long after that they gave considerable assistance to the fleet. As was befitting "their wealth, their situation and their fleet," they were accorded confirmation of their liberties and free customs by Magna Carta and by a more comprehensive charter of Edward I, confirmed reign after reign. Further recognition of their unique role is the fact that the representatives of the five ports in parliament were dignified with the title of "barons."

Some towns were important then as now — London and York, ports like Southampton and Bristol, industrial centers like Norwich and Coventry, cathedral towns like Canterbury and Lincoln. By the end of the fifteenth century these had all attained the special status of "shires incorporate," as had three others, Hull, Nottingham, and Newcastle.

Norwich served as a staple town for a time under Edward III, and its importance in the trade in wool and worsted dates from his reign. The town walls, begun in 1294 and completed in 1342, were so notable as to receive honorable mention in histories of architecture, for they "enclosed the largest area in the kingdom in a roughly circular enceinte, broken by forty towers and twelve gates." Norwich elected able representatives and paid them well. Coventry in Warwickshire, a large industrial center at the present day, was known for its trade in wool, cloth, and caps. Its guilds were numerous and wealthy, and along with those of Chester and York were famous for putting on each year one of the great cycles of mystery plays. At the time it attained county status in 1451, the government consisted of the court of ten aldermen and a common council of twenty, but election returns were witnessed in full county court by as many as twenty to forty burgesses.[19]

Lincoln in modern times is an important county seat in the heart of a rich agricultural area. It has a large trade in corn and other produce and also manufactures agricultural machinery and implements. The great cathedral on its hill above the town still dominates the countryside for miles around, reminding us that in the Middle Ages Lincoln was notable as the cathedral city of a large and populous bishopric, distinguished for such notable scholar-bishops as Robert Grosseteste. However, midway between Westminster and the north, Lincoln was also a convenient sojourn of kings, who favored the city with charters granting liberties and customs comparable to those of London. Parliaments were held there in 1301, 1316, and 1328, with the cathedral serving as meeting place for the formal sessions. Lincoln, too, was famous for its scarlet cloth, its craft guilds, and its pageants. It returned its two citizens to parliament from 1295 to 1885. It was a separate unit with county status from 1409, and parliamentary elections took place in the full county court of the city, held in the Guildhall. The electors were the mayor and about twenty-five of the more substantial burgesses, " 'with the consent of other worthy citizens then being present.' "

Bristol, over in the southwest on the Avon, about eight miles above the point at which the river enters the Bristol Channel, has been called "one of the best examples of a town that has owed its greatness entirely to trade." When the Chamberlain's Company of actors on tour in 1597 visited Bristol, they found it in some ways "a miniature version of London, with its Cathedral and the beautiful houses that had been built by its merchants. Its stone bridge over the Avon was nearly as good as London Bridge over the Thames, for it was lined with houses in the

---

[19] Oddly, in view of its importance, Coventry, which had sent representatives to the Model Parliament, sent none for a hundred years before 1451. At the time of the Great Reform Bill the franchise of Coventry was vested in the freemen, i.e., in "those persons not being paupers, who had served seven years' apprenticeship to one trade, and it is possible this custom dated from the fifteenth century." McKisack, p. 54.

same way and even had a chapel on it. The Avon at this point was tidal, and the ships could be brought 'under sail into the very heart of the city.' " [20]

Naturally Bristol's great day came only with the era of exploration and discovery, and the swing of trade west to the "ocean sea." The tourist may recall as one of modern Bristol's most striking features the tower on Brandon Hill west of the cathedral, commemorating the fourth centenary of the Cabots. The records of the Society of the Merchant Venturers begin in 1467, some years before John Cabot's first voyage. However, in early days the borough was not negligible. In the Domesday Book it appears as a royal borough with a mint. In the thirteenth century it was exporting wool to the Baltic, had a wine trade with southern France, and such local industries as soap-making and tanning. In 1337 an enterprising burgess with the suggestive name of Thomas Blanket set up looms and employed foreign workmen in the making of woolen cloth. The charter of 1373 extended the boundaries of the town and raised it to the status of county, the first besides London to receive that honor. Typical among its notable citizens was William Canynges (1399–1474), who was five times mayor and twice represented Bristol in parliament. He is said to have carried on "a huge cloth trade" with the Baltic, and became wealthy enough to rebuild the Church of St. Mary Radcliffe. Better known in parliamentary history is the barrister Thomas Yonge, of whom we shall hear more presently.

In the fourteenth century, London, though not yet technically the capital, was well aware of its prestige and importance to the nation. A petition of the Commons, 1354, describes the city as the abode, as nowhere else in the realm, of "our Lord the King, and of all the great ones, a great part of his commons, merchant strangers and others." Later in the century a passage in the *Letter Books* refers to London as the safest place within the realm, "whither the most people resort for business, and more particularly, seeing that it is the capital city and the watchtower of the whole realm and that from the government thereof other cities and places do take example." There is no lack of physical description of London, with details ranging from the first use of "sea coals" to the red tile roofs replacing thatch, and the hundred churches, the chief architectural glory of the city. Though the walls of the houses were still of mud and timber, the number of stone mansions built by great

[20] Marchette Chute, *Shakespeare of London* (New York, 1949), p. 199.

lords or wealthy citizens was on the increase. Such was John of Gaunt's Savoy on the way between London and Westminster. Several of the bishops came to have houses in or near London.

From 1355 on London sent not two but four members to parliament, paying considerably more than the customary wages and providing lavishly for their expenses. For the Cambridge Parliament of 1388 these included special clothing for the members and their servants, the repair and refurnishment of lodgings, gifts to minstrels, laundry, and wine! In the next century, however, expenses were limited to wages, and an allowance for cloth and fur — in other words, costumes that would worthily reflect the wealth of the city. Extra expenses were allowed only when parliament was meeting at a distance.

In theory the official and proper place for holding elections was the Husting, the county court of the city held at the Guildhall. In the course of the fourteenth century the function was assumed by the Courts of Aldermen and Common Council.[21]

From early days London was able to send notable citizens to the Commons. A certain John de Grantham who sat in three parliaments (1328, 1330, and 1338) owned property in eight London parishes and in the town of St. Omer. John de Causton owned a brewery, houses, and shops, and at his death left money for the maintenance of several chantries. After the middle of the century London merchants were wealthy enough to replace the Italians and Gascons as the king's "bankers." Such was John Philipot, celebrated, Plucknett says, "as the first Englishman who has left behind him the reputation of a financier" and who served Edward III as paymaster. In 1377 he equipped a squadron of 1,000 armed men and in 1379 provided ships for an expedition to Brittany. While mayor he financed one of the two stone towers built below London Bridge, and on his death "bequeathed lands to the city for the relief of three poor people for ever."

Admitting that "the parliamentary burgesses of medieval times produced no great political leaders," that they were inferior to the knights in status and influence, and that no burgess held the office of Speaker

[21] The statute of 1406 had little effect. "The aldermen and common councillors, in order to satisfy the requirements of the King's Chancery, revived the proclamation and formal election in the Husting, but themselves retained the real choice of representatives which they made in either or both of their courts, at the Guildhall, generally during a session of the Husting. The names were probably submitted to the Husting for formal approbation before being entered on the return." McKisack, p. 51.

until the reign of Henry VIII, still their role was neither insignificant nor uninteresting. It is important to realize the twofold aspect of their position in parliament: general public functions, and those of private or local interests.

It was the first, of course, that was important to the king and his officials. "The burgess comes to parliament in order that the borough may be bound by the measures to which he there gives assent." [22] The *Parliament Rolls* do not make much specific reference to the citizens and burgesses, but it is not well to lay too much stress on the silence of the rolls, which are not concerned with the private deliberations of the Commons. There are recorded some appointments of burgesses to committees. On occasion they serve as collectors of subsidies and as auditors of accounts. They advise as to the amount of tax grants and the rate of customs, help frame Commons petitions. On matters of trade and finance the information and advice of the greater merchants must have been invaluable.

From the local point of view the burgess is his town's attorney. His presence at parliament enables him to present petitions for confirmation of charters, the increase of local liberties, and redress of grievances, and to undertake private business in or near London for constituents. City and borough charters usually contained sweeping clauses assuring permanence and inviolability, but in practice eternal vigilance was required. Especially was confirmation felt necessary on the accession of a new king, usually in return for substantial payment. In the first parliament of Richard II the members for Norwich presented a petition "whereby the poor citizens of Norwich asked for a confirmation of the charters, privileges, and customs granted and confirmed to them by former kings." Lynn got an *inspeximus* and confirmation of its charter at the beginning of Henry V's reign. Again in 1439 the charter of Lynn was delivered to the parliamentary burgesses for confirmation " 'if by the advice of the said burgesses of parliament it can conveniently be done'; and in 1442 the charter was confirmed 'by the labor and industry

[22] The writ of summons asked that the elected come with full power (*plena potestas*). "For a considerable time after 1294 the borough representatives commonly appeared in Parliament bringing with them a formal document, sealed with the borough seal, stating that the mayor and the whole community of the borough concerned had given them full power to act." J. G. Edwards, "The *Plena Potestas* of English Parliamentary Representatives," in *Oxford Essays in Medieval History Presented to Herbert Edward Salter* (Oxford, 1934), p. 144.

of Walter Curson, one of the burgesses of parliament.' " In the quaint words of a Norwich record, its representatives were expected "to increase our liberties as they may be able."

Grievances to be redressed were as often economic as political. In 1413 Lynn instructed its burgesses to collect a debt of forty marks owed the mayor and commonalty by the king's serjeant-at-arms, and in 1425 to secure repayment of a loan from Henry V's executors. Others asked reduction of their *firma burgi*. In 1413 Salisbury directed its representatives to "try to obtain an amendment of the Assize of Cloth, and advanced to them the sum of 100s. for this and other business."

There were keen interurban rivalries. A Londoner called a merchant from York or Southampton "stranger" no less than one from Paris or Ghent. One town's liberties interfered with those of another. Typical of intercity conflicts was the protracted quarrel in the early years of Edward III's reign between the lusty fisherfolk of Great Yarmouth on the one hand and London, Norwich, Little Yarmouth, and Gorleston on the other over fishing rights. Both sides resorted to direct reprisals. As time went on, cooperation in the Commons and opportunities for peaceful interurban conferences on the side softened animosities. Lynn gave its representatives to the second parliament of 1413 "letters of attorney empowering them to conclude an agreement with the mayor, bailiffs, and burgesses of Southampton, in the matter of tolls." In 1423 Norwich's two burgesses "remained in London for two days after the dissolution to discuss the question of exemption from tolls and customs with the 'mayor and council' of the city of London." In the Good Parliament of 1376 cities and boroughs presented strong petitions embodying common municipal grievances.[23]

"Now to treat of the great and notable franchises, liberties, and customs of the City of London would require a whole volume of itself," exclaimed Sir Edward Coke, writing in the seventeenth century. Even in the fourteenth the list was a long one, increased by charters of Edward III and Richard II.[24] But although London had more liberties, it also had more occasion to defend them. The proximity of the court and of the law courts lent prestige and was good for trade, but had its disadvantages also. There was always danger of the extension of royal

[23] See p. 103.
[24] Besides the usual "liberties," there were the conservancy of adjacent rivers, restrictions on "merchant strangers," exemptions from tolls throughout England, its own court at fairs, etc., and in imitation of the gentry, even hunting grounds in the nearby Chiltern Hills.

jurisdiction at the expense of London's courts, of the use of commissions armed with unusual powers, and occasionally of the extreme measure of being "taken into the king's hands." Royal purveyors could walk the city at their pleasure, bearing their white wand of office, and mark with the broad arrow whatever goods were required for the king's use. Sometimes the citizens took matters into their own hands, especially in regard to their conservancy of the Thames. Again defense of their rights was handled by direct negotiation with the king or Council or by suits in the central courts.

Petition in parliament, however, afforded the support of the Commons as a whole and gave the desired publicity. Such petitions sponsored by the Londoners included requests for the confirmation of their charters, protests against government concessions to foreign traders, control of rivers, and disputes over jurisdictions and immunities. London always played an important role in national crises and was sure to be on the popular side. Its citizens helped turn the tide for Isabella and Mortimer against Edward II, had their part in the crisis of 1340–1341 led by Archbishop Stratford, displayed open hostility to John of Gaunt in the 1370's and 1380's, and in 1399 received Henry IV with enthusiasm.

Another important service of the burgesses was that of reporting on the session to the folks back home, who were without benefit of newssheets or radio. Here again most fascinating and instructive are the records of Lynn, which contain many examples of such parliamentary reports. Of course the reading or explaining of the acts passed was a duty, an aspect of the promulgation of statutes. But the descriptions from Lynn suggest that "the return of the representatives from parliament was regarded as an event of some importance, bringing numbers of burgesses to the Gildhall to hear the news and to learn what they were to be asked to pay."

In 1413 the burgesses delivered their report on the first parliament of Henry V: "William Hallyate and Master John Tylney, burgesses of parliament in this year, arose and stood by the window in the northern part of the hall, and worthily declared the acts of the last parliament before the mayor and commonalty, point by point, from the beginning to the end, opening with the sermon of the reverend father the Bishop of Winchester, Chancellor of England, which he preached in the presence of the lord king of England, the text of which was *Ante omnem actum stabile consilium,* of which sermon he made three divisions. . . .

Then the mayor asked William and John to restore to the commonalty the muniments and evidences which they had in their possession. And they delivered the royal charter . . . to the chamberlains. . . . Then the mayor asked the parliamentary burgesses why the charter of liberties had not been ratified. They answered that no charter in the whole of England had been ratified or confirmed by the Friday after St. Barnabas last past, not even the charter of the city of London, and they added that whereas the ratification of charters used to be granted for ten marks or £10, now £100 or one hundred marks is asked, which seems excessive. . . ."

Again, on their return from the parliament of May, 1421, the two members for Lynn "published their report on the news and acts (*nova et actus*) of parliament, 'as well as they were able to remember them'. . . . Bartholomew, who was the spokesman, gave a description of the assembling of the members, 'saying that he entered the Star Chamber with great difficulty and discomfort because of the multitude of people, noble lords, citizens of cities and burgesses of boroughs; and they were among the first boroughs called because such was the order of the sheriff's return.'" The manner of giving the reports varied. In 1421 the two members divided the labors, each giving a half of the report. Again in 1425 "Thomas Burgh read aloud from a roll containing the acts of parliament, and John Copnote added explanatory comments."

IV

Powers, Procedure, and Privileges

✿✿

MORE effective than generalizations, if we are to form a lively picture of parliament in action, is a reconstruction of certain actual sessions as complete as our evidence permits. But first a summary of the powers and duties usually exercised in the fourteenth century may serve as an introduction. For the convenience of the modern student a classification such as the following will best serve our turn: (1) judicial functions, (2) administration and matters of state, (3) control over taxation, and (4) legislation. The first two continue to belong more properly to the Lords; the third and fourth will be shared increasingly by the Commons. The relative importance of each varied from session to session, reign to reign. The "King in his Parliament" was concerned with immediate practical needs and circumstances, as were his Lords and Commons. Much depended on the personality of the monarch. Governmental functions were not sharply differentiated or defined. Incidentally some notable advances in procedure were made and the conception of parliamentary *privilege* formulated. Concerning constitutional theory, we shall hear more in a later chapter.

Parliament labored under the disadvantage of its short and intermittent sessions. Parliaments might come and go, but Council and Household, a kind of permanent civil service, went on forever. In the course of the fourteenth century the Council becomes a definite group with its own traditions, and eventually its own clerk. Its members take a prescribed councillor's oath and receive annual salaries or annuities or, for the lesser clerks, day wages. The Council continues to be the king's advisory body with respect to all aspects of government, though policy and administration are most important. It still includes, of course, the great heads of departments like Exchequer and Chancery, which had "gone out of court," and some of the judges. Perhaps nothing reveals so perfectly the status of these ministers as the councillors' oath. (1) They are responsible to the king but pledged to preserve the rights of the king *and of the Crown* — the distinction is clearly recognized. (2) Like their royal master in his coronation oath, they promise to do justice to all "of whatever estate or condition." For the judges there is an additional clause: "And that you will take nothing from anyone for doing wrong or delaying justice." [1] These great ministers of state and the judges continued, of course, to be appointed and paid by the king, but they were inclined to acquire a certain independence, to uphold the traditions and customs of their departments. Yet the separation of parliament and Council is not too complete. There will always be a few peers who are councillors. In the Commons may be found some elected knights of the shire who have served in the Household and bear the curial stamp.

But what of the court, or Household? In modern times, the reign of Queen Victoria, for instance, the royal household was complicated and expensive, but not a factor in government. Readers may recall Strachey's rather amusing account of Prince Albert's determination to institute reforms and the problems involved. He describes how control was "divided in the strangest manner between a number of authorities, each independent of the other," nominally under the Lord Steward or the Lord Chamberlain, neither of whom resided at court. The divisions of authority "extended not only to persons but to things. The Queen observed that there was never a fire in the dining-room. She enquired why. The answer was, 'The Lord Steward lays the fire, and the Lord Chamberlain lights it . . .'"

The medieval Household was complicated and costly, as we know from the *Ordinance* of 1318. Devised by the baronial reformers, this document enumerates and authorizes the various officials, servants, and servants' servants and their perquisites. Including the thirty serjeants-

---

[1] The oath (in 1307 form) reads in part: "That well and loyally, according to your knowledge and ability, you will counsel the king. That well and loyally you will keep his counsel; and that you will not accuse another [on account] of anything that he may say in the council. And that, to the best of your ability, you will give and devote your care, aid, and counsel to keep and maintain, to safe-guard and restore, the rights of the king and of the crown, in so far as you can without committing wrong. . . . And that for no one, through love or hate, for good will or ill will, you will abstain from having right and justice done to every man, of whatsoever estate or condition, according to your knowledge and ability." Stephenson and Marcham, pp. 176–177.

at-arms and eight footmen, they number well over a hundred, a list which suggests the vast equipment and supplies needed, not just for the royal family, but for all these persons entitled to "eat in the hall." For instance: "The king should have a fit steward of the household, who, if he is a banneret, is to have a knight, three squires, and a clerk for the pleas that pertain to the stewardship, [all of them] eating in the hall. . . . A treasurer of the wardrobe, who is to have a chaplain, a clerk and two squires eating in the hall. . . . Item, a clerk of the spicery, chief usher of the wardrobe, who shall receive from the clerk purveyor of the great wardrobe, the wax, napery, linen, cloth, canvas, spices, and the other things of all sorts that pertain to his office . . ." [2] And so on *ad infinitum* with a porter, a squire fruiterer, several chaplains and their clerks, a physician, surgeon, clerk of the market, baker, launderer, cooks, poulterer, etc.

It was a temptation to medieval kings to exalt the functions of certain of these Household servants at the expense of the great ministers of state. The Keeper of the Wardrobe [3] was a kind of Household treasurer who cared for jewels, money, documents, and valuables. Funds paid in and handled by him without passing through the Exchequer were virtually in the royal pocket. Similarly the controller (counter-roller) served as a private secretary. As keeper of the privy seal he might be asked to authorize letters unbeknownst to the chancellor with his great seal. As the privy seal came to be used officially by the Council, there was substituted a royal secretary in charge of the king's *signet*.

Most notorious in his attempts to enhance his power through the Household was Edward II. Edward III's attempt to do the same was confined mainly to the early years of the French wars, when Household officials crossed the Channel with him as a kind of wartime government. Richard II gradually built up a courtier and curialist element in the latter part of his reign. The Household thus served as a means of evading policies urged by parliaments in their brief, intermittent sessions.

Powers: "The High Court of Parliament"

Some years ago Professor McIlwain, in his notable *The High Court of Parliament*, emphasized the importance of its judicial role in early

[2] Stephenson and Marcham, p. 204.

[3] In the early days the *wardrobe* housed arms and armor, saddles and harness, horses, boats, chests, etc., used to accompany the king on his travels about the realm. Housed in the Tower of London, this was dubbed the Great Wardrobe. *Wardrobe* or at times *Chamber* was the term applied to the Household staff described above.

years, a needed corrective to overemphasis by earlier writers on its legislative capacity. Here it was the Lords, not the Commons, who constituted the highest court in the land. This is true, of course, down to the present time, though the actual judges are the special "law lords," not the whole body of peers.

We have seen the importance of judicial work in the session of 1305, typical in that respect of Edward I's reign, and how at that time judges and other councillors were in and of parliament. An analysis of sessions in the first decade of Edward III indicates little change as yet. "There is every cause for believing that while parliament was sitting, the council regarded itself as part of parliament, and its acts might therefore be described as the acts of parliament." Judges and councillors (with some peers if their interests were involved) served as a panel of discussion to which courts of first instance would adjourn difficult points, and handled matters involving the king's rights and other public business, a kind of administrative law and justice. There are a few assertions of the "dignity of parliamentary judicature: a decree of parliament ought not to be revoked save by a parliament; it is 'the highest place in the realm' and the tampering with its endorsement is a serious offense . . ."[4]

With the separation of the Council and the House of Lords during the reign of Edward III, the jurisdiction of the two ceased to be identical and was better defined. To the House of Lords remained (1) trial of peers by peers for treason or felony, (2) appeals on writs of error from the common law courts, and (3) after 1376, impeachment. Parliament followed the common law, while the Council continued to act as a court of equity, inclined to handle criminal equity itself and to leave civil equity to the chancellor and his able staff.

Trial by peers was abolished by act of parliament as recently as 1948 as a result of the problems suggested by its revival, after long disuse, in the de Clifford case of 1935. In its origin it was purely feudal — the right of any vassal, even the simple knight, to trial in a court of his equals; that is, fellow vassals of the same lord. It was in the reign of Edward II that the barons began to be called, and to call themselves, peers. In some instances peers meant counselors, again judges. It was the factional strife of the reign that publicized and made of the right a coveted privilege. Real lawful *trial* had been virtually in abeyance. Each party on

[4] Plucknett, "Parliament," in *The English Government at Work*, pp. 109–112.

coming into power condemned its opponents by alleging that their misdeeds were "notorious" and recording the judgment. When opportunity offered, the victims or their heirs protested acts done without the consent of the *peers of the realm,* i.e., *judges,* and claimed the *judicium parium* of Magna Carta. This right was publicized and defined in the constitutional crisis of 1341, and seldom questioned thereafter for actual peers. When a peer was tried on a charge of treason or felony, the Lords were judges of both fact and law.[5]

Proceedings on review of error, available in both criminal and civil cases, closely resembled those in the common law courts and were argued by counsel. In the fifteenth century it was settled that the function of the Lords was to correct errors in matters of law, not fact. Apparently there were not many such appeals in the later Middle Ages, but such a case is hard to spot: "Such trace as it may have left would normally be on the roll of the lower court, for . . . parliament soon abandoned the attempt to keep a plea roll." Even in the eighteenth century Blackstone could still write of the "nobility of this realm as being not only by birth hereditary counsellors of the crown, and judges upon their honour of the lives of their brother-peers, but also arbiters of the property of all their fellow-subjects, and that in the last resort. In this their judicial capacity they are bound to decide the nicest and most critical points of the law; to examine and correct such errors as have escaped the most experienced sages of the profession, the lord keeper, and the judges of the courts at Westminster. Their sentence is final, decisive, irrevocable; no appeal, no correction, not even a review, can be had. . . ."

It was in the first parliament of Henry IV, which offered opportunity for clarifying relations with the new ruler, that the Commons formally disclaimed any part in the judging function: The Commons "set forth to the king that, whereas the judgments of parliament pertained solely to the king and to the lords, and not to the commons except in case it pleased the king of his special grace to show them the same judgments for their satisfaction, no record should be made in parliament concerning the said commons to the effect that they are or shall be parties to any

---

[5] In the sometimes rather long intervals between sessions the Lord Steward presided and acted as judge of law, with twenty-three peers as judges of fact only, i.e., a jury of peers. We know of such a procedure in 1415, and again in 1499. "Whatever may have been its origin, the custom . . . was finally established by the precedent of 1499." Holdsworth, I, 389–390.

judgments henceforth to be given in parliament. To which, at the king's command, response was made by the archbishop of Canterbury, to the effect that the commons are petitioners and demandants, and that the king and the lords have always had and of right shall have the [rendering of] judgments in parliament, after the manner described by the same commons . . ." [6]

In the process of impeachment, of course, the Commons figured as accusers and eventually as prosecutors, never as judges. There is no evidence that knights and burgesses served on committees for the hearing of private petitions, a semijudicial procedure, until the Tudor period. Only in Elizabeth's reign did they take advantage of the fact that they were part of the "high court of parliament" to claim power to enforce certain of their privileges.

Powers: Administration and Matters of State

Ways in which parliament occasionally sought to direct policy through control of the king's ministers included: (1) afforcing the Council with men of baronial or high ecclesiastical status and point of view, (2) asking a voice in the nomination of certain key posts, and (3) devising some means of removing objectionable officials, eventually by impeachment. The attempt to force parliamentary appointments upon Edward III, 1341, and the first use of impeachment, 1376, to remove corrupt officials will appear in the notable parliaments of those years to be described below. During the minority of Richard II there were the inevitable disputes among the barons as to control of the Council, but parliament did nominate to office and prescribe policies.

As we have seen, the Commons were the source of useful information on local government and administration. Occasionally the power of the purse strings served as an indirect opportunist means of control over royal policies.

The last resort was deposition. In the fourteenth century this was a "modernized" form of the old feudal *diffidatio,* or withdrawal of allegiance — a sort of homage and fealty in reverse. It inevitably involved extralegal measures, even violence. In the case of the ne'er-do-well Edward II the initiative came from his neglected Queen Isabella, Baron Mortimer, and their adherents. Parliament concurred in a *fait accompli.* There was more theorizing in 1399. The deposition of 1327 was cited as

[6] Stephenson and Marcham, pp. 255–256.

a precedent, the role of parliament, or at least of the estates that usually composed parliament, was emphasized, though the personal factor was not wanting — the disinherited Henry of Lancaster.

Back in August Richard had issued writs of summons for a parliament to meet Tuesday, September 30. But the very day before, Henry's supporters secured Richard's abdication and absolved all his subjects from their allegiance. On Tuesday Westminster Hall witnessed a dramatic scene, described in the *Parliament Rolls*. Two bishops appointed by Richard as his proctors read the renunciation to all "the estates of the kingdom." "Estates and people" heard and accepted the renunciation, framed a list of charges, and authorized the deposition.

"And immediately, as it appeared from the foregoing [actions] and their result that the kingship of England, together with its appurtenances, was vacant, the aforesaid Henry, duke of Lancaster, rising from his place and standing so erect that he could be well seen by all the people, humbly signing himself on the brow and breast with the symbol of the Cross and first invoking Christ by name, laid claim to the said kingship of England, thus declared vacant, together with the crown and all its members and appurtenances; [and this he did] in his mother tongue by the form of words following . . .

"After which declaration and claim the lords both spiritual and temporal, and all the estates there present, were asked singly and in common what they thought of that declaration and claim; and the same estates, together with all the people, unanimously agreed with out difficulty or delay that the aforesaid duke should reign over them. And immediately . . . the aforesaid archbishop, taking the said King Henry by the right hand, led him to the royal throne aforesaid. And after the said king, kneeling before the said throne, had made a short prayer, the same archbishop of Canterbury, with the assistance of the aforesaid archbishop of York, placed the said king and caused him to sit on the aforesaid royal throne, while the people in their excessive joy loudly applauded. . . ." On October 1 came the last step, the announcement to Richard through proctors of the action of the estates.[7]

In matters of state naturally King and Council exercised the greater authority. Yet for the perennial problems of the Scots and the French wars it was essential to have the support of the Lords on policy and the Commons for financial backing. In the parliament of 1332 the proposal

[7] Stephenson and Marcham, p. 254. — See Note A at the end of this chapter.

of the French King Philip VI that the young Edward III accompany him on a crusade was referred to prelates and magnates, not to the Commons. Again, when the king by his chancellor asked "whether it were best to treat with the French by way of amity or marriage according to the offer of the French," the Commons, it is noted, "think the way of marriage best." On subsequent occasions in connection with the French wars the Commons were consulted,[8] but it would be hard to determine from the brief recordings of the clerk how much weight was placed on their opinion and advice. The attitude of the Commons themselves changed as the war progressed and burdens multiplied. When it appeared that the king was taking the line that it was up to the parliament which had favored the war to finance it, they replied: "Most dread lord, as to your war and the array thereof, we are so ignorant and simple that we cannot give you advice. We therefore pray your gracious lordship to excuse us, and that it please you, with the advice of the great men and sages of your council, to ordain what shall in this matter seem best to you for the honour and profit of yourself and your kingdom; and whatever shall be thus ordained by the consent and agreement of you and of the great men aforesaid, we readily assent to and will hold it firm and established."

From the king's point of view it was sometimes desirable to assume the backing of the entire nation as presented in parliament. This attitude is reflected particularly in antipapal policy and legislation. A letter from Edward III to the pope, 1343, protesting reservations, provisions, and collations granted by him and his predecessors, reads: "To the very holy Father in God, Sir Clement, by divine providence sovereign bishop of the holy church of Rome and of the church universal, his humble and devout sons, the prince, *dukes, earls, barons, knights, citizens, burgesses and all the commune of the realm of England in the parliament* held at Westminster on the quinzaine of Easter last past devoutly kissing his feet with all reverences and humilities . . ."

In 1366 all the estates were consulted before the momentous step was taken of ending the tribute money to Rome conceded by King John. "On the said morrow, first the prelates by themselves, and then the

[8] In 1343, for instance, Lords and Commons, after separate deliberations, advised the king to make peace if a truce could be obtained "honourable and advantageous to himself and his friends." If not, the Commons promised to "aid and maintain his quarrel with all their power." In 1368, when David Bruce offered peace with Scotland, the Lords alone were consulted. On some occasions the clerk merely records that "Parliament advised."

other dukes, earls, barons, and great men answered and said, that neither the said king John, nor any other could put himself nor his realm nor his people in such subjection, without their assent and accord. And the commons having been questioned upon this and having taken counsel answered in like manner." Letters of Henry IV and Henry V to the pope (to be described below) assert that acts could not be changed or revoked without the assent of the estates in parliament.

Powers: Control over Taxation

In early days any form of direct taxation was occasional and unusual — extraordinary revenue. In normal times the king, like other great landholders, was expected to "live of his own." Such additional income as he received — feudal dues, tallage, etc. — was based on private contract, proprietary relations. There was some income from fines in the courts and such occasional gifts of nature as wreck and treasure-trove. In modern times true national taxation is characterized, in White's words, by "fixing attention upon kinds of property rather than classes of men, by taxing at one time all of a certain kind of property irrespective of who holds it. Its scope is the nation, not the class, and its basis is public, not private."

When the increasing needs of government made it necessary to supplement the "king's own," a source for the idea and a practical form were found in the feudal *aid* which became the tax on moveables — the *tenth and fifteenth* — and was extended to all the propertied classes.[9]

The first half of the fourteenth century saw the establishment of the theory of parliamentary consent for such a grant, the setting of a fixed rate and method of assessment, and at least the beginnings of appropriations, conditional grants, and audit of accounts. Because of active preparations for the French wars, 1339 and 1340 were key years. In the parliament of October 1339 the Lords showed willingness to make a grant, but the Commons insisted on consulting their constituents first! In the session of January 1340 both made grants, but the Commons attached such stringent conditions that officials felt compelled to consult the king, still on the Continent. After Edward's return to England, the spring parliament made a grant on conditions.[10] Their petitions

[9] See Note B on Taxes at the end of this chapter.

[10] The landed class — prelates, earls, barons, and knights — granted the "ninth sheaf, the ninth fleece, and the ninth lamb from all their sheaves, fleeces, and lambs for the two years next to come." Citizens and burgesses granted a ninth of their moveables. Another miscellaneous group paid a fifteenth.

were embodied in four statutes (prepared by a committee of Lords and Commons), one of which stated emphatically that the people should not "be from henceforth charged nor grieved to make common aid or to sustain charge, if it be not by the common assent of the prelates, earls, barons, and other great men, and the commons of our said realm of England, and that in Parliament." Seldom afterward was this principle called in question. The ingenuity of kings was exerted rather in evading it, as did Richard II and Richard III with their forced loans and benevolences.

The victory for parliament as to indirect taxes was slower in coming. Medieval customs were not protective tariffs — they were imposed on exports as well as imports. Later, as "impositions," they served occasionally to wring concessions from foreign merchants or to put pressure on their governments, but commonly tolls were imposed for revenue. These became standardized. There was first the Old Custom (*antiqua custuma*), so called because it was set by the parliament of 1275, on exports of wool, wool-fels, and hides. The New Custom (*nova custuma*) of 1303 was negotiated by King Edward I with alien merchants, Gascons and Italians, granting them increased trading privileges in return for customs duties on most imports and some exports. After various protests and experiments, English merchants, too, were obliged to accept the New Custom. It served as a model for the later well-known subsidy of *tunnage and poundage,* paid by both denizens and aliens, which in the form set in 1373 was to last for centuries.

Under the pressure of war costs Edward III did successfully at times raise even the Old Custom by agreements with the "estate of merchants" outside parliament, such as that of 1342 imposing an additional 40s. per sack of wool! It was justified on the grounds that it was the alien exporter who would pay. In their remonstrance the next year the Commons showed that "they possessed some rudimentary knowledge of the principles of political economy," pointing out that the merchant strangers would retaliate by reducing prices paid English producers! Protests in 1339–1340, 1343, and 1346 had little effect. Sometimes the Commons adopted the device of voting the rate already arranged by the king, thus making it appear that such arrangements must have their approval. No wonder the seventeenth century precedent-hunters found a bewildering and contradictory supply, and selected from it to fit their cause, royalist or parliamentary. Finally an act of 1362, confirmed in 1371, conceded that no grants of subsidies on wool be made without the consent of parliament, and the Crown's private dealings with the merchants ceased. It was a victory for both sides: parliament maintained its principle, but had to recognize the justice of the king's claim for higher rates. As it was not feasible for customs rates to be changed from year to year, from the middle of the reign of Henry VI right down to 1625, the first year of Charles I, the customs were voted the king for life.

In modern times all funds are *appropriated*; that is, granted for specific purposes, whether by parliament in Britain or Congress and the state legislatures in the United States. This was not true in fourteenth-century England. It might be assumed that a grant would be used for the needs presented by the chancellor at the opening of the session, but there was no assurance that this would be the case. Hence appropriation of supplies was a novel and for long only an occasional practice. In 1348 in their grant of three *fifteenths* to be levied during three years for the French wars, the Commons specified "that this aid shall be assigned and kept solely for the war of our lord the king and shall in no way be assigned to pay old debts," and begged that if peace or a long truce was made, the third year's assessment should not be levied, together with the practical proviso that if the war came "towards the parts of Scotland," the aid paid by the taxpayers north of Trent should be assigned to the defense of those parts. In 1353 an increased custom on wool was approved on condition that it be applied solely for the purposes of the war. During Richard II's minority the Commons were always careful to tack conditions to their grants. In succeeding years (1389–1397) the practice continued. Some subsidies were actually remitted by proclamation, when the condition of an expedition against the enemy was not fulfilled.

A natural corollary when things did not seem to be going well was the desire of a parliament to check up on the collection and expenditure of funds voted in a previous session. One can imagine the Commons grumbling, "Wonder what they did with the money we gave them last time!" In both 1340 and 1341 the king permitted an examination of accounts — in the first instance by a committee, in the second by commissioners. The parliament of October 1377 went further. It secured the appointment of two notable London merchants, William Walworth and John Philipot, as sworn parliamentary treasurers to receive and disburse the war grants. When the next parliament met at Gloucester in 1378, the government produced Walworth's accounts, "but only as an act of grace and without creating a precedent." The practice was not so well established but that Henry IV could retort to the Commons in

1406 that "kings do not render accounts," but he eventually relented. Disused under the Yorkists and Tudors, the claim to audit was revived in 1624 and 1641, and established as a regular practice only in the reign of Charles II.

Normally the government brought pressure on parliament for prompt action on the desired money grants, and postponed answers to petitions until the end of the session. It was natural for the Commons to want to reverse the order — let redress of grievances *precede* supply. Evidence does not enable us to assign this happy thought to any particular knight or burgess — some hard-headed London merchant, perhaps — but it was to prove a useful lever on occasion. Richard's judges condemned the claim as a form of treason: the king, not the Lords and Commons, has the power to determine the order of business in parliament, they agreed.

The situation of the Lancastrian kings was such that with only occasional restraints the Commons were able to exercise and more precisely to define all these practices: voting taxes, conditional grants, appropriations, and audit of accounts. For instance, in 1404 a grant was designated for the defense of the kingdom only with two treasurers of war, Thomas Lord Furnivall and Sir John Pelham, appointed and sworn in parliament to receive it and to account to the Commons at the next parliament.

One definite gain for the Commons, secured under Henry IV, was recognition of the rule, in modern times an axiom of parliamentary law, that all money bills must originate in the Commons. True, peers were not exempt from direct taxes as were the first and second estates in France, but the knights and burgesses represented the taxpayers of small means, those upon whom the burden weighed most heavily.

Powers: Legislation

Today we are apt to think of parliament primarily as a legislature. In early medieval times there was little conscious law-making, even little distinction between a court judgment and the act of "legislating." Law was conceived of as immemorial custom, not man-made, not makable, nor easily changed. An *ordinance, establishment, statute* — the words were used loosely — reaffirmed, publicized, clarified, and to some extent elaborated on existing law. The King in Council issued directions to officials which did unwittingly introduce new law and procedure. Any fundamental change required approval of the *community of the realm,* in its early meaning of the prelates and barons in the

Great Council. It is the fashion among some modern historians to ignore the chronicles in favor of official records only, but at times a chronicler put things most aptly, witness what the author of the *Annals of Osney* writes of Edward I as a lawgiver: "Certain statutes the king published very necessary for the whole realm, by which he stirred up the ancient laws that had slumbered through the disturbance of the realm; some which had been corrupted he recalled to their due form; some which were less evident and clear of interpretation he declared; some new ones useful and honourable he added."

In Edward I's statutes the enacting clauses vary suggestively. *Quia Emptores,* permitting free alienation of land and checking subinfeudation, matters of vital interest to all great landholders, begins: "Our Lord the King in his Parliament . . . at the instance of the great men of the realm, granted . . ." Westminster I, a veritable little code with its some fifty items, has broader authorization: "These be the acts of King Edward . . . made at Westminster at his first parliament general after his coronation . . . by his council and by the assent of the archbishops, bishops, abbots, priors, earls, barons and the community of the realm, being thither summoned. . . ." Even the modern formula does not eliminate the crown. With legislation as with other functions, it is still the *King in his Parliament*: "Be it enacted by the King's most excellent Majesty, with the assent of the Lords spiritual and temporal and the Commons in this parliament assembled . . ."

In the course of the fourteenth century the representative elements come increasingly to *share in,* we dare not say *control,* legislation. There may still be measures sponsored by the King and Council or by the Lords. The petitions of Commons may be amended or rejected by these, their superiors. The comprehensive *Commons' petition* of the fourteenth century was really not one petition but many. Still, the singular is justified, for collectively "it" comprised all the Commons' requests for a given session. At the beginning of the century such petitions were rare. We found none in the parliament of 1305. Apparently there were two in Edward II's reign which were the basis for statutes.[11] Typical for the future was the comprehensive Commons' petition from the first parliament of Edward III, forty-one articles, each of which begins "Prayen the Commons" (*Prie la Commune*). Sixteen of these gave rise to some statutory enactment.

[11] The Articles of Stamford, 1309, and a short act of 1320 sometimes called Westminster IV.

The over-all potential value of the petitioning practice in contrast to the ruder ways of the preceding era has been effectively estimated by Joliffe as follows: "Common and frequent petition, without the threat of force, took the place of prolonged discontent and the abrupt presentation of a complex cahier of grievances at the point of the sword. Reform no longer proceeded by violent crises divided by long periods of years, but by the steady pressure of successive parliaments. . . . [Thus] crown and nation kept steadily informed of each other's needs." Some Commons' petitions may have been prompted from above. There continued to be bills which originated with the Crown, yet the consent of both Houses in their passage emphasized the fact that Parliament shared in the work of legislation.

King and Council might use their discretion, selecting from the Commons' petitions some items which should become statutes. Of course not all Commons' petitions required to be made statutes. In many instances it was enough to direct officials to obey and enforce existing laws, to follow customary procedure. Sometimes the royal answers are evasive, again opportunist and practical. A sampling culled from the *Rolls* includes: "This article was answered in the last Parliament." "It seems to the council that the law formerly ordained ought to suffice." "The King will consider [advise on] the matter until the next Parliament." "The time is too short to act on this matter before Easter. The King is willing that it be handled after Easter." "Let him who feels aggrieved declare his case in particular [individually] and appropriate remedy will be afforded." "That would be *to make new law* which could not be done due to lack of time." This suggestive phrase, "to make new law," occurs in answer to three petitions of the 1348 parliament.

Matters of a temporary nature were handled by *ordinances,* considered less solemn and permanent than *statutes,* and sometimes made, not in parliament, but in a Great Council.[12] Neither clerks nor chroniclers were consistent in their use of these terms. Professor Chrimes warns us

---

[12] Evidence comes from the *Parliament Rolls.* The Ordinance of Labourers, issued in 1349 while no parliament was in session, was in 1351 made into the more effective Statute of Labourers in parliament. At the request of the Commons the Ordinances of the Staple of 1353 were in the next parliament confirmed "to be holden for a statute to endure always." Plucknett (edition of Taswell-Langmead, p. 182) says: "In 1363, when it was proposed to enact the first sumptuary laws, the lords and commons were asked 'inasmuch as the matter agreed upon in the parliament was novel and unheard of before,' whether they would prefer an ordinance or a statute. They decided to proceed 'by way of ordinance and not by statute, in order that, if anything should need amendment, it might be amended at the next parliament.' "

that we make "insufficient allowance for the medieval habit of indulgence in synonyms." Nevertheless, by the middle of the fourteenth century Chancery is the abode of an official *statute roll,* the term *statute* comes readily to the lawyers' lips, and the Commons conceive of a *statute* as something relatively permanent. Approved by King, Lords, and Commons, it may be repealed only by the same. That repeal was a recognized procedure in the latter half of the century is evident from the customary formula which stands at the head of the Commons' petitions, to the effect that "all the good ordinances and statutes made in the time of our said lord the king, and in the time of his progenitours, *not repealed,* be firmly holden and kept."

In 1409 Henry IV explained in a letter to Pope Alexander V that statutes and ordinances could be revoked or changed only "after first taking mature counsel, as is right and fitting, with the nobles and estates of our realm in parliament to be summoned especially on that account, without the calling of which or the assent of the estates aforesaid, since it touches their interest, no statutes or ordinances previously made can be revoked or changed." Similarly Henry V in 1419 informed the pope that the Statute of Provisors could not be repealed without the consent of the three estates.

Once a petition was selected as the basis of a statute, worthy of formal enactment, it was turned over to the judges for *engrossing* — that is, rewording and inscribing on parchment — as H. L. Gray puts it, "changing an appeal to an imperative." [13] It has been assumed that through the influence of the king or Council this process led to unwarranted changes in the sense. But we must remember that the Commons' requests "were often ill-conceived and badly presented." Of the various methods by which petition and answer were combined to make a statute, there were three which effected little change: (1) simple assent — the statute is the petition in affirmative phraseology; (2) most common, a rephrasing of the petition to make it clearer and simpler; and (3) the adding of a clause prescribing a penalty for violation; in other words, "putting teeth into it." Three others went further, for the response (1) might add a restriction or reservation, (2) might refuse or postpone some part of the petition, while granting most of it, and (3) might greatly modify the petition, in which case the statute is the response rather than the petition.

[13] See Note C at the end of this chapter.

On the whole, Professor Gray concludes, changes were not so numerous or radical as has been supposed. The parliament of 1413, which made considerable changes in six of the ten statutes based on Commons' petitions, was an exception. But it is significant as leading to another bit of conscious claim and theorizing which goes down in the record, as the Commons insist: "We be as well assenters as petitioners."

Some statutes have informative preambles, explaining the problem to be dealt with or the evil to be redressed — "the great damages and mischiefs which have happened and daily do happen in the realm." This type is well illustrated by the Statute of Labourers with its lament over the "grievous incommodities" through the lack of ploughmen, and how "many seeing the necessity of masters, and great scarcity of servants, will not serve unless they may receive excessive wages, and some rather willing to beg in idleness, than by labour to get their living."

The Statute of Treasons, 1352, was a popular measure, in answer to repeated petitions of the Commons to protect the subject against dangerous extension of the offense, even to the killing of a king's messenger: "Whereas the king's justices in different counties adjudge persons indicted before them to be traitors for sundry matters not known by the Commons to be treason, it would please the king by his counsel and by the great and wise men of the land, to declare what are the treasons, in this present parliament." The petition (repeated in the statute) thus calls for a definition of the law. The king's answer, "A Declaration which Offences shall be adjudged Treason," constitutes the body of the act.[14]

We do not have to wait for Henry VIII for the propaganda preamble, witness the statutes of Provisors and *Praemunire* from which that monarch was later to derive considerable inspiration. The first quoted an earlier act as to the purpose of kings and nobles in past ages in granting endowments to "the holy Church of England," namely, "to make hospitalities, alms, and other works of charity, in the places where the churches were founded, for the souls of the founders, their heirs, and all Christians." Further, how the "said kings in times past were wont to have the greatest part of their council, for the safeguard of the realm when they had need, of such prelates and clerks so advanced." The second Statute of *Praemunire* contains a virtual declaration of independence from papal overlordship, and anticipates Henry's assumption

---

[14] For the act on the use of English in the courts, see below, p. 98–99.

of sovereignty: ". . . so the crown of England, which hath been so free at all times, that it hath been in subjection to no realm, but immediately subject to God in all things touching the regality of the same crown, and to none other . . ."

So much for public bills, but what of the host of private petitions which figured so prominently in early parliaments like that of 1305? Throughout the fourteenth century the Commons sometimes sponsored and included in their comprehensive petitions the bills of a group, such as a county, a borough, or special economic interest, but not those of individuals. The distinction was made clear in 1346, when it was emphasized that private petitions be given the receivers to pass on to triers or auditors, while Commons bills were to go to the Clerk of the Parliament. By the fifteenth century private *petitions* had become private *bills* in the modern sense of the term. Such could be introduced at the will of the petitioner into either House, but there was evident preference for the Commons.

The issuance of ordinances, like the later "orders in council," sometimes offset or modified the effect of statutes temporarily. Only once did a king presume to annul a statute.[15] The *suspending power* — that is, declaring inoperative for a set period a statute or group of statutes — was not used in the Middle Ages. The *dispensing power* was frequently used. It consisted in the exemption of particular persons under special circumstances from the operation of a law. One useful aspect was the king's power to pardon. Sometimes the royal clemency was exercised with dangerous generosity, as in the comprehensive pardons attendant on coronations and jubilees or the blank pardons granted to favorites, checked by a law in Richard II's reign. If wisely used, pardons served to mitigate the harshness of the criminal law. By the fourteenth century it had become a rule of the common law that one convicted of manslaughter committed in self-defense or through misadventure (accident) might have his sentence suspended while he sought a pardon from the king.

More significant here is the dispensing power in the form of an exception — permission to an individual or group to do something *in spite of* or *notwithstanding (non obstante)* any law to the contrary. Both the idea and the phrase are believed to have been adopted by Henry III from the practice of the popes in issuing papal bulls. Most common

[15] See below, p. 97.

in our period were such as these: a grant of land to the Church in spite of the Statute of Mortmain (many such licenses were issued!); after the Act of Provisors became law, permission to place an alien ecclesiastic in an English benefice, notwithstanding the statute. Occasionally the exception related to crafts or commercial regulations, an anticipation of the monopolies and patents of the Tudors. But though it was admitted that the king, in certain cases, had a discretionary power to apply or not to apply statutes, he could not dispense with common right, nor change common law on his own authority.

Parliament sometimes specifically conceded the power in a statute, again attempted to exclude it, but the crown continued to exercise it. On the whole the dispensing power was accepted as a lawful and useful prerogative. Even the great Bill of Rights, 1689, ruled against it merely "as it hath been assumed and exercised of late."

Procedure: Clerks and Records

The Clerk of the Parliaments was really the Clerk of the Lords. His duties were to keep the *Rolls,* cause formal proclamations to be read, and to receive and read replies to the petitions of the Commons. The Commons came to have three officers, each in the pay of the Crown — the Speaker, the Clerk, and the Serjeant-at-Arms. Their clerk was the Under-clerk of the Parliaments, appointed and assigned to them by the Crown. His tasks were apparently to draft the Commons' petitions and their answers to the king's commands, and possibly to keep some record of attendance as a basis for the writs of expenses. The first known was a certain Robert de Melton, 1363.[16] The Serjeant-at-Arms, who dates at least from 1388, was an officer of the Crown lent to the Commons.

In modern times the Speaker is the able and experienced chairman of the House. Whatever his party affiliations at the time of his election, thenceforth he maintains an attitude of strict impartiality. The Commons must have had a *spokesman* from earliest times. His task at first has been compared not inaptly to that of the foreman of a jury — to collect their opinions and to declare the result in the name of the whole body. The first recorded reference to such a spokesman comes from the *Parliament Rolls* of 1343: "Then came the knights of the shires and the

[16] "The first appointment by letters patent of an 'under-clerk of the Parliaments,' as the Clerk of the Commons is still styled in his patent, was that of Robert de Melton in 1363. Like his superior, the under-clerk was a chancery clerk, but his emoluments and subsequent career were on a much more modest scale. . . . We know little of the duties of Commons Clerks before Tudor times." Mackenzie, p. 55.

commons and replied by Sir William Trussell." It was in the Good Parliament of 1376, as we shall see, that Sir Peter de la Mare emerges as the first Speaker about whom we have much information. From this time on the Speaker of nearly every parliament is known. Six knights, including Sir Peter, served in the office in the reign of Richard II, two each in two parliaments, and one in three.

As to freedom of access to the sovereign, each peer had the right individually as a counselor of the crown, a survival of the personal relationship of lord and vassal in the old feudal council. The Commons were represented collectively by their Speaker. Through him the king spoke to the Commons and the Commons to the king. It was important to be able to reach the king's ear to petition, to advise, or to remonstrate, to have their interests presented correctly, and a favorable construction put on their words.

From 1377 on the Clerk records on his *Rolls* the ceremony of the Commons presenting their Speaker to the king and Lords. It is tempting to see in his wording the progressive importance of the office. In the parliaments of 1377, 1378, 1380, 1381, and 1382, for instance, the knight chosen by the Commons is designated as their "spokesman" — literally, "he who has the words for the Commons." In 1393–1394, 1397, and 1399 he is their "speaker" or "common speaker," while in the first parliaments of Henry IV he is their "speaker and procurator in Parliament." [17]

The *protestation* made by the Speaker in the presence of the king and Lords is not yet the formal request of Tudor days for all the privileges. It is a request that a favorable construction be put upon the official utterance of the Commons through their Speaker, and a plea for a certain immunity for the spokesman himself in the exercise of his difficult role. It took real courage in those days to voice criticism or dissent. Evidently there was no precise formula as yet. The Clerk seems to be putting down as well as he can what was said on each occasion. After what he had suffered for his role in the Good Parliament, it is not surprising to find Sir Peter de la Mare, in 1377, declaring that what he has to say will not be of his own initiative, "but on the motion, assent and express wish of all the Commons there present." In 1378 Speaker Pickering makes his protestation "as well for himself as for the whole Commons of England there assembled." First, for the Commons, if he

[17] In the French of the *Rolls* these are respectively: *q'avoit les paroles de par la Commune; lour commune parlour;* and *lour parlour et procurator en Parlement.*

should say anything which "sounded as if it were to the prejudice, damage, slander, or hurt of the King or of his crown, or to the diminution of the honour and estate of the great Lords of the realm," it should be held for naught and as if it had never been said: "The Commons have no other wish but that the estate of our Lord the King and the rights of his crown be maintained and guarded in all points." More particularly for himself, though it must have advantaged the Commons, too, he asks that if through lack of discretion or otherwise he says "too much or too little," or anything that does not have the assent of his fellow members, it may be corrected by them before their departure, or when it pleases them.

In this period, as in the sixteenth century, parliamentary business was apt to move more smoothly with a Speaker acceptable to the king. It was the policy of Richard II, as old knights of the household died, to replace them, says Steel, by "new men of ability, daring and lack of scruple." Such were Sir John Bushy (who served as Speaker), Sir William Bagot, and Sir Henry Green, special links to coordinate Council, parliament, and court with the minor gentry of the countryside. As pictured in Shakespeare's *Richard II*, Bushy (Bussy in the *Parliament Rolls*) is a somewhat sinister figure, one of the three flatterers who have misled their king.

> Where doth the world thrust forth a vanity —
> So it be new, there's no respect how vile —
> That is not quickly buzz'd into his ears?

From Henry of Lancaster comes the scornful comment on

> Bushy, Bagot and their complices
> The caterpillars of the commonwealth
> Which I have sworn to weed and pluck away.

And directly: "You have misled a prince, a royal king."

Actually Bushy was probably a fairly diligent and adroit courtier knight. He was sheriff of Lincolnshire, 1383–1386. His parliamentary career was more notable than Chaucer's, for he sat for Lincolnshire in ten parliaments! [18] Such service was not a novelty in the family, for his father, Sir William Bushy, sat for the same shire in four parliaments between 1368 and 1380. Sir John had shown his shrewdness and ability by first serving the king's interests in his own shire. He was "employed

[18] Actually M.P. for Cambridge in 1388, for Lincolnshire in the parliaments of 1386, 1390 (two), 1391, 1393, 1394, 1395, and 1397 (two).

to direct municipal elections at Lincoln so that the 'contrary opinions' of the citizens of that city might be guided to choose mayor and bailiffs 'pleasing to God and good for the king,' and subsequently to appease the feud between the 'high and mighty persons' of Lincoln and the king's 'midling subjects'."

This power of managing men, thinks Professor Tout, may well have been what secured him, by royal favor, his position as Speaker, which he held in 1394, in the two parliaments of 1397, and possibly in 1395.[19] It was Bushy who, in September 1397, presented in full parliament, as suggestions emanating from the Commons, Richard's measures for the undoing of his political enemies, and secured their acceptance by acclamation. There was also the type of Speaker who was *persona grata* to both king and Commons, notably Sir Arnold Savage, of whom we shall hear more below.

Our contemporary sources of information on medieval parliaments are not as complete as could be wished. We have to wait until the Tudor period for the *Lords and Commons Journals* (1509 and 1547), and still later for the parliamentary diaries and news letters. Such unofficial sources as chronicles are of some value, especially as meetings of parliament begin to arouse public interest. There are political poems, bits of satire, and an occasional treatise.[20]

The two great official sources are the *Parliament Rolls* and the *Statute Roll*. The first is a brief narrative account of the session drawn up by the Clerk at its close. It records the time and place of meeting, the main business transacted, the taxes voted, the Commons' petitions with the royal answers, and occasionally the record of certain pleas (cases). The Clerk, as Clerk of the Lords, was not in a position to make more than occasional reference to the Commons; that is, when they were present in "full parliament." The under-clerk assigned to the Commons kept no official record. There was no set form for the *Rolls*. The earliest are incomplete, "an unsystematic putting together of odds and ends."[21] Those for the latter part of the fourteenth and early years of the fifteenth centuries are most vivid and instructive. They may include a description of the formal opening, quote the chancellor's address, de-

---

[19] The *Parliament Rolls* do not name the Speaker for 1395, but Tout suspects that Bushy served. At least we know he remained in England and did not accompany Richard to Ireland.

[20] See Chapter 6.

[21] See Note D at the end of this chapter.

scribe the Commons' presentation of their Speaker, and even record his speeches!

The *Statute Roll,* though more authoritative, was narrow in scope, recording only the text of enacted laws. It too was casual in its beginnings, and only gradually attained its formal status. From the reign of Edward I until the introduction of printing, private collections of statutes (little manuscript volumes, many of which have survived) were circulating among members of the legal profession. At first for official use, loose copies of statutes were kept in Exchequer and Chancery, but increasingly Chancery emerges as the home of the *Great Roll of the Statutes.* By 1340 this was recognized as authoritative.

Privileges

The conception of parliamentary privilege emerges in the late fourteenth century and is developed under the Lancastrian kings, though not yet in its modern form. Privileges are claimed and sometimes exercised, but not completely or formally recognized by the Crown. The peers had certain privileges not only as individuals but also as Lords of Parliament, but there was less need for protection in their case. For the Commons three privileges are of special importance: (1) freedom of access to the king through their Speaker, (2) freedom from arrest and protection against assault, and (3) freedom of speech. Only in Elizabeth's reign did the Commons also claim the right to determine contested elections and the power to commit for *contempts,* i.e., breaches of privilege.

American readers not familiar with the term *parliamentary privilege* may nevertheless have read in their papers of some episode involving *legislative immunity* in Congress or their state legislature. They may recall the clause in the United States Constitution (Article I, section vi): "They [the senators and representatives] shall, in all cases except treason, felony, and breach of the peace, be privileged from arrest during their attendance at the session of their respective Houses, and in going to and returning from the same: and for any speech or debate in either House they shall not be questioned in any other place." This rule is the lineal descendant of the English privilege, coming by way of the thirteen colonies. In England immunity from arrest, except for treason, felony, or breach of the peace, was claimed for the members of both Houses, and also their servants, horses, and other property, not only during but forty days before and after the session. The horse and servant were not the mere luxuries of a gentleman, but necessities of travel and protection on the journey up to Westminster. There were still plenty of hazards, even on the king's highway.

Freedom from arrest was a natural corollary of the concept of the king's peace and royal safe conduct, essential for those whom *he* had summoned to *his* parliament. Though not embodied in any bill of rights or statute in the later Middle Ages, it was conceded by the king in individual cases and implicitly recognized in principle. Some historians give the impression that arrests were trumped up by the king or political opponents to exclude a bold or captious member. While this may have been true occasionally, we must remember that arrest was the process used for trespass and, in the fourteenth century, extended to debt. It takes the legal historian like Plucknett to remind us that what is involved is "the relief of members from certain lawful constraints to which the generality of the public were subject, *i.e.,* extra-judicial distress, and arrest by court process in civil litigation." There was a real problem here — the conflict between the claims of privilege and the rights of the subject seeking to recover debts or damages. It was recognized by the judges in Thorpe's case: "Ther be many and diverse Supersedeas of Privelegge of Parlement brought in to the Courtes, but there ys no general Supersedeas brought to surcesse of all processes; for if ther shuld be, it shuld seeme that this high Court of Parlement, that ministreth all Justice and equitee, shuld lette [check] the processe of the commune lawe, and so it shuld put the partie compleynaunt withoute remedie, for so much as actions atte commune lawe be not determined in this high Court of Parlement."

The procedure was for members to be released either by a special act of parliament or by a writ of privilege issued by the chancellor. There are extant records of several individual cases, all dating from the fifteenth century.[22]

"In the history of Parliamentary liberties freedom of speech," says Notestein, "makes about the longest story. One of the first rights assumed, it was almost the last important right to be won." As late as 1689 it had to be reaffirmed in the Bill of Rights.[23] Under Edward III, says Elsynge, the Commons "did oftentimes discuss and debate amongst

[22] See Chapter 6.
[23] "That the freedom of speech, and debates or proceedings in parliament, ought not to be impeached or questioned in any court or place out of parliament."

themselves many things concerning the king's prerogative and agreed upon petitions for laws to be made directly against his prerogative, as may appear by divers of the said petitions, yet they were never interrupted in their consultations, nor received check for the same, as may appear also by the answers to the said petitions." Written in the seventeenth century, this presents too rosy a picture, yet it has an element of truth for much of that reign, owing to the relative harmony between Edward III and his parliament. Friction was sure to arise over the misgovernment at home and failure abroad in the old king's dotage, and then in the minority and ultimate despotism of his grandson.

The issue over freedom of speech appears in various forms. Besides the aspect of access through the Speaker, discussed above, there are (1) the scope of parliamentary business — the subjects with which the Commons may deal — and (2) freedom of debate.

As to the first, must the Commons keep to the royal agenda, the program laid before them by the King and Council at the beginning of the session? Such a rule would have nullified the use of petition as a means of initiation. In fact, Professor Notestein has aptly called this aspect of the Commons' long struggle "the winning of the initiative." This was one of the questions which Richard II put to his judges in 1387, and to which he received the answer he sought.

Had parliament a right, he asked, when the king had assigned certain subjects for discussion, to neglect those matters and deal with others? No, ruled the judges. This opinion was rejected next year by the Lords Appellant, reaffirmed by Richard in 1397, and finally repudiated at the beginning of Henry IV's reign. Never again did a ruler impose such complete limitations on his Commons. King and Council did on occasion monopolize the time of the Houses with official business, or warn the Commons away from certain subjects, such as matters of state.

The second question is the one that most readily comes to mind: Was it possible for members to debate freely among themselves without fear of reprisals should bold speaking give offense to King or Lords? Here reproof or even arrest might be justified on the grounds that the words or sentiments were treasonable. However, there were plenty of ways short of arrest and imprisonment by which a monarch or great lord could visit displeasure on a commoner or his constituents.

The striking cases of Peter de la Mare, Thomas Haxey, and Sir Thomas Yonge all occurred in novel circumstances, in times of strain and stress.[24] Perhaps for this reason they have been minimized by cautious scholars, yet each did lead to conscious definition of the privilege, and remained as precious precedents for later generations.

At the risk of offending those who claim to "have laid the ghost of Haxey," it is maintained that his case merits some attention here. Haxey was one of the victims of Richard's *coup d'état*. It was in the parliament of January 1397 that the Commons, just as the king with the help of Speaker Bushy seemed to have won them to the support of his French alliance, presented to the Lords a petition under four heads. The first three dealt with administrative grievances of a routine sort. The fourth, "couched in uncourtier-like language," boldly criticized the king's costly entourage: "That the excessive charge of the king's household should be diminished to wit, of the multitude of bishops, who have lordships, and with their retinue are supported by the king; and also of many ladies and their attendants who dwell in the palace of the king and at his cost." When it was learned that the bill had been handed in by one Thomas Haxey, the Commons in "full parliament" apologized. King and Lords condemned Haxey as a traitor, though as a "clerk" he was released to the Archbishop of Canterbury, eventually pardoned, and restored to some of his pluralities.

Haxey was long a puzzle to historians. What was a *clerk* doing in the Commons? Was he a clerical proctor, an isolated survival of the representative clergy in parliament? It is now clear that Haxey was not a member of the Commons at all, but had merely presented his bill for their sponsorship. Actually he was a senior civil servant of fifteen years' standing, preferred through royal favor, and at this time Keeper of the Rolls in the Court of Common Pleas. No wonder Richard was angered by criticism from such a source.

The judgment was reversed in Henry IV's first parliament. It has been pointed out that the reversal was based on the unfair procedure against Haxey and the dangerous expansion of the law of treason, not on the threat to the liberties of the Commons. There are two versions of Haxey's petition, one concerned exclusively with the misjudgment, the other with clauses significant for the Commons who had sponsored

[24] Peter de la Mare was imprisoned by the "reactionaries" whom he had offended, John of Gaunt and the courtier clique, and released when his friends regained influence. Haxey, condemned as a traitor by Richard II, was pardoned by Henry IV. Thomas Yonge offended the Lancastrians only to be rescued by the Yorkists whom he had supported. See Chapter 6.

his bill, such as the concluding ". . . as well for the enforcement of right as for the salvation of the liberties of the said commons." [25]

NOTE A. THE TITLE OF HENRY IV

Justice William Thirning, for himself, his co-proctors, and all the "estates and people," named 6 proctors for these estates; archbishops and bishops; abbots, priors, and all other men of Holy Church, secular and regular; dukes and earls; barons and bannerets; "bachelors and commons of this Land by south," and bachelors and commons "by north." When on the following Monday, parliament met in response to writs issued by Henry September 30, the Archbishop intimated that until that moment no lawful parliament had met, since Richard's summons was nullified by his abdication.

Some recent historians have defied tradition by denying that Henry IV had a *parliamentary* title. They point out that in the official Lancastrian account in the *Rolls* it is always the *estates,* not *parliament,* that is said to act. For instance, Professor Gaillard Lapsley maintains that the old view needs considerable revision: "To that end, I suggest, that our evidence is best interpreted by supposing that Henry could have had a complete and technically correct parliamentary title, that his supporters intended that the revolution should be accomplished in that way, and that Henry by a *coup de main* at the last moment was able to obtain the Crown on the grounds of conquest, inheritance, and some loose form of acceptance." *English Historical Review,* XLIX (1934), 423–449, 577–606.

Professor Chrimes is content with a more moderate re-evaluation: "It is possible that Henry was, in lieu of the parliamentary sanction, craftily using the idea of the estates for his own purposes. But more probably the reiterated use of the term 'estate' throughout the episode was not due to any very deliberate forethought. It was the natural word to spring to mind in describing the groups of persons there gathered. No great subtlety was needed for such a use; but the usage certainly had its consequences. It clearly made current a notion that the estates of the realm, though not assembled and operating in the ordinary legal form of parliament, could nevertheless perform the important constitutional functions involved in the occasion. There could be no doubt henceforth that the estates of the realm authorized the substitution of one monarch for another." *English Constitutional Ideas,* pp. 114–115.

NOTE B. TAXES

In 1332 cities and boroughs were accorded the right to pay the *aid* instead of the more arbitrary *tallage.* The rate was set at a *tenth* from

---

[25] Earlier in the petition also we read: ". . . on account of which bill, at the desire of the said king, the said Thomas was adjudged traitor and forfeited everything that he had, in violation of right and of usage that had hitherto prevailed in parliament

the urban and a *fifteenth* from the rural population. After 1334 the amount raised in that year, roughly £38,000, became the standard, that is, what the government might expect to collect on such a grant. For convenience it was the practice to assign a definite sum to local units — township, village, and borough. "Eventually some of these charges came to be attached to certain parcels of land, and the tax became virtually a real property one."

The authorized customs rate was "half a mark from each sack of wool and half a mark from each three hundred woolfels [sheepskin] which make a sack and a mark from each last of hides [bundle of 200 cowhides] that issue from the realm as well in Ireland and Wales as in England."

The *new custom* of 1303 imposed 2s. per tun on imported wine and 3d. per £ value on most other imports and many exports. In 1373, as *tunnage and poundage,* the rate was 2s. per tun on imported wine and 6d. per £ on general merchandise imported or exported (exclusive of wool etc. which had its own rates). In this period *subsidy* was applied to an increase in the customs. Only in the Tudor period was it commonly used to denote the direct tax of the *tenth and fifteenth.*

NOTE C. LEGISLATION

Our knowledge of the role of the Commons in legislation was enriched by the publication in 1932 of the researches of Professor H. L. Gray. While making full use of the *Parliament* and *Statute Rolls,* he went back of these to the original petitions and bills, so many of which have been preserved in the Record Office. His findings throw light on the various technical steps in legislation, such as the successive readings, amendments, and the relations of Lords and Commons. Actually he proceeds in reverse, starting with the fuller evidence of the *Lords Journals* of 1509 and then back to earlier periods. Gray concludes that between about 1350 and 1423 the Commons' petitions were the main basis for legislation, modified, of course by the responses of the king and Lords. Critics maintain that he has exaggerated the role of the Commons, pointing out that many measures seeming to be based on Commons' petitions were really prompted from above. But, as Lapsley well puts it, reviewing Professor Gray's book: "Surely, the vital point is not the extent to which the Commons initiated legislation, but their constitutional position as forming an indispensable part of the parliament whose authority was essential to the enactment of a statute."

NOTE D. THE PARLIAMENT ROLLS AND STATUTE ROLL

The first good narrative of a session, with short, dated minutes of proceedings day by day, is that of the Lincoln Parliament of 1316, com-

---

and to the undoing of the customs of the commons . . ." Two versions of the petition are included in the Roll. The phrases in italics are added in the second version. — Stephenson and Marcham, pp. 256–257; *Rot. Parl.,* III.

piled by William Armyn, Chancery clerk. There is a similar good record for a parliament of 1332, included in a roll for six sessions 1330–1333; a continuous roll for parliaments of the years 1339–1355 and 1362–1377. The set of printed *Rolls (Rotuli Parliamentorum)*, 6 volumes, contain a number of items included by the editors, not part of the manuscript roll.

For the statutes Richardson and Sayles have worked out an ingenious analysis of the evolution of the official roll. Already, in the early years of Edward I's reign, they surmise, *statute* "must have become a common word upon lawyers' lips; and, a certain sign of its popularity, it was beginning to be applied retrospectively . . . all the major enactments of Edward I were cited in Court very speedily after their issue." Their study of the manuscript roll seems to indicate a "strict contemporaneity" of the entries at least from 1299. Oddly enough, these scholars conclude that the original basis of this roll was not the collection of authentic texts preserved in Chancery, but "a private collection of statutes such as was circulating among the legal profession in the thirteenth century." In the reign of Edward III, perhaps by 1340, just as parliament was acquiring responsibility for law-making, so was Chancery for official recording, and its roll now became one of authority. The Parliament Roll for the mid-Lent session of 1340 includes directions for the enrolling in Chancery of the statutes, those "points and articles which are to be permanent" (*les points et les articles qi sont perpetuels*), and for putting into letters patent other matters of a temporary nature. That the authoritative character of the Roll was recognized is apparent when it appears that henceforth the early relationship was reversed: any judge or lawyer would seek assurance that his private unofficial volume of statutes had been collated with the Roll. — "The Early Statutes," *Law Quarterly Review*, L (1934), 201–223, 547–571.

V

Parliament at Work: Actual Sessions

❁❁❁

IN AN age of such tremendous energies, long swords, and short tempers, it is surprising that parliaments functioned as smoothly as they did. Even in Elizabeth's reign, members were warned not to wear their spurs in the House. In the Lincoln Parliament of 1316 at a full session in the cathedral and in the presence of the king, Sir John Ros and the younger Hugh le Despenser passed from hot words to blows with sword and fist "in contempt of the Lord King . . . and in breach of the peace, and terror of the people in the said parliament." But trouble might come from outside, the turbulent populace of London and Westminster, curious onlookers, or mischievous prentice lads. Hence it became customary from 1328 on to read a proclamation forbidding the carrying of arms, including swords, long knives, or other suspected weapons, in or near the Palace of Westminster or in the City of London and suburbs, except for officials assigned to keep the peace. Yet it was "not the intention of our lord the King, that each earl and baron can not have his sword carried with him, except when actually in the presence of the King, or in the council chamber." Furthermore, children were not to play at "bars" or other games, nor knock off people's hats, nor touch hand to them, nor make any other hindrance by which anyone cannot peaceably pursue his affairs.

Parliaments were not always held at Westminster. Within the years 1274 to 1338 an incomplete list shows thirty-three at Westminster, two at London, and twenty-five elsewhere, including such notable cathedral towns as Winchester, Salisbury, Lincoln, and York. At Lincoln in 1316, formal sessions were held in the great cathedral, while for other occasions the chapter house or the hall of the dean's hospice served. It was trouble with the Scots in the 1330's that brought to the north, York, not only meetings of parliament, but the court with Chancery, Common Bench, and Exchequer as well. The return to Westminster was complete and permanent (with rare exceptions) about 1339. It was the Hundred Years War, suggests Professor Tout, which "finally secured for Westminster the permanent position of 'capital' of England." While military strength lay in the north, financial resources were in the southern counties.

Today Westminster is a part of greater London. One can go from St. Paul's to the Abbey in a few minutes by bus or tram, as many a tourist may recall. In the fourteenth century Westminster was a separate community, clustering around its Abbey and its Hall, two miles from London. "Westminster had become the recognized center of royal administration, law and Parliament, although it had no commerce and no municipal privileges of its own, and was only a village at great London's gate. There was no royal foothold inside the English capital corresponding to the Louvre in Paris. When the King came up to town, he lived sometimes at Westminster on one side of London, sometimes in the Tower on the other." [1]

It was William Rufus who had built on the south side of Old Palace Yard a great banquet hall. It remained for Richard II to have two feet added to the height of the stone walls and to cover the whole with a superb Gothic roof (built by Hugh Herland, his master-carpenter), made of great oak beams supported by springing arches. The Hall, the only surviving part of the old Westminster Palace, measures 240 feet in length from north to south, and 68 feet in width from west to east. It has been the scene of many famous events, ranging from the festivity of coronation banquets and national rejoicings, such as the victory of Agincourt, to the tragedy of treason trials and impeachments, and even the trial and death sentence of a monarch, King Charles I.

For our purpose, it is increasingly the meeting place of parliament — "full parliament" — in its formal opening and closing sessions at least. For the various separate sessions of the estates other rooms of the Palace to the south of the Hall served — the Painted Chamber, the White Chamber, and the Little Hall. We have little information as to the meeting place of the Commons in early days. In 1352 they were defi-

[1] Trevelyan, *English Social History*, pp. 31–32.

nitely assigned the chapter house of Westminster Abbey, and by 1376 this was referred to as their "ancient" and "accustomed" meeting place. After about 1395 the refectory of the Abbey seems to have replaced the chapter house. Only in 1547 was the Chapel of St. Stephen's within the Palace assigned to the Commons to be their "house" for nearly three hundred years until it was destroyed by fire in 1834.

The opening address was comparable in a way to the modern Speech from the Throne. Professor Pollard suggests that "the somewhat monotonous series of addresses with which parliaments were opened in the middle ages played no small part in the slow education of the Commons in the sense of political responsibility." While some were routine, others were eloquent, even dramatic. As we might expect with a bishop chancellor, the "cause of the summons" was often preceded by a short sermon. Thanks to the zeal of the Clerk, the texts of many such sermons have been preserved. Professor Chrimes quotes forty-one Latin texts culled from the *Rolls,* with the dates of the parliaments in which they were used!

In the jubilee year of Edward III, Chancellor Adam Houghton assumes a tone of loyal enthusiasm and gracious praise of the royal family: "Behold, Lords, whether there was ever Christian King or Lord that had so noble and gracious a lady to wife, and such sons as our Lord the King has had, both Princes, Dukes, and others. For of the King and his sons all Christian peoples have had fear, and by them the Realm of England has been most nobly amended, honoured, and enriched, more than in the time of any other King. . . . But if we his subjects desire and will to prosper in his grace in this year of Jubilee, and to take comfort from him who is the Vessel of Grace or chosen Vassal of God, needs must that we set ourselves in all virtue to receive that grace and to flee all wrongdoing." [2]

In Henry IV's second parliament, the emphasis is on orthodoxy, and on the good intentions of the new sovereign to fulfill his coronation oath to the letter. Later in the century political theory and philosophy are introduced, as in 1467: "It was shewed [runs the report] by the Kyngs commaundement and in his name by the mouth of the Ryght Reverent Fader in God, the Bysshop of Bathe and Welles, Chaunceller of Englond, unto the seid Lordes and Commons, that Justice was grounde well and rote of all prosperite, peas and pollityke rule of every Reame, whereuppon all the Lawes of the world been grounde and sette,

[2] Joliffe, p. 409.

which resteth in thre; that is to say, the Lawe of God, Law of Nature, and posityfe Lawe; and by seying of all Philosophers, felicite or peas in every Reame is evermore caused of Justice, as it appereth by proba-bill persuasions of Philosofers. Wherfore first be asked, what is Jus-tice? . . ."[3] And so on with practical applications of his definition of justice.

Harmony and cooperation between Lords and Commons appeared not only in times of crisis, but in routine business. The four statutes of the spring parliament of 1340 were drawn up by a committee of bishops, barons, knights, and burgesses, led by the Archbishop of Canterbury. Occasionally the Commons in their chapter house were visited by a committee of Lords now at the king's initiative, again at the Commons' importunity. Parliaments, like the early Great Councils, continued to have their social side: special festivities such as characterized the con-ferring of titles on the king's sons in 1362 to be described below, and the concluding feasts which Professor Tout assumes were a regular thing. An extract from a memoranda roll of 1312 orders payment to the king's butler for wine for the autumn parliament at Westminster. A chronicler describes "the great and excellent feast held in the name of our lord the king and several great lords of the realm" in 1376.

For purposes of illustration four actual parliaments will be described in the following pages. Those of 1341 and 1376 come in time of crisis, occasions on which the Lords in the first instance and the Commons in the second interfered with boldness in matters of administration. The others, 1362 and 1401, are of the routine type, by far the more common, though not without some novelty.

1341. Crisis and Conciliation

To understand the Easter Parliament of 1341 we must rehearse the events of previous months. The whole makes a dramatic story. In the fall of 1340 King Edward, on failing to receive expected money and supplies for the prosecution of the war, had reluctantly concluded a truce, then secretly left Ghent, where his allies fairly held him hostage. He took ship from Sluys, and after a stormy crossing of three days and nights, sailed up the Thames to arrive before cockcrow (the night of St. Andrew's Day) at the water-gate of the Tower. Then followed by torch-light the summoning of frightened scapegoat ministers and immediate dismissals and arrests.

[3] Chrimes, pp. 121–122.

The chancellor and the treasurer, both bishops, were dismissed from office, but escaped imprisonment. Others not so fortunate were five clerks, three leading merchants, and such lay ministers as the warden of the Tower, the keeper of the Channel Isles, and several judges. In January three justices were commissioned to arraign these officials at the king's suit. This meant, in some instances, that commissioners were to sit in judgment on peers and on members of the clergy. It was a quarrel, as one of the chroniclers tells us, "between the King and his confidants and the ministers serving in the great offices."

But the royal wrath did not stop with central government officials. All the escheators and most of the sheriffs were dismissed, and writs issued for the election of new coroners. To the dismay of the citizens a general eyre was to sit at the Tower of London. Sixteen commissions (one for each of a group of shires), armed with special powers, were sent out to hear and determine "oppressions and extortions" by the king's ministers. But the remedy proved worse than the disease. The strong-arm methods of such commissioners were sure to evoke bitter protests. They did not follow due process of law — the famous "law-of-the-land" clause of Magna Carta. They prosecuted on mere rumor and common fame without the safeguard of the grand jury. They imposed exorbitant fines, not in accordance with the gravity of the offense.

It was no less a person than the great Archbishop of Canterbury John de Stratford, chief of the recent Council of Regency, who became leader of the opposition. He successfully eluded the king by taking refuge in his own church of Canterbury, where he remained until his appearance at the parliament in April. He was accused of misdemeanors in office, in particular that he had assumed responsibility for the war with France, then failed to make good with the necessary money and supplies. Later he was charged with having "traitorously" stirred up the people against their king. Indeed, he proved a master of propaganda. By means of sermons, letters to the king and Council, letters to his diocesan clergy, and sentence of excommunication, he became the spokesman of clerk and layman, peer and commoner, in a real constitutional struggle.[4]

He, too, had a sense of the dramatic. He waited until the holy day of his famous predecessor Becket (December 29, St. Thomas's Day) for his first public pronouncement. After celebrating mass, he preached a ser-

---

[4] For himself Stratford asked trial by peers to the extent of investigation in parliament of his official conduct. He maintained the traditional attitude of the clergy in regard to more serious charges.

mon in praise of the martyr who in his days had not feared the prince (his text, *in diebus suis non timuit principem*), and proclaimed his own intent henceforth to champion the rights of the Church.

He was rewarded when in the Easter Parliament clergy, barons, and Commons rallied to his cause, against the king and his courtiers. The temper of this parliament suggests that of Charles I's parliament of 1628. Just as many a member of that body had recently suffered in person or seen his neighbors suffer from forced loans and arbitrary arrests, so many now present had felt or seen the heavy hand of the commissioners.

For nearly a week the king, by means of two of the Household officials, excluded the archbishop and two of the bishops from taking their seats. Professor Tout has paraphrased for us the chronicler's dramatic story of the outcome:

"The second week of the session had begun. A 'full parliament' was assembled, with the king on his throne, presiding over the general gathering, but Stratford was still kept out of his seat. A representative of the ancient houses, earl Warenne, had marked with disgust the absence of the three bishops and the presence of such men as Parving, Stafford, Kilsby, Darcy and others [royal clerks] 'not worthy to sit in parliament.' . . .

" 'Sir king,' he cried, 'how goes this parliament? Parliaments were not wont to be like this. For here those who should be foremost are shut out, while there sit other men of low rank who have no business to be here. Such right belongs only to the peers of the land. Sir king, think of this.'

" 'Then John Darcy quietly got up and went out, and was followed by Kilsby and the rest without a word.' In this silent abdication of their seats, the servants of the household abandoned the struggle. Other magnates associated themselves with Warenne's request, and the earl of Arundel demanded from the king the immediate admission of the archbishop. Edward could no longer resist, and granted what was asked."

Not long after, a personal reconciliation took place in full parliament in the Painted Chamber. As reported by the Clerk: "And the said archbishop humbled himself before the lord king and besought his favour, and the king received him back into his goodwill."

Each of the estates, clergy, magnates, and Commons drew up a group of petitions, conditions for grants of supply. From the point of view of parliamentary history three demands are of special interest: (1) The Lords asked assurance of trial of peers by peers, extending to alleged misconduct in office. (2) Both Lords and Commons asked that ministers and judges be appointed in parliament and sworn to observe Magna Carta and other statutes, a hint of ministerial responsibility. (3) They requested that auditors be appointed to inquire into the accounts of those who had handled the war funds. The king conceded only that as certain offices became vacant he would appoint "with the advice of magnates and councillors near at hand." These would be sworn in at the next parliament, and in each successive parliament be held responsible to answer complaints against them. With some modification as to appointments, these were embodied in the famous but short-lived statute of 15 Edward III. It is disconcerting to discover that this was the act which Edward presently presumed to repeal.[5] Nevertheless the results of this dramatic parliament were not altogether negligible. The young king had learned his lesson, and was usually willing to make concessions. There followed years of relative harmony, a policy of live and let live. The barons did not press their claims too far. The great ministers of state and the household officials effected a degree of governmental division of labor and cooperation.

1362. Peace and Pageantry

An attractive parliament, routine but not colorless, was that which met in the fall of 1362 (October 13 to November 17), the first important session since the conclusion of peace with France. The Treaty of Calais inaugurated a decade of "peace, retrenchment and reform" during which the harmony of curials and magnates continued. True, there was some difference in point of view. Lords and Commons felt that now peace was made, the king should again "live of his own." Officials were aware of war debts to be paid, and the king was concerned about house-

---

[5] The act of repeal by which parliament later supported the king's action (17 Edward III) contained the proviso, "because some articles are comprised in the same statute which are reasonable, and in accordance with law and reason," that "of such articles and others agreed on in this Parliament there be made a statute anew, by the advice of the justices and other learned men, and kept for ever." No such act was made. Magna Carta remained the only "statutory" basis for trial by peers. Although the claim as to trial for misdemeanors was lost, somewhat the same end was effected by impeachment later.

holds to be set up for his children. The ransom of French King John helped temporarily, and a subsidy was conceded.[6]

There was novelty in the hint of patriotism, of emphasis on things English, even British. This appeared at the outset in the opening address delivered by Sir Henry Green, C.J., *in English* (though the Clerk recorded it in the usual French), urging the use of English in the royal courts. Further, there was a new arrangement for the handling of petitions. For the first time were assigned to one group of receivers all petitions coming from any part of the British Isles — "England, Ireland, Wales and Scotland" — and to another group those of "Aquitaine and other lands and islands beyond the sea."[7]

Even more than usual the Commons' petitions dealt with administrative grievances: the ever recurring abuses of purveyance, excessive demands of escheators, encroachments of mayors of the Staple, defining of the duties of justices of laborers and of the peace. The whole administration was passed in review, and promises were secured of amendment.

Of the twenty-four articles of the Commons' petitions, fifteen became statutes.[8] Some of these are distinctive, even famous. There was an emphatic confirmation of Magna Carta, a reiteration of the rule for annual parliaments, and the institution of the useful and permanent Quarter Sessions for justices of the peace. The happy thought of the Commons to change the name *purveyor* to the hopefully suggestive one *buyer* was adopted. Provision was made for commissions — two "good and loyal men" of each shire with a third from the king's Household — "to inquire of buyers and takers," and enforce rules. Purveyance of victuals by a subject was declared felony. Finally reasons were declared "why the laws should be pleaded in the English tongue":

"Item, because it is often showed to the king by the prelates, dukes, earls, barons, and all the commonalty, of the great mischiefs which have happened to divers of the realm, because the laws, customs, and statutes of this realm be not commonly known in the same realm, for that they be pleaded, showed, and judged in the French tongue, which is much unknown in the said realm; so that the people which do implead, or be impleaded, in the king's court, and in the courts of other

[6] Twenty s. per sack of wool and per 300 woolfels, and 40s. per last of hides for 3 years.

[7] The previous division was between English and non-English petitions, Wales, Scotland, and Ireland being grouped with "the lands from beyond the sea."

[8] Five of these, numbers 2 through 6, relate to some aspect of purveyance.

have no knowledge nor understanding of that which is said for them or against them by their sergeants and other pleaders; and that reasonably the said laws and customs shall be the more soon learned and known, and better understood in the tongue used in the said realm, and by so much every man of the said realm may the better govern himself without offending of the law, and the better keep, save, and defend his heritage and possessions . . ."

There was a touch of glamor and festivity in the conferring of titles upon the king's sons. Few kings could boast of such a family, yet by the irony of fate, not one was to wear the crown! Marriages with English heiresses had already provided landed estates. For the Prince of Wales it was a veritable love match with Joan of Kent, but as heiress of the king's uncle, Edmund of Woodstock, she brought with her the estates of an English earldom. For Lionel it was a marriage with the heiress of Ulster, and for John of Gaunt, Blanche of Lancaster. With the approval of some of the Lords, Edward chose the closing days of this parliament as the fitting occasion and scene for the conferring of titles. In full parliament of Lords and Commons the chancellor explained the king's pleasure — to do honor to the sons with which heaven had blessed him. The Prince of Wales was created Prince of Aquitaine; Lionel, Duke of Clarence; John, Duke of Lancaster; and Edmund, Earl of Cambridge. Then followed by the king's own hand the girding with the sword, the giving of "charters" of creation, and for John as Duke the conferring of the cap of maintenance, circlet of gold, etc., all of which is duly recorded by the Clerk.

He concludes: "And then our Lord the King thanked the Lords and Commons for the great benefits which they often had shown and done him in their labors. And he gave permission to the said Commons to depart, except for some of the said Commons who were to remain for certain matters the King wanted to discuss with them. And so finished the Parliament."

1376. The Good Parliament

The "Good Parliament" was so called by contemporaries because of its valiant attempt at reforms, short-lived though these proved to be.[9]

[9] *De parliamento facto Londoniis quod bonum a pluribus vocatur* (the parliament held at London which is called good by many), *Chronicon Angliae*, p. 68. *Parliamentum quod bonum merito vocabatur* (the parliament which was rightly called good), Walsingham's *Chronicle*, I, 324.

It is included here rather because we know so much about it, especially the role of the Commons, and because it marks the first use of impeachment. The session was unusually long for those days, lasting from April 28 to July 6, ten full weeks. There was a large attendance: the four princes, two archbishops, fourteen bishops, and many abbots and priors; the earls of March, Arundel, Salisbury, Warwick, Suffolk, and Stafford, with "all the barons and bannerets of worth in the land," and "two hundred and four score knights and esquires, citizens and burgesses, for the commons of divers cities, boroughs and shires."

The unusually complete and detailed contemporary accounts reflect the importance of the session and the interest it aroused. Besides the Clerk's record, which covers nearly sixty pages in the printed *Rolls,* there are two remarkable chronicles. The *Chronicon Angliae* comes from St. Albans, the monastery on the great north road some miles from London, and noted for its chroniclers. Its tone is prejudiced in favor of the popular cause, but on the whole it agrees with the official record, and also gives interesting sidelights on personalities and episodes. The *Anonimalle* (Anonymous) *Chronicle* comes from St. Mary's York, a Benedictine abbey. It is believed that the account of the Good Parliament was lifted by the compiler from the report of someone who was an eyewitness, or at least in close touch with the events he records. He is acquainted not only with procedure in "full parliament," but with that of the Commons apart in the chapter house, and gives for the first time a circumstantial report of the debates.[10]

Though the situation has not been so honored, it was dramatic enough for a play by Shakespeare or a novel by Scott. Affairs were going badly at home and abroad. After his futile attempt to return to France in 1372 Edward III fell into sedentary habits. Windsor castle was his usual residence, with occasional excursions to nearby royal manors, rarely to Westminster. The seriousness of the old king's condition was evidenced by the fact that his physicians came to be in constant attendance. Meetings of the Council were generally held at Westminster without the king.

Administration had fared badly under the direction of the king's second son, the ambitious Duke of Lancaster, who unfortunately allied with the most unscrupulous of the curialist element — Sir John Neville,

[10] The editor, Professor Galbraith, is sure the writer was an eyewitness of the events in the Parliament House; not so sure as to his presence with the Commons in the chapter house.

the steward; William Latimer, acting chamberlain since 1371; and their accomplices. Last but not least, there was Alice Perrers, one of the ladies of Queen Philippa's household, who had taken the king's fancy even before the queen's death in 1369, and who continued to exercise influence over him for the rest of his life. As late as 1374 the king had held a great tournament at Smithfield at which Alice appeared as "the Lady of the Sun." Unfortunately she did not confine her charm to such festive occasions, but took her seat on the judges' bench and "maintained" (supported) her friends in their suits. The Commons were presently to charge that "a certain lady" was receiving two or three thousand pounds a year from the king's treasury. Even the elements seemed to conspire to ill ends, what with bad harvests, high prices, a murrain of cattle, and in 1374 and 1375, local recurrences of the black death.

But now to turn to the heroes of our tale, the leaders of the popular opposition. These included the two households nearest to the throne. Foremost, of course, was that of the Black Prince, who lay ill at Sheen; his wife, the beloved Joan of Kent; and little Prince Richard. The other was the household of the Earl of March, whose son by Philippa, daughter of Lionel of Clarence, was next heir after Richard. Amongst the prelates and magnates hostile to John of Gaunt were several whom we shall meet presently as members of the Lords committee named by the Commons.

The real hero was to be Sir Peter de la Mare, a knight from the march of Wales. Some would have us believe that it was by design that the first two known speakers were stewards of great lords — Peter de la Mare of the Earl of March and Thomas Hungerford of the Duke of Lancaster: the managers of the Commons on behalf of their masters in the Lords. Even so, it is cooperation rather than coercion that should be stressed. Lords and Commons shared many of the same grievances. It was sometimes connections of this sort that enabled them to work effectively together.[11]

Sir Peter has evoked enthusiastic support from both contemporary and modern writers. No student deeply versed in the sources of the

[11] "The Good Parliament . . . represents in fact the temporary triumph over Gaunt and his faction of a rival coalition consisting of the church party, the magnates jealous of Gaunt, and especially, the two households nearest to the throne. These were those of the dying Black Prince and the Earl of March, whose son by Philippa, daughter of Lionel of Clarence, must have been widely held to be the next heir after Richard of Bordeaux. Yet this coalition could hardly have effected much without the sudden, violent and unexpected encouragement of the commons." Steel, pp. 23–24.

period has seen fit to minimize his talents and leadership. As lord of the manor of Yatton in Herefordshire, he was vassal as well as steward of the earl. One modern admirer of Sir Peter's has gone so far as to suggest that in such a relationship, as between the inexperienced young earl and his mature and capable steward, the latter was probably the better man of the two. The St. Albans chronicler describes him "as one whom God had endowed with profound wisdom, boldness in utterance of his opinions, and more than common eloquence." It "has been suggested, but without proof, that the very favorable character which he there receives may have been due not only to political sympathy, but also to a relationship with Thomas de la Mare, the Abbot of that house" (*D.N.B.*). But this same chronicler gives ample testimony of Sir Peter's popularity with the Londoners. During a tumult in the city protesting the policy of Lancaster, a priest "who dared to utter abusive language of the popular speaker was so roughly handled that he died of his wounds." Again, when on the accession of Richard Sir Peter was set at liberty from his political imprisonment, he was welcomed by the Londoners "with special demonstrations of joy," not less, says the chronicler, "than those with which they hailed Becket's return from exile." Verses were composed in his honor. His parliamentary career did not terminate with 1376. In the October parliament of 1 Richard II, as knight for Hereford, he again served as speaker, and he also sat for the same shire in five successive parliaments, 1380–1383 (3–6 Richard II). As we shall see, the best testimony comes from the account in the *Anonimalle Chronicle*, by one who evidently saw him in action.

King Edward was present in person for a few days, but soon left the Duke of Lancaster as his lieutenant in dealing with the estates. Sir John Knyvett, one of the few instances of a lay chancellor, set forth three "causes for the summons," to provide for (1) the good governance and peace of the realm; (2) defense as well by land as by sea against enemies, "of which there were a great plenty"; and (3) continuance of the war with France and other enemies. The next day the Lords went as usual to the White Chamber, the Commons to the chapter house of the Abbey, which the chronicler now calls their "ancient place of meeting."

The program of reform that was worked out did not attack the king, nor find fault with government departments and offices as such. It secured removal of the miscreant Household officials and their agents, and the afforcement of the Council by three bishops, three earls, and three barons, "to be constantly at hand so that no business of weight should be dispatched without the assent and advice of all." The Commons, says Tout, drew up and presented at the close of the session "the most comprehensive series of petitions that ever a medieval parliament presented to its king." These petitions (141 items) included a great variety of matters, most of which look to enforcement of existing law rather than new legislation.

Many have a familiar ring, such as the request for annual parliaments and the appointment of sheriffs for one year only. More novel is the suggestion that justices of the peace be elected for each county by the lords and knights in parliament, sworn before the Council, and removable only with parliament's consent. Characteristically, the northern counties are suffering from storms, famine, and the Scots, and to make matters worse, purveyors are not paying enough for sheep. Cities and boroughs unite in a vigorous protest against the free-trade concessions to merchant strangers and demand that their liberties be observed as guaranteed by Magna Carta. The supply of that most essential of foodstuffs, fish, is endangered — people with manors along river banks are actually taking fry of salmon to feed their pigs! The commons of several shires (nine are named) complain of the scarcity and dearness of herring due to the monopoly accorded the fisherfolk of Great Yarmouth in their herring fair.

Usually when the Commons retire to the chapter house, "in which they could take their counsel privately without disturbance or vexation from other people," the historian, too, is excluded. But now, thanks to the remarkable *Anonimalle Chronicle,* he can almost fancy that he is sitting in a reporter's gallery, for we read:

"And on the said second day all the knights and commons aforesaid assembled and went into the chapter house and seated themselves about [the room] one next another. And they began to talk about their business, the matters before the parliament, saying that it would be well at the outset for them to be sworn to each other to keep counsel regarding what was spoken and decided among them, and loyally and without concealment to deliberate and ordain for the benefit of the kingdom. And to do this all unanimously agreed, and they took a good oath to be loyal to each other. Then one of them said that, if any of us knew of anything to say for the benefit of the king and the kingdom, it would be well for him to set forth among us what he knew and then, one after the other [each of the rest could say] what lay next his heart.

"Thereupon a knight of the south country rose and went to the reading desk in the centre of the chapter house so that all might hear and, pounding on the said desk, began to speak in this fashion: '*Jube domine benedicere, etc.* My lords, you have heard the grievous matters before the parliament . . .'"[12]

The grievous matters he then set forth included the complaint that the people were too impoverished to bear the new taxes imposed, urged that the king "live of his own," and hinted at guile and extortion in high places. A second knight called attention to the removal of the Staple (the official wool market) from Calais "without the knowledge or consent of Parliament, but for the benefit of a few," i.e., Lord Latimer, Richard Lyons, and others.[13] A third suggested that it would be wise to ask for a committee of the Lords to advise them as had been done in 1373. Two or three others spoke on various subjects, and then came the climax:

"About the same time a knight from the march of Wales, who was steward to the earl of March and was named Sir Peter de la Mare, began to speak where the others had spoken, and he said: 'My lords, you have well heard what our companions have had to say and what they have known and how they have expressed their views; and, in my opinion, they have spoken loyally and to good purpose.' And he rehearsed word for word, all the things that they had said, doing so very skilfully and in good form. And besides he advised them on many points and particulars, as will be more fully set forth below. And so they ended the second day.

"Then on the third day all the knights and commons assembled in the said chapter house and day after day until the next Friday held discussion concerning various matters and [particularly] the extortions committed by divers persons, through treachery, as they were advised. During which discussion and counsel, because the said Sir Peter de la Mare had spoken so well and had so skilfully rehearsed the arguments and views of his companions, and had informed them of much that they did not know, they begged him on their part to assume the duty of expressing their will in the great parliament before the said lords, as to what they had decided to do and say according to their conscience. And

---

[12] He begins his speech with a conventional Latin grace and ends it the same way: *Tu autem domine mesere nostris.* — Stephenson and Marcham, p. 220.

[13] Richard Lyons was a London vintner who had become a member of the king's Household and Council, farmer of the subsidy and customs granted by the parliament of 1373, and collector of the "petty custom" of London. Latimer was acting chamberlain.

the said Sir Peter, out of reverence to God and his good companions, and for the benefit of the kingdom, assumed that duty." [14]

Most dramatic was the scene in the Parliament House on May 9, when the Commons appeared to request a committee of the Lords. Sir Peter and a few others were admitted, but the rest were "repulsed and shut out and went where they would," at which Sir Peter and his companions "marvelled greatly." The duke, on learning that Sir Peter was spokesman for the day tried in vain to induce him to proceed. "My lords," he retorted, "you know well and well understand that all the Commons who have come here have come by [order of] our lord the King and by writ and by election of the sheriffs of the various shires, and what one of us says all say and assent to; wherefore at the start I demand the reason why some are held without, and for certain I won't touch on any business until they have all entered and are present." Only when the duke had them sent for and rounded up after a two hours' search did Sir Peter proceed.

After consultation with the king, the committee was conceded — the identical four bishops, four earls, and four barons and bannerets named by the Commons.[15] These included the Earl of March; Henry Percy, the future Earl of Northumberland; and two young bishops of the magnate class, William Courtenay of London and Henry Depenser of Norwich. On Monday, May 12, the joint committee, after a conference in the chapter house, returned to report in full parliament. Again Sir Peter was the spokesman, boldly denouncing the curialists, especially Latimer and Lyons.[16] It was in connection with his graphic account of the evils resulting from the removal of the Staple from Calais that he so effectively emphasized the role of parliament in lawmaking and the permanence of a *statute*.

" 'My Lords, a statute was made in Parliament by common assent that the entire staple of wools and other merchandise should be at Calais . . . and now the said staple has been dispersed for some time to different cities and towns in England without the common assent of Parliament, and against the statute made thereupon . . .' And when Lord

[14] Stephenson and Marcham, pp. 221–222.

[15] "Thereupon the Duke said to Sir Peter 'whom do you want?' 'Sir,' said he, 'the bishops of London, Norwich, Carlisle and Bath, the earls of March, Warwick, Suffolk, and Stafford; among the barons and bannerets the lord Percy, Sir Roger Bewchampe, Sir Gui de Brian and Sir Richard Stafford.' "

[16] Other charges included how the two had made a great loan to the king and repaid themselves with interest, although two London citizens had offered a loan interest free, and how they had profited by transactions with Crown debtors.

Latimer had heard their words he said: 'When the staple was removed from Calais it was done by the king and his council.' And Sir Peter replied that this was against the law of England and against the statute made thereupon in parliament, and what is made in parliament by way of statute cannot be unmade without parliament and this I will show you by the written statute. And the said Sir Peter had a book of statutes near him and opened the book and read the statute before all the lords and commons so that it couldn't be denied."

A week later, May 19, with the king's consent, two former treasurers, questioned on oath before the Lords, confirmed the main charges. It was then that the Commons "cried out" against the accused, demanding their arrest and trial by the Lords. Thus did the Good Parliament initiate proceedings which later legal theory regards as the origin of impeachment, judicial procedure for the removal of officials guilty of acts detrimental to the public welfare. The Commons indict and prosecute, the Lords, in keeping with their role as a high court, judge. Here it may be well to remind the American student, familiar with the clause in the United States Constitution, that in England impeachment did not extend to the king, as it may to the president of the United States.[17] Preserving the fiction that "the king can do no wrong," it was a happy device for reminding him by peaceful and lawful process that he ought to appoint good ministers and direct them to follow the law of the land. This was an improvement over the cruder earlier devices of feudal revolt or putting the government in commission.

Eventually the Commons impeached at the bar of the Lords the two peers, Lord Nevill the steward, and Lord Latimer the chamberlain, and four commoners (Lyons, Ellys, Peachy, and Bury), farmers of the customs and of certain monopolies. These early impeachments were not conducted with the formalities of later days, such as the famous case of Thomas Wentworth, Earl of Strafford, in the seventeenth century, but as in that case, it was a temptation to heap up the charges and equate them with treason. Thus Latimer was accused, like the favorites of Edward II, of "notoriously accroaching royal power," and of having traitorously abandoned two towns in Brittany to the French. Still there

[17] Of course the founding fathers in the new world were inspired by the British procedure in prescribing in the Constitution that "the House of Representatives . . . shall have sole power of impeachment. . . . The Senate shall have the sole power to try all impeachments." In the United States this is properly defined as *judicial* procedure by a *legislature*, but in England the Lords were already cast in the role of a high court.

was actual trial. Witnesses were called, and the accused were allowed to appear and to defend themselves as they could.

Latimer objected that there was no specific accuser for him to answer. He tried to eliminate the Commons by claiming trial by peers alone. Lyons characteristically sought to win over the king and the Prince of Wales with gifts of money. "Edward took the bribe, cynically suggesting that it was only some of his money come back again, but the Prince refused the barrel of gold disguised as a barrel of sturgeons, which Lyons sent to Kennington 'for love of his good lordship.'" [18]

Equally futile was Lyons' defense that he had acted with royal warrant. But let the official record speak for itself:

"And the said Richard was told that for it he ought to produce the warrant under the authority of which he had done the said things. But no warrant nor authorization was produced in parliament under the seal of the king, nor otherwise; save only that he said, that he had commandment therefor from the king himself and from his council to do it. And upon this, testimony was given openly in parliament, that our lord the king had said expressly the day before to certain lords here present in parliament, that he did not know how nor in what manner he had entered into such an office with regard to him; and furthermore, he did not recognize him as his officer."

At the end of the session all the estates went to Eltham, where the king in person pronounced the responses to their petitions. There was the usual concluding feast. In the words of the chronicler: "Sir Peter de la Mare and the knights of the shires held a great and excellent feast in the place and in the name of our lord the King and several great lords of the realm." It was well attended, there being present several bishops, seven earls, several barons, and knights of the shires, the mayor and most notable citizens of London, as well as the representatives of some of the other cities and boroughs. A gift of choice wines from the royal cellars, as well as gold and wine from some of the lords, helped to make the occasion a success. A note of seeming amity and satisfaction prevailed. "But," concludes the chronicler, "the decrees of the said Parliament were undone within a half year thereafter, as you shall hear." [19]

[18] Tout, *Chapters in Administrative History*, III, 300–301.

[19] Lancaster resumed control and the special council was dispersed. The supporters of the duke, even the impeached courtiers, returned to court, and Sir Peter de la Mare was imprisoned in Nottingham Castle. When Edward's last parliament met in January 1377, it reversed the judgments of its predecessor.

Yet scholars have been rightfully impressed with the importance of the Good Parliament. To Professor Plucknett it is the fact that "there remained the new and dangerous weapon of impeachment, and still more important, a great impression upon public opinion which now became deeply interested in parliament." To Professor Tout it is the role of the Commons: "Politically, it was no new thing for a parliament, at one with itself, to carry all before it and to proceed on its course regardless of the king and his ministers. But it was both a political and a social development for the commons to take the leading part they played in the proceedings of this parliament. Not only does Sir Peter de la Mare stand out as its hero. The commons held set debates in the chapter house, and these debates were thought worthy of record in the chronicles of distant monasteries. Many of the knights shared the oratorical gifts of their Speaker, and some, at least, of the representatives of the boroughs were called upon to speak in full parliament, notably two of the London members."

1401. Parliamentary "Rules of Order" and "Precedents"

Attractive from many angles is the second parliament of Henry IV, held at Westminster January 21 to March 10. For the general historian or the biographer of kings, it is perhaps most notable for the business transacted. Hostilities of the crisis years just past were resolved. Reconciliations were effected between great persons, lords of rival factions. The earls of Rutland and Somerset were reinstated in their lands and possessions as loyal subjects of the new sovereign.

Already acute was the problem of Wales and the border counties. Only in Shakespeare's lines does the "irregular and wild Glendower" boast, "I say the earth did shake when I was born," and "I can call spirits from the vasty deep." But in 1401 he was calling many a loyal Welshman to his standard. "Welsh students in England," Wylie says,[20] "had left Oxford at the call of Owen, to further the rebellion, and Welsh labourers were returning without warning to their own country, and arming themselves with bows and swords. In Wales the fields were neglected, stock was sold, and with the proceeds the Welshmen were procuring 'sadles, bowes and arowes, and other harnys.' . . . Already, negotiations had begun with some of the chiefs of the islands off the West of Scotland, to effect a landing at Barmouth and Aberdovey before

[20] J. H. Wylie, *History of England under Henry IV*, I, 169 (London, 1884). Chapter 10 is a good narrative account of this parliament and current events.

the coming summer." King Henry was inclined to be conciliatory. Parliament urged strong measures, though the Commons successfully protested, as unprecedented, orders of the Council for all towns and villages on or near the coast to man and equip for sea, at their own cost, a fleet of fifty-two ships, called "barges and balingers." Emergency measures, certain Ordinances for Wales, were enacted, but as events were to prove, Glendower was not easily checkmated.

More startling, perhaps because nearer home, was the problem — acute even in London and Westminster — of the Lollards. Under this name were included not only bona fide followers of John Wycliffe, but many a malcontent or free lance. If ever King and Parliament prided itself on its orthodoxy, it was this one. The pronouncement or cause of the summons delivered by Chief Justice of Common Pleas Sir William Thirning, sounds the keynote. It includes not merely the usual promise on the part of the king to confirm the liberties of the English Church (*Ecclesia Anglicana*), but the assurance that "Holy Church be maintained and sustained as it had been in the time of his noble progenitors and predecessors, Kings of England, *and as it is approved by the Holy Fathers and Doctors of Holy Church and by Holy Scripture.*" The handling of the problem affords an effective picture of the relationship and the cooperation between parliament and Convocation.[21] On January 29 three councillors, the constable, chamberlain, and treasurer, as commissioners for the king, presented themselves in Convocation and asked, as was usual, for prayers for the public weal and for the clerical vote of taxes. They then directed attention to the Lollards and promised the king's cooperation in steps to suppress them.

The official records of this convocation include details on the questioning of four heretics, with a full statement of their opinions. Three recanted, but the fourth, one William Chatrys, who remained obdurate, was degraded by Convocation. Archbishop Arundel secured from King and Council an authorization, i.e., order to the "secular arm" — in this instance the mayor and sheriffs of London — for the burning of Chatrys. The order was signed February 26. Apparently formal sanction of the Lords was secured, but not of the Commons. The sentence was carried out March 2. "The first fagot fire quenched the zeal for martyrdom," says Wylie, "and London witnessed many edifying recantations." Before Convocation was dismissed the clergy sent to the king and parliament

[21] This was, of course, the Convocation of the Province of Canterbury, but comprised the majority of English bishoprics.

the petition on which the famous statute *De Haeretico Comburendo* was based.

In his request for a generous grant of taxes Judge Thirning detailed a formidable array of his government's necessities. Expenses already incurred, including loans to be paid off, were incident to Henry's original coming to the realm "for the salvation and recovery of the same," the coronation, and expeditions against rebellious subjects. The future called for adequate protection of Calais and Guienne against the French and possible difficulties with Ireland and Scotland. Most novel was the task of returning to her homeland Richard's widow, the little French princess Isabelle, "Madame the Queen, with all her jewels, and other sums received with her at the time of the marriage," not to mention the expenses of the transfer. In response the Commons "with the assent of the Lords Spiritual and Temporal" granted a *tenth and fifteenth,* and a subsidy "for the defense and good government of the realm."

To the student of parliamentary history the session is important for both theory and practice. The situation was such that both the new king and his Commons were sticklers for forms and precedents. Further, the Clerk of the Parliament kept an unusually complete record of what was done and said — the formalities of procedure and the rather unusual parleys between king and Commons.

For instance, for Thursday January 20, the Clerk records how the newly elected members appeared in Westminster Hall before the chancellor and the steward to answer to roll call and verify their returns. They were then instructed to appear in person before the king in the Painted Chamber next day at ten o'clock. The opening address, ably handled by Thirning, began with the most emphatic assurances on behalf of the king that he intended to observe his coronation oath and to respect the liberties of all — clerks and laymen, Lords and Commons. Furthermore (and this must have pleased the judge) good laws made in the past were to be kept, justice done alike to poor as well as rich, and no one impeded from suing at Common Law. In conclusion, Thirning recalled how in previous parliaments several of the Lords and Commons had been more concerned with their individual and special affairs than in the "common profit and aid of the realm": "And finally the King wills and commands that no lord, knight of the shire, citizen, or burgess, who has come to parliament by virtue of summons, shall absent himself from the same parliament or depart from it out of the city until it is finished; and that they shall come on time every day to their places assigned for the parliament." [22]

Through their Speaker, Sir Arnold Savage, the Commons desired and received of the king assurance that they might have ample time for deliberation and not be pressed to decide important matters at the close of the session. A few days later, January 25, Sir Arnold proffered a number of practical requests conceived in the interests of his fellow knights and the citizens and burgesses. These urged the king not to listen to idle tales or unfair reports of the Commons' proceedings by any one of their number; that the business done and to be done in the parliament be enacted and engrossed "before the departure of the justices and while they had it in their memory," and that answers to their petitions *precede* supply! But kings too, can cite precedents. After consultation with the Lords the royal response to this last claimed "that such procedure had been unknown and unaccustomed in the time of any of his progenitors or predecessors . . . And, in conclusion, the king wished in no way to change the good customs and usages of ancient times."

The closing on March 10 was harmonious. The clergy, content with the statute on heretics, had voted subsidies; the king was in a gracious mood; and the Commons "thanked God for the King's wisdom, justice and humanity, for his destruction of evil doctrine, and of the sect which preached it, and for the good and complete agreement between all estates of the realm."

It was on a Saturday, January 22, the second day of the parliament of 1401, that the Commons presented to the king Sir Arnold Savage — as events were to prove, a Speaker extraordinary! He too, came of a parliamentary family. For six generations heads of the house served as knight of the shire for Kent, as did Sir Arnold in five parliaments, in two of them as Speaker.[23] He had also been sheriff (1381, 1385), had journeyed to Spain with John of Gaunt, and held the important post of Lieutenant of Dover Castle. He was obviously *persona grata* to the king,[24] but also supported the interests of the Commons, and played his role with zest and enthusiasm.

[22] Stephenson and Marcham, pp. 257–258, 259.

[23] Knight of the shire for Kent in the parliaments of January and November 1390, January 1401, October 1402, January 1404; Speaker in the third and last.

[24] In 1404 the king consulted him shortly before the meeting of parliament as to the arrangement of business. He had attended councils during the previous year.

Contemporary chroniclers and modern historians alike have outdone themselves in praising his ability and eloquence. The St. Albans chronicler records that he managed the business of the Commons with "such prudence, tact, and eloquence as to win universal praise." According to Ramsay he "had the art of dealing effective thrusts under cover of a cloud of polished verbiage." Chrimes comments on "his well-known verbal energy." Walter Savage Landor (a descendant) includes in his *Imaginary Conversations* a chat between the king and the knight.

In making the customary protestation Sir Arnold included, as the Speaker of Henry's first parliament had done, a request that the Commons "have their liberty in Parliament as they have had before these hours; And that this protestation be entered of record in the Roll of Parliament." Instead of the usual formula asking for forbearance if he should say too little or too much, his rich vocabulary served to embroider it to "too little for default on his part, or *superfluity by folly or lack of knowledge . . .*" We may feel sure that if he erred, it was on the side of superfluity. A more novel feat followed which must have astonished his hearers, for Sir Arnold proceeded to prove his capacity and fortify his memory by summing up what the Chief Justice had set forth, "clearly and in a few words."

The Clerk records at least three other examples of that "polished verbiage," conveying a practical thrust. When on Tuesday the 25th, the Commons again appeared before the King in Parliament, their Speaker prefaced the requests for the safeguards described above with gracious thanks to his Majesty for his support of the true faith and his promise to respect all the "liberties." Again, a warning against acceptance of the challenges of the French directed against certain of the Lords followed a philosophical discourse on the three things necessary for the good governance of any realm — understanding, humanity, and riches, virtues "with which providence has richly endowed our Lord the King." It was this speech that fascinated Landor, especially the passage on riches: "the said Commons showed our Lord the King that the greatest treasure and wealth of the world is for each King to have the heart of his people. For it follows that if he has the heart, it is likely that he will have what he needs of their goods."

Even so, there was a limit to the royal patience. When a few days

He was one of the knights named by the Commons in 1404 to serve on the king's "great and continual council." His name appears as a member of the Council in 1405 and 1406.

later the Commons reappeared with more verbal requests, they were instructed to include these in their *written* petitions as was customary

Still, the formal closing offered Speaker Savage another opportunity His comparison of parliament to the Mass, perhaps fantastic to modern minds, suited the temper of this assembly in its staunch orthodoxy. As paraphrased by Professor Chrimes, Sir Arnold's "analogical speculation" runs as follows:

"It is recorded that the commons, in Parliament showed to the king how it seemed to them that 'le fait de parlement' could well be likened to a Mass. The commencement of the Parliament, when the archbishop read the epistle and expounded the Bible, was like the commencement of the office. The king's repeated declaration that it was his will that the faith of Holy Church should be sustained and governed as it had been by his progenitors, and that the laws should be held and kept in all points, as well by rich as by poor, to the great pleasure of God and comfort of his subjects, seemed like the sacrifice in the Mass to be offered to God by all Christians. Then at the end of the Mass, it was necessary to say 'Ite, missa est,' and 'Deo gratias'; and at that time it seemed to the commons that they had come to the point when 'Ite, missa est' was the appropriate form of words, and for three reasons all the people ought to say 'Deo gratias'. For God had given them a gracious king, who wished to do justice and was endowed with humanity; moreover, he had destroyed the 'malvoise doctrine' and the sect which was threatening the church; and finally the lords and commons of the realm and the king were possessed of good and whole hearts towards each other."

VI

The Contributions of the "Men of Law"

✿✿✿

IN THE reigns of Henry IV and Henry V, king, Council, and parliament worked in a harmony almost suggestive of later ministerial responsibility. During the Lancastrian-Yorkist strife of the mid-century, parliament and Council were apt to be dominated by the faction temporarily in the ascendant. Yorkist parliaments anticipate those of the Tudors in less frequent sessions and in rather able control by the king. One historian goes so far as to exclaim: "Under Edward IV and Richard III Parliament has no history."

However, it is the purpose of this chapter to show that even the fifteenth century witnessed practical advances in parliamentary procedure, privilege, "vocabulary," and theory. Some of these probably came from those obscure but indispensable clerks and under-clerks of the parliaments, an efficient and relatively permanent civil-service element. Others are obviously due to the judges and lawyers. Some, perhaps, may have come from a hard-headed merchant or financier M.P. A combination difficult to beat was the lawyer-merchant, such as Sir Thomas Yonge, to be described below.

Constitutional theory, we are told, lagged behind advances in practice. More accurately, we may say that there is constitutional theorizing, but it is not fully established or generally agreed upon, as would be the case with a written constitution or definitive statutes. One view may be enunciated by the chancellor in his opening address, another by the Commons through their Speaker, still another by the judges and the gentlemen of the Inns of Court.

Before turning to fifteenth-century concepts and theories we may well consider the astonishing little anonymous fourteenth-century treatise, "The Manner of Holding Parliaments" (*Modus Tenendi Parliamentum*).[1] This was probably not widely circulated or accepted in its own day, but survived to puzzle and deceive seventeenth-century parliamentarians. Stubbs called it "a somewhat ideal description of the constitution of parliament," and again, "a theoretical view for which the writer was anxious to find a warrant in immemorial antiquity."

Ancient, indeed, is the lineage the *Modus* assigns to Parliament, including the Commons: "Here is described the mode how the Parliament of the King of England and his Englishmen used to be holden in the time of King Edward, the son of King Ethelred; which mode indeed was recited by the more select men of the kingdom before William Duke of Normandy, both Conqueror and King of England, the Conqueror himself commanding it, and by him approved, and used in his own times and also in the times of his successors Kings of England."

The account which the *Modus* gives of the "business" of the parliament accords with known practice, except perhaps for the ideal picture of harmony and unanimity and the precise calendar of procedure. There is no slighting of his Majesty, the King in his Parliament, for we are told: "The King is the head, beginning, and end of Parliament, and so he has no peer in his degree, and so the first degree consists of the King alone." Then comes a list of the other "degrees" (the term which this author uses instead of the more usual *estates*), five in number: archbishops, bishops, abbots and priors; procurators of the clergy; earls, barons, etc.; knights; citizens and burgesses. Within each grade members are peers each of the other.

Most novel for its time is the emphasis on the importance of the elected representative elements. Following a statement about the granting of an aid (tax) comes the surprising assertion: ". . . and be it understood that the two knights who come to the Parliament for a shire have a greater voice in Parliament in agreeing or dissenting than an earl of England who is greater than they are, and in like manner the procurators of the clergy of a single bishopric have a greater voice in Parliament, if they all agree, than the bishop himself, and this in all things which by Parliament ought to be granted, refused or done.

"And by this it is evident that the King can hold a Parliament with the commons of his kingdom without bishops, earls, and barons, pro-

[1] See Note A at the end of this chapter.

vided they have been summoned to Parliament, although no bishop, earl, nor baron obey the summons, because formerly there was neither bishop, nor earl, nor baron, yet then Kings held their Parliaments; but still on the other hand, although the commons — the clergy and laity — are summoned to Parliament, as of right they ought to be, and for any cause will not come, as if they pretend that the Lord the King does not govern them as he ought, and assign special cases in which he has not governed them, then there is no Parliament at all, even though the arch-bishops, bishops, earls, and barons, and all their peers, be present with the King."

Whether or not members of the Commons were familiar with the *Modus*, in an age when custom and precedent meant so much it was only natural that they should assume for themselves an ancient lineage. In 1388, for instance, they claim that impeachment is among the "ancient ordinances and liberties of parliament." In their famous petition to Henry V, 1414, their claim to a share in law-making is based on the as-sumption "Consideringe that the Commune of youre land, the which that is and evere hath be a membre of youre Parlement . . ." In Ed-ward IV's reign they affirm that the privilege "that they should not be impleaded in any action personal" had existed "whereof tyme that mannys mynde is not the contrarie."

Parliamentary Procedure

From about 1423 on comes a change modernizing legislative proce-dure, the substitution of individual *bills* for the collective Commons' petitions.[2] Each such bill was drafted as a unit and in proper formal terms, "containing in itself the form of an act" (*formam actus in se con-tinens*), according to a later expression. It was long one of the legends of parliamentary history, popularized by Stubbs, that this was a device hit upon by the Commons to enforce acceptance of their measures *in toto* and avoid the risk of changes in the process of engrossing. The best view seems now to be that the Commons merely adopted the form devised and used by the government for certain official and private bills, as an improvement in business method.[3] Even so, the practice must have

[2] The following account of parliamentary procedure is based on Gray, pp. 177–183.

[3] For instance, "grants of taxes were technical documents whose 'form' was care-fully drawn and adopted — in the fifteenth century invariably drawn as indentures. The same development went on in the council, where petitioners seeking grants, franchises, and the like would submit a draft of the document they desired. In 1423 a petitioner introduced into parliament the exact text of the letters patent she wanted, and in 1439 the crown presented to the commons a 'schedule or bill' con-

had advantages from the Commons' point of view. It marked a form of maturity, a sort of legislative coming of age on their part. It gradually became the rule that bills might originate in either House with two exceptions: money bills must come from the Commons, bills affecting the peerage, such as for the restitution of forfeited honors, from the Lords. However, the Clerk's captions are deceptive — he includes in the *Rolls* under his heading Commons Petitions "all bills of general import the provisions of which would have to be widely observed." Experts examining the many original manuscript bills preserved in the Public Record Office can usually distinguish between Lords' bills and Commons' bills by the wording and by the endorsement indicating that the bill is to be sent to the other House for consideration (i.e., *baillées aux Seignurs*).

It has been pointed out that in the fifteenth century, especially in the Yorkist period, few statutes of great import were enacted. Although not weighty enough to merit inclusion in our textbooks, they were of practical value, beneficial to the little farmer and artisan and the merchant class. Of the approved bills in the two sessions of Edward IV's parliament (1463–1466), Gray instances the following: "One forbad imports of grain when prices fell below specified figures; one required good cobbling of shoes; one formulated regulations touching the manufacture and sealing of cloths and the payment of clothworkers; one forbad the purchasing of futures in wool except by clothworkers during a period of three and one-half years; one prohibited the importation of Burgundian merchandise so long as Burgundian markets were closed to English cloth; two succeeded, where bills of 1453–4 and 1455–6 had failed, in insisting that wool be shipped to Calais, but avoided the delicate subject of royal licenses; finally, approval was given to a bill limiting the costliness of apparel, which was presented on the ground that 'excessive Arayes' impoverished the realm, enriched strange realms and destroyed husbandry."

Parliamentary Privilege

Several interesting cases of privilege — freedom from arrest — are recorded for the second and third quarters of the century. Four of them

taining technical changes in the settlement of certain crown lands to the uses of Henry V's will."

"The first known document containing the actual words '*formam actus in se continens*' was the attainder of Henry VI in 1461, which was followed by other attainders and by acts of resumption." Gray.

relate to citizen or burgess M.P.'s, and in each instance release was granted. That legitimate civil process was involved seems to be indicated by the care of the government to safeguard the interests of the plaintiff at whose suit the arrest was made.

In 1429, for instance, one William Lark, a servant of William Melreth, member elect for the city of London, was arrested on a charge of trespass at the suit of one Margery Janyns, and on judgment given, was imprisoned in the Fleet. Yet, as the Commons complained,[4] he was in the service of the said William Melreth at the time of the arrest "and truly supposed that, by the privilege of your court of parliament, he was quit of all arrest during (the session of) your said court, except for treason, felony, or surety of the peace." Lark's release was authorized with the assent of the counsel of the Margery Janyns named in this petition, saving to the plaintiff the recovery of damages after the session. The significance of this case has been minimized. It involved a mere member's *servant*. The future guarantee asked by the Commons was not conceded — "and as to the remainder of the petition, *le roi s'avisera*" (the king will consider it, be advised). Yet the Commons' petition was explicit enough to have encouraged similar claimants as well as to have caught the eye of later precedent-seekers. They prayed the king not only to release Lark but also to grant "that none of your said lieges — that is to say, lords, knights of your shires, citizens, or burgesses in your parliaments to come, together with their servants or menials — shall in any way be arrested or detained in prison during the time of your parliaments, except for treason, felony, or surety of the peace, as aforesaid." [5]

The others, burgesses arrested on process for debt, were all released without question, even in two instances in the reign of Edward IV. Only in the case of William Hyde of Chippenham is there any implication of malice or foul play. "Hyde was arrested at Lambeth at the suit of John Marshall, a London mercer, seeking to recover an alleged debt of £69, and taken to London 'by myschevous men, murtherers, unknown for any officers,' cast into Newgate, 'as and he had bee a Traitour,' brought before the Bench and remitted to Newgate." Chippenham was a small borough, but its representatives have been identified as rather important people charged with considerable debts. Walter Clerk, mem-

---

[4] Only in 1543 did the Commons assume the right to deliver a member out of custody and to imprison the offending officials who had effected the arrest. See below, pp. 153–155.

[5] *Parliament Rolls*, IV, 357, and, briefly, McKisack, p. 122. The following cases, Hyde, Clerk, and Atwyll, are based mainly on McKisack, pp. 123–124.

A parliament of Edward I

Section of a view of London (about 1638)

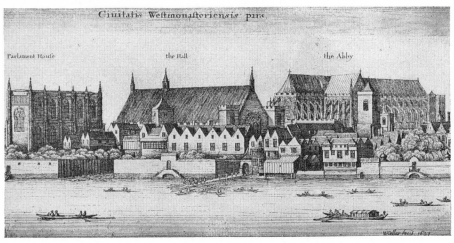

Ciuitatis Weftmonafteriensis pars

Parliament House   the Hall   the Abby

A part of Westminster: the Parliament House, the Hall,
and the Abbey (about 1647)

ber in 1460, was probably the man who sat for Southampton in 1455 and was its mayor in 1457. William Hyde (M.P. 1472) may have been not a resident burgess, but one William Hyde *esquire*.

In the case of John Atwyll (Exeter, 1478) the Commons play up the plight of the poor member who "may not have his free departing from this present Parliament to his home, for doubte that booth his Body, his Horses and his other Goodes and Catalles necessarie to be had with hym, shuld be put in Execution in that behalfe, contrarie to the Pryvilege due and accustumed to all the membres usuelly called to the forseid Parlementes." [6]

The Commons' petitions are interesting for their emphasis, not on the personal disability of the burgesses, but on the importance of their presence in parliament. Clerk, it is urged, should be released "so that he may tend daily of this youre parliament as his dute is to doo." Hyde's arrest is leading to "grete delay and retardation of procedyng and goode expedition of such matters and besoines as for your Highness and the commen wele of this your Reame in this present Parlement were to be doon and speede."

Most famous was the arrest of Speaker Thorpe, a baron of the Exchequer and a staunch Lancastrian. This was the case which parliamentarians of James I's reign characterized as "begotten of the iniquity of the time." Failure to secure release was due to partisan bias — the plaintiff was none other than Richard, Duke of York! But let us hear the story as the legal historian tells it.[7] During a prorogation of parliament Thorpe "was imprisoned in the Fleet on an execution issuing out of his own court of the Exchequer, for non-payment of a fine due to the king for trespass committed in seizing certain goods of the Duke of York. The commons sent some of their members to complain to the king and lords, and demand the release of the Speaker, and of Walter Rayle, another imprisoned member. As in Larke's case, counsel for the plaintiff in the previous action was heard, who opposed Thorpe's release since the Duke would be deprived of his legal remedy."

The Lords consulted the judges, but disregarded their opinion, and ruled " 'that the seid Thomas, accordyng to the lawe, shuld remayne

[6] "While attending Parliament daily," he was arrested on a judgment in the Exchequer by default, obtained by one "calling himself merchant of the said city of Exeter." He was released on a writ of *supersedeas*, saving the rights of the suitor after the session.

[7] Plucknett, ed., Taswell-Langmead, pp. 220–221, and quoting the *Parliament Rolls*, V, 239.

stille in prison for the causes above-said, the Privelegge of the Parlement, or that the same Thomas was Speker of the Parlement, notwith-
stondyng'; and the commons were directed in the king's name to proceed 'with all goodly hast and spede' to the election of a new Speaker,
which they did the next day."

Yet the Commons won a theoretical, if not a practical, victory from
the judges. They disclaimed any authority to "determine the Privilege
of this high Court of Parlement," the determination and knowledge of
which belongs to the Lords. While reluctant to check the process of the
common law, they nevertheless asserted that " 'if any persone that is a
membre of this high Court of Parlement be arrested in suche cases as be
not for treason or felony, or suerte of the peas, or for a condempnation
hadde before the Parlement, it is used that all such persones shuld be
released of such arrestes and make an Attourney, so that they may have
their fredom and libertee frely to entende upon the Parlement.' "

Another case in which the issue of privilege was also beclouded by
factional interests was that of Thomas Yonge. This involved freedom
of speech and action in the Commons. In June 1451 Yonge was arrested
and imprisoned in the Tower "for matters by him showed in the
House." Yonge, a staunch Yorkist, supported by a number of the Commons, had made the constructive, but to Somerset and the Lancastrians
unwelcome, motion, that as the king had no issue, Richard, Duke of
York, be declared heir apparent to the crown. In April of the next year,
on the temporary reconciliation of the two parties, Yonge was released.
In 1455, when the duke became Protector, Yonge presented a petition
to the Commons which was sent on to the Lords. As a result, the king
willed "that the Lords of his council do and provide for the said suppli-
ant, as by their discretion shall be thought convenient and reasonable."
Yonge asked compensation for himself in heavy damages, but his
petition also contains the most effective statement to date as to privilege.
He reminds the Commons that all members "ought to have their freedom to speak and say in the house of their assembly as to them is
thought convenient or reasonable without any manner of challenge,
charge or punition therefore to be laid to them in anywise." [8]

Yonge's case is more interesting than Haxey's, for he was an actual
member of the Commons and an important one. He represented Bristol
in six parliaments (1435–1449) before the fatal motion, and again in

[8] The *D.N.B.* cites the king's order to the Lords, but concludes: ". . . no further
proceedings in the matter are recorded." Plucknett assumes he secured the desired
redress.

1455–1456; and sat for Gloucestershire in 1460.[9] Bristol, like most trading centers, was Yorkist in sympathies. Thomas was following in the family tradition, for his father and brother were also active in politics. Thomas was both a merchant and a lawyer, a man "entitled to speak with authority," and to be a leader in the Commons. He was a barrister who had received his legal training at the Middle Temple. From 1439 on his name frequently occurs in the *Year Books* (the ancestor of the modern law *Reports*). With the triumph of the Yorkists, his ability was recognized. He was made Serjeant-at-Law, King's Serjeant, and Judge of Common Pleas in 1467, and of King's Bench in 1475.

Parliamentary "Vocabulary"

An English scholar, Professor Chrimes, has recently undertaken to "investigate the spirit behind the forms" — to deal with constitutional theory as distinct from constitutional practice — and in conclusion to give us an account of the constitution in the form in which an observer at the end of the fifteenth century "*could* have given it *if* he had tried."

As to parliament, he seeks to learn from the sources "how parliament was in fact being *thought of,* as an institution, by the men of the century. . . . not so much parliament itself, as parliament's image in men's minds." His method is to notice, in order of time, in the phraseology of such sources as the *Parliament Rolls* and *Year Books* key terms like "the high court of parliament," "estates of the realm," the "three estates," or "by authority of parliament." It is surprising to find that constitutional ideas and the institutions to which they relate seem to be gaining precision not only in the early Lancastrian period but in the course of the very years which we are wont to associate with the Wars of the Roses, livery and maintenance, factional councils and packed parliaments, and finally the reigns of the strong Yorkist monarchs.

The conception of Parliament as the king's high court, of course, has been with us from the days of Edward I and the little treatise *Fleta*. In the later Middle Ages it is being used on all sides. To cite only a few examples: The chancellor in his opening address refers to "Parliament which is the most high court of the realm" (1384 and later). The Lords use the phrase to emphasize their own authority as peers of the realm.

[9] He was probably also in the parliaments of 1461 and 1462–1463, for which the returns are lost. His father, John Yonge, mayor of Bristol in 1411, represented the city in parliament in 1411 and 1413–1414. A younger brother, John, settled in London, represented that city in parliament, and served it as sheriff in 1455, and Lord Mayor in 1466. The 1435 election indenture calls him *mercator*.

The judges in Thorpe's Case refuse to determine the privileges of that high court of parliament; for it is "so high and so mighty in its nature that it might make law and unmake that which was law." Increasingly the Commons refer to themselves as "the comens that been comen to this your high court of Parliament" (1453, 1455, 1461, and others). Most effectively, the king himself, Edward IV, so addresses the Commons and their Speaker (1467): "John Say, and ye sirs, comyn to this my court of Parlement for the comon of this my lond."

The conception of "estates of the realm" received considerable emphasis in connection with the deposition of Richard II and the accession of Henry IV. Then there were named, not just three, but several estates, like the "grades" of the *Modus*. From this time on, reference to the "estates of the realm" or to "all the estates" come from various elements within parliament itself — Lords, Commons, the king, the chancellor. Increasingly as the century wears on, the emphasis on three estates prevails. For instance, in 1429 it was recorded that the articles for procedure of the Council were read "before the Lord King in his Parliament, in the presence of the three estates of the kingdom." It becomes common form in the wording of prorogations,[10] and appears in some rather notable opening addresses of the chancellors. Bishop Russell, addressing the first parliament of Richard III, comments: "In thys grete body of Englonde we have many diverse members undre oone hede. Howe be hyt they may alle be reduced to iii chyef and princypalle, whyche make thys hyghe and grete courte at thys tyme, that ys to seye, the lordes spiritualle, the lordes temporalle, and the commens."

The phrase "the authority of parliament" appears from the late fourteenth century on, and at first in times of crisis: a change of ruler or a minority, an occasion when parliament is exercising some unusual power. For instance, in the charges framed against Richard II, it was claimed that statutes were binding until revoked by "the authority of another parliament." At the beginning of the reign of the infant King Henry VI, the action of the Council in summoning parliament and commissioning officials was presently "held good and effectual" by the "authority of parliament." In 1461, on the victory of the legitimist Yorkist, Edward IV, the Commons asked that the judicial acts of his *de facto* predecessor be declared lawful by the "authority of parliament." Meanwhile, the phrase was adopted and standardized in the ordinary process of legislation. In 1433, "for the first time, the statute of the year was sanctioned

[10] So used in 1433, 1449, 1450, 1459, 1473, 1488, 1489, 1491.

by the assent of the lords spiritual and temporal, at the instance and request of the commons, and *by authority of parliament.*" From 1444–1445 on, with one exception, this clause was used regularly in recording parliamentary sanction to legislation.[11]

A veritable summation, using all the key phrases, comes, oddly enough, in an official recognition of the usurper Richard III, a clear-cut and effective statement of parliament and its role. When Richard's *coup d'état* had been accomplished and his parliament had assembled, an explanation was inscribed in the *Rolls.* It relates how a parchment containing certain articles in the name of the three estates was presented and accepted by the king. The estates had acted outside of parliament, but as their authority is greater in the form of parliament their action is now ratified in and by the same! Finally the *Rolls* state: ". . . howe that the Courte of Parliament is of suche auctorite, and the people of this Lande of suche nature and dispocion, as experience teacheth that manifestacion and declaration of any trueth or right, made by the Thre Estates of this Reame assembled in Parliament, and by auctorite of the same, maketh, before all other thyngs, moost feith and certaynte, and, quietyng mens myndes, remoeveth the occasion of all doubts and seditous language. Therfor, at the request, and by assent of the Thre Estates of this Reame, that is to say, the Lordes Spirituelx and Temporelx, and Commoens of this Lande, assembled in this present Parliament, by auctorite of the same, bee it pronounced, decreed, and declared that oure said Soverayne Lord the Kyng, was, and is, veray and undoubted Kyng of this Reame of Englond, with all things therunto . . . as well by right of Consanguinite and Enheritaunce, as by lawefull Elleccion, Consecration and Coronacion." [12]

The Lawyers in Parliament

The role of the judges in the drafting of statutes has already been described. It is naturally in the legal literature — the pronouncements of the judges and pleaders — that we find theories as to fundamental law, the relation of statutes to the common law, the extent to which the king through his judges may interpret or even modify the law. Recent studies based on the *Plea Rolls* and *Year Books* [13] indicate that in the reigns of the three Edwards the judges exercised wide discretionary

[11] Chrimes, pp. 72–73, 116–123, 138–139.
[12] Chrimes, pp. 124–125, quoting *Rot. Parl.*, VI, 240–242.
[13] Plucknett, *Statutes and Their Interpretation in the Fourteenth Century*; Chrimes, *English Constitutional Ideas in the Fifteenth Century*.

power in "making exceptions out of the statute," extending or restricting the application of certain statutes. In this period they were rather jealous of the common law: it was not to be modified more than necessary. By the fifteenth century the supremacy of statute law over common law was unquestioned. Statutes were classified as introductory of new law or declaratory of old, affirmative or negative, general or particular. If declaratory of old law, a statute might be interpreted equitably. If introductory of new law, negative or particular, it should be interpreted strictly. Sometimes attempts were made to discover the original intention of the legislature, a method so much insisted on later by Sir Edward Coke.

Instructive comments from the "men of law" are recorded in the *Year Books*. For instance, the part played by the judges in engrossing statutes is suggested by a case back in 1305. When counsel argued for a certain construction of the Statute of Westminster II, "he was cut short by the Chief Justice with the remark: 'Do not gloss the Statute; we understand it better than you do, for we made it.'"[14] Chief Justice Thorpe in 1365 pointed out that everyone is bound to know at once what is done in parliament, for parliament represents the body of the whole realm. Littleton, as Judge of Common Pleas, is quoted as emphasizing the majority principle in parliament: "Sir, in the parliament if the greater part of the knights of the shires assent to the making of an act of parliament, and the lesser part will not agree to it, still it will be a good law to last forever."

As might be expected, the lawyers emphasize parliament as a court. Chief Baron of the Exchequer Fray said in 1441: "The parliament is the king's court and the highest court that he has; and the law is the highest inheritance that the king has, for by the law he himself and all his subjects are ruled. And if the law were not, there would be no king and no inheritance." But when Fray went on to argue that *tenths and fifteenths* were revenues of the court of parliament like attainders and forfeitures, he was promptly corrected by the Chief Justice of Common Pleas: "The fifteenth granted to the King by his people cannot be called a perquisite or profit of his Court of Parliament, for the perquisites or profits of his courts are things which accrue to him through a forfeiture to his law."

---

[14] McIlwain. The following passages quoting Thorpe, Littleton, and Fray, are based on *Year Books* cases quoted in the original French by Chrimes, Appendixes 8, 60, and 25 respectively.

As to the exclusion of lawyers from the Commons, the statute of 1372 was evidently not long operative. One chronicler, at least, thought it worth recording that the Coventry Parliament of 1404 (*omnino illiterati*, or "entirely unlearned") contained no lawyers, as if this were unusual, although the writs of summons he describes may not have been as novel as he thought.

In the fifteenth century many boroughs began to send their recorders. London was probably the first to have such an official. A description of the office and its services for the city will serve to indicate its importance and potentialities and how ably such a member might serve his city or borough in parliament. Originally he was a clerk who sat with the mayor and aldermen in the Court of Husting at the Guildhall, where he pronounced or *recorded* by word of mouth the judgments given, hence the name *recorder*. In the fourteenth century "he was selected from among the most skilful and vertuous of the law apprentices of the whole kingdom, and had other duties added to the original one of pronouncing the judgment of the court, for he acted as general legal adviser to the Mayor and aldermen, and on most occasions as the mouthpiece of the city. When the Mayor and his brethren attended a Court of the King's Justices at the Tower, or St. Martin-le-Grand, or Westminster, it was the Recorder who recited the liberties of the city, and similarly on ceremonial occasions, when kings or princes visited the city, it was he who pronounced the address of welcome. On assuming office the Recorder had to take oath to do equal justice to all, to come readily at the warning of the Mayor and sheriffs, to give them good and wholesome counsel, to ride with them to keep and maintain order in the city, and to accept nothing in the way of fees or robes from anyone except the Chamber of London."[15]

One of London's lawyer M.P.'s became a Judge of Assize in Yorkshire, another Chief Justice of King's Bench. Norwich and Winchester sent their recorders to parliament on occasion. Richard Page, who sat for Plymouth, was King's Solicitor. In 1450 we find a certain William Wayte writing to John Paston urging the election of William Jenny, a lawyer, and citing various precedents for such a choice: "Telle them that he may be yt as well as Yonge is of Brystowe, or the Recorder is of

---

[15] "He appears to have been summoned by Royal Writ to the court for gaol delivery of Newgate for the first time in 1368, and thus started that career which has led to his becoming to-day the chief judge in city criminal trials." Charles Pendrill, *London Life in the Fourteenth Century* (London, 1925), p. 240.

London, and as the Recordour of Coventre is for the city of Coventrie, and it is so in many places in Ingland."

Yonge of Bristol was indeed worth "honorable mention." A practising barrister, a member of the Middle Temple, and later a justice of the Common Pleas and of King's Bench, he was returned eight times by Bristol and once by Gloucestershire!

Professor Holdsworth, that great master of legal history, has effectually portrayed the role of the lawyers in parliament. Their presence meant that the "best legal talent of the day was ready to assist in the development of its powers. It meant that men who were accustomed to the working of the procedural rules of the courts were ready to assist it to devise a rational system of procedure. . . . just as the procedural rules of the common law were the foundation upon which that law was built, so the acquisition by the English Parliament of a reasonable set of procedural rules is the secret of its capacity to develop into an organ of the government of the state."

He lists several features, some as definitely, others as "probably," derived from the law and lawyers, including the committee system, real argumentative debate (not mere oratory), "minute attention paid to matters of form," customs and precedents including privilege, and its separate rolls.[16] The extension to the "high court of parliament" of the idea of "contempt of court" came from the lawyer members. It was the Commons who, in the parliament of 1472, criticized riotous conduct in Southwark and deplored the fact that those guilty of the disturbances "no consideration take to that that youre high presence is had here at youre Paleis of Westminster, ne to that youre high Court of Parlement is here sittyng . . . and it is in a manere a contumelious contempt of your Highness and youre Courtes here hold and kept." This, of course, is closely akin to the "king's peace," but in the Tudor period the Commons were to adopt the idea effectively for the protection of their own members and privileges.

Amongst members of parliament who eventually became judges, most interest attaches to Sir John Fortescue, since he was to write a striking description of the assembly in which he served. He was long known as Chief Justice of King's Bench (1442–1460) and as author of notable treatises, but his parliamentary career has been obscure. His latest editor, Professor Chrimes, reveals that before 1437 he had been eight

---

[16] Holdsworth, II, 429–434. For the lawyers in Tudor parliaments, see Chapter 9.

times elected a member of parliament. He was returned for various boroughs of his native Devon and finally as knight for Wiltshire. He also served a number of times as justice of the peace and on various commissions.

Fortescue, as a staunch Lancastrian, shared the exile of the royal family and as "chancellor," with Queen Margaret and the young prince over in France (at the Castle of Koeur near St. Mihiel in Bar), constituted a veritable "government in exile." It was here in the years 1468–1471 that he wrote *The Praises of the Laws of England (De Laudibus Legum Angliae).* This takes the form of a dialogue, instructing the prince in his future role of kingship by comparing English and French institutions. The treatise has been characterized as "the first deliberate attempt at an essay in comparative jurisprudence," and the first to base political theory on direct observation of contemporary conditions, "in some degree anticipating the standpoint of Machiavelli." The picture is somewhat idealized, as we have seen in the description of the jury quoted above. But his later essay on the *Governance of England* proves that he was aware of the defects of government in this troubled era, and the remedies he advanced were practical, the very ones the Tudors were to adopt.

For our present purpose, interest lies in his contrast between the French kingship as a regal power solely (*dominium regale*) and the English kingship as regal and politic (*dominium regale et politicum*). Fortescue recognizes that the English king is under God and the law, as Bracton had affirmed two hundred years before, but what Bracton could not have said, he is also limited by parliament. His doctrine is one of limited monarchy, but not yet parliamentary sovereignty. Fortescue does not give a precise origin or lineage to parliament, but does assume that "the customs of England are very ancient, and have been used and accepted by five nations successively" — Britons, Romans, (Britons again), Saxons, Danes, (Saxons again), and finally by Normans. "And throughout the period of these nations and their kings, the realm has been continuously ruled by the same customs as it is now, customs which, if they had not been the best, some of those kings would have changed for the sake of justice or by the impulse of caprice, and totally abolished them, especially the Romans, who judged almost the whole of the rest of the world by their laws."

The description of parliament is introduced in order to show "with what solemnity statutes are promulgated in England." An earlier passage has indicated the share of parliament in taxation.[17]

As to the statutes in England: "These, indeed, do not emanate from the will of the prince alone, as do the laws in Kingdoms which are governed entirely regally, where so often statutes secure the advantage of their maker only, thereby redounding to the loss and undoing of the subjects. Sometimes, also, by the negligence of such princes and the inertia of their counsellors, those statutes are made so ill advisedly that they deserve the name of corruptions rather than of laws. But the statutes of England cannot so arise, since they are made not only by the prince's will, but also by the assent of the whole realm, so they cannot be injurious to the people nor fail to secure their advantage. Furthermore, it must be supposed that they are necessarily replete with prudence and wisdom, since they are promulgated by the prudence not of one counsellor nor of a hundred only, but of more than three hundred chosen men — of such a number as once the Senate of the Romans was ruled by — as those who know the form of the summons, the order, and the procedure of parliament can more clearly describe. And if statutes ordained with such solemnity and care happen not to give full effect to the intention of the makers, they can speedily be revised, and yet not without the assent of the commons and nobles of the realm, in the manner in which they first originated. Thus, prince, all the kinds of the law of England are plain to you. You will be able to estimate their merits by your own wisdom, and by comparison with other laws; and when you find none in the world so excellent, you will be bound to confess they are not only good, but as good as you could wish."

But for Fortescue, concludes Professor Chrimes, "we might perhaps be tempted to accept the views of those historians who have imagined that the fate (as well as the destiny) of parliament was still in the balance at the end of the fifteenth century. Such views, usually based upon misleading statistical data, are utterly unconvincing when we realize that parliament, in the eyes of this doughty champion of monarchy and common law, was as inevitable and indispensable as that very monarchy and that very common law. The institution could not have faded, because the *principle* of it has become firmly rooted."

[17] Chapter 16: "The king of England does not by himself or his ministers impose on his subjects any tallage or burden, nor change their laws nor make new ones, without the express consent or concession of his whole kingdom in his parliament."

NOTE A. THE MODUS TENENDI PARLIAMENTUM

There are extant copies in fourteenth-century manuscripts. Within that period historians' guesses, based on internal evidence, range from Edward II to the end of Richard II's reign. In the seventeenth century Sir Edward Coke, misled by the preamble, assigned it to a pre-Conquest origin, while Prynne gave it too late a date, Henry VI. The distinguished lawyer and legal historian, John Selden, assigned it to the reign of Edward III. Among recent scholars, the learned Professor Tout concurs with Selden, inclining to the view "that it was drawn up not before 1340, but probably not very long afterwards." The treatise fills about twenty pages in a modern printed edition, and as in the original, is neatly divided into paragraphs with topical headings, twenty-five in all. These are surprisingly complete, covering membership, the clerks, and even the doorkeeper and crier; the ceremonies of the opening and closing, "the business of the Parliament" in general, and in particular "difficult cases and judgment," the "King's aid," and even "transcripts and Records of the Parliament."

PART II. PARLIAMENT IN THE TUDOR PERIOD

VII

England in the Age of the Tudors

✿✿

"WHEN Henry VII ascended the throne," writes Lunt, "much in England was medieval and little was modern; when Elizabeth ended the line of Tudor in 1603 the proportion had been reversed." In emphasizing the century of the Tudors as an era of transition, the historian, of course, is not thinking of "modern" in terms of the machine age, the fruits of science and invention. He is concerned rather with the passing of such "medieval" features as feudalism, the handicraft system with its guilds, the all-pervading universal Church, and the scholastic philosophy of the universities. In their place come centralized authority and efficiency in government, the expansion of commerce supported by a royal navy, enclosures (mainly for conversion of arable into pasture), the domestic or "putting out" system in industry, individualism and a critical faculty in scholarship. There come to mind several *isms* which conveniently epitomize the new era: absolutism, nationalism, and sovereignty; mercantilism; humanism; and in foreign relations the "game of the balance of power."

When Henry VII assumed the crown in 1485, he became King of England and Wales, and Lord of Ireland. Wales was to be further organized along English lines by Henry VIII, who first invited Welsh representatives to parliament. Through Poynings' Acts[1] Henry VII had instituted a more effective control, but it remained for his son to take the title of King of Ireland. Scotland, of course, was completely inde-

[1] Named after Sir Edward Poynings, an Englishman whom Henry sent to replace the Earl of Kildare as deputy in 1494.

133

pendent. The only English possession left on the Continent was the staple town Calais, though loss of the French fiefs had never been officially recognized. New world colonies were a thing of the future, but as early as 1497 John Cabot was to reach Cape Breton Island. One may read in the accounts, "To him that found the new isle — £10."

The population was between two and three million, with the greater part still living in rural areas. Sheep "may have numbered about eight millions, that is, there were about three sheep to every human." [2] Except for imported luxuries, England was largely self-sufficient. Society was still stratified. Villeinage was soon to disappear, and the status and prosperity of the small farmer, whether freeholder or customary tenant, were to improve. The "sturdy yeomen" of this class were not to be found in any other land. As to the *political nation*, we shall hear more presently in connection with parliament.

It is interesting to compare with Fortescue's earlier *Praises* the impressions of an Italian visitor, Polydore Vergil,[3] as he describes Britain — "an Ilonde in the ocean sea buttinge over agaynste the Frenche shore." He is impressed with the great estuary of the Thames and its value for commerce, London bridge "of stone of wondrous artificiall workmanshippe," the temperate, healthful climate, and the effects of so northern a latitude — "the nighte is scarslie five houres in lengthe in soomer."

Further, "the grounde is marvellous fruitefull, and abundantlie replenished with cattayle." There is plenty of game for hunting, "so the nobilitie is much delited and exercised therein." The beef is peerless, and "in fine, the cheefe foode of the Englisheman consisteth in fleshe." As to wool, "this fleece maie justlie be alluded to [as] the golden fleece wherein the chefe richis of the people consistethe."

According to ancient usage, the nobles "do not so greatlie affecte citties as the commodious nearenes of dales and brookes, . . . wherebie it comethe to passe that the ruralls and common people, bie the entercourse and daylye conference which they have with the nobilitie, confuselee dwellinge amonge them, are made verie civile, and so consequentlie their citties nothinge famous."

England was in advance of the Continent in political and economic changes, but lagged behind in the renaissance of letters and art. A cul-

---

[2] "Today England and Wales contain about twenty million sheep, or one sheep to every two human beings." Bindoff.

[3] Coming to England about 1501 as a papal collector, Vergil remained to become naturalized. In 1508 he was commissioned by Henry VII to write a history of England, which appeared in 1534, in twenty-six books dedicated to Henry VIII.

tural map of sixteenth-century Europe indicates in concentric circles three great areas. First are the Latin nations, Italy and France, at the heart of civilization. Second, less advanced in culture but superior in some respects, are the areas of the Netherlands, Switzerland, the south and central German states and free cities, and *England*. Last in an outer circle lie the less advanced lands of Spain and Portugal, Poland and Hungary, North Germany and Scandinavia, and in the British Isles, *Scotland and Ireland*.

A Who's Who for about 1500 would include many a famous name, familiar even to those who have not studied the history of the era. Italians predominate in the arts: princely patrons like the Medici and Sforza; masters of statecraft like Cesare Borgia and Machiavelli; artists like Leonardo da Vinci and Raphael. In exploration and discovery, of course, the outstanding names are Portuguese and Spanish, or Italians sailing under the flags of Portugal and Spain.

Even when Henry VIII came to the throne, we are reminded, "Italy was the Mecca of progressively-minded Englishmen in every walk of life." However, in the England of about 1500, signs of promise were not wanting. Caxton had set up his press at Westminster in 1477. In three years thirty different books had been printed. Other presses soon appeared in London, with Fleet Street — newspaper row today — the printers' row of the sixteenth century. The scholars Linacre and Grocyn, recently returned from Italy, had introduced Greek at Oxford University, where Colet joined them in 1497. The latter was presently to establish his Boys' School at St. Paul's in London, while Linacre, as Royal Physician, was to found the College of Physicians, and dedicate his translation of Galen to the pope. Erasmus was in England more than once, visiting his friend Lord Mountjoy. Young Thomas More was sometimes with this older group, but occupied mainly in studying law at Lincoln's Inn, and hesitating between law and holy orders.

At court it was the queen mother, Margaret Beaufort, who was the patroness of Caxton and founded the Lady Margaret professorships at Oxford and Cambridge. Henry himself was on friendly terms with the dukes of Ferrara and Urbino and had Italians in his service — a Genoese physician, a master of ceremonies, and the scholar historian Polydore Vergil quoted above. The king also employed the best available tutors for the young princes, Arthur and Henry, including Skelton, who as poet laureate wore the green and white Tudor liveries. It was Henry VIII who was to bring king and court more fully into the swing of the

Renaissance, thus justifying Lord Mountjoy's enthusiastic letter to Erasmus on the young prince's accession: "I have no fear but when you heard that our Prince, now Henry VIII, whom we may well call our Octavius, had succeeded to his father's throne, all your melancholy left you at once. . . . But when you know what a hero he now shows himself, how wisely he behaves, what a lover he is of justice and goodness, what affection he bears to the learned, I will venture to swear that you will need no wings to make you fly to behold this new and auspicious star." [4]

Tudor chroniclers outdid their medieval predecessors in their enthusiasm for the great city on the Thames, and rightly so, for striking developments were taking place. "An Apology of the City," about 1575, calls London "an ornament to the realm by the beauty thereof, and a terror to other countries by reason of the great wealth and frequency [population]. It spreadeth the honour of our country far abroad by her navigations, and maketh our power feared even of barbarous princes." [5] Westminster, though linked to London by a line of great houses along the Strand, was still a separate community. It was the political capital — the home of the Chancery, Exchequer, and Law Courts, and the usual meeting place of parliament. London was the economic and social capital, yet not without great political importance. The Apology calls it "a mighty arm and instrument to bring any great desire to effect, if it may be won to a man's devotion." Pollard goes so far as to say that "Tudor despotism consisted largely in London's dominance over the rest of England."

The proximity of the two "capitals" was mutually advantageous. "A merchant in a French port was a hundred to five hundred miles away from Paris when he had a grievance to voice or a proposal to make; but a Londoner had only to go two miles up the Thames to reach the government offices or houses of parliament." [6] The Londoners were to become the best parliamentary lobbyists of the day.

London in Henry VII's reign was in area still little more than the one square mile of the modern "City," but striking changes were imminent. The walls, though not demolished, were no longer needed for defense. City life was free to extend west to Charing Cross and Holborn, north and east. South of the river Southwark was presently to attain the fea-

[4] Quoted by A. F. Pollard, *Henry VIII* (London, 1905), pp. 40–41.
[5] "An Apology of the City," printed in John Stow's *Survey of London*.
[6] Herbert Heaton, *Economic History of Europe* (New York, 1948), p. 309.

tures we associate with it in Shakespeare's time. In a bird's-eye view the scene would still be dominated by the Tower of London, old Gothic St. Paul's (minus its steeple after the fire of 1560), and London bridge, impressive now with houses from end to end, and its tall chapel in the center.

In the early years of the sixteenth century there were in London twenty-three important religious houses with their churches and cloisters, halls, gardens, and orchards. Some also had property which they rented, as, for instance, Christchurch Aldgate (one of the Austin priories) which had within the city tenements in sixty parishes, which produced over £300 yearly income. The dissolution of the monasteries (1536–1539) thus added space advantageous for residential and business purposes and made possible a large increase of population. "For the monastic precincts in London were — to use the language of a modern state agent — 'eligible building sites, ripe for development'." [7]

The greatest growth in population came after the middle of the century — from 60,000 consumers in 1540 to more than 300,000 in 1640, a fivefold increase. But quality as well as quantity was involved, for the newcomers included immigrants skilled in craft techniques, the noted seamen at Wapping from whom Hakluyt gathered the material for his *Principal Navigations,* able writers and actors attracted by the press and the stage, both centered in London.

London was the hub of foreign as well as domestic trade, and was also associated with the new maritime adventures. The Royal Exchange, built in 1566, served as London's bourse. There was yet no bank such as those of Genoa and Venice, but in London brokers, scriveners, and notably the goldsmiths served both government and private individuals.

The five Tudor rulers hardly need an introduction, popularized as they have been in biography, fiction, drama, and cinema. Yet their dramatic qualities have led to sensationalism, obscuring their virtues as rulers. Their absolutism was relative — they were not *despots* in the usual sense of the term. "At the top Tudor rule might savour of despotism," Bindoff says, "but at the bottom it rested upon a broad basis of self-government; and under kings who were masters of their craft the English people went on quietly serving their long political apprenticeship."

[7] E. Jeffries Davis, "The Transformation of London," in *Tudor Studies . . . Presented to Alfred Frederick Pollard* (London, 1924), pp. 287–311, an attractive, detailed account of the change.

The monarch depended upon and needed the active cooperation of the governing classes, and this could best be secured through parliament. Usually leadership, not coercion, sufficed.

Perhaps the greatest compliment that can be paid to Henry VII is to record amongst his biographers no less a person than the great scholar-statesman Francis Bacon. Henry Tudor was not quite Bacon's ideal of the "philosopher king," yet the fruits of his rule were such as might have come from such a monarch. The prince who was so "disciplined by adversity" during his exile that even on the throne he kept his own accounts, the man with "wide eyes" and a "tight mouth" who saw all and said little, was the king whose rule was summed up in Bacon's cryptic phrase — "What he minded he compassed."

Besides giving his land twenty-four years of peace and good government, Henry worked effectively with the new industrial and mercantile elements in the population. Early in the reign (1486) he courted them by a progress which took him to some of the key cities. At Bristol he made careful inquiry of the mayor and burgesses as to the causes of the town's poverty (loss of ships and merchandise in the last five years), encouraged them to build new ships, and promised help. "He thus won the hearts of the Bristol merchants, the mayor declaring that they had not received such words of comfort from any king for a hundred years." [8]

Henry VIII was truly a Renaissance prince, not unlike the Italian Medici and Sforza. His state was larger, his title hereditary, unlike the despots who climbed various ladders of fortune. Still, he shared their egotism and ruthlessness. He had the versatility of "Renaissance man," with talents ranging from mathematics and music to horsemanship and tennis. For contemporary confirmation we have only to turn to the best reporter of his day, the Venetian ambassador Sebastian Giustiniani, who on September 10, 1519, wrote to the Venetian Senate:

"His majesty is twenty-nine years old and extremely handsome. Nature could not have done more for him. He is much handsomer than any other sovereign in Christendom; a great deal handsomer than the king of France; very fair and his whole frame admirably proportioned. . . . He is very accomplished, a good musician, composes well, is a most capital horseman, a fine jouster, speaks good French, Latin and Spanish, is very religious, hears three masses daily, when he hunts, and sometimes five on other days. . . . He is very fond of hunting, and never takes his

---

[8] James Gairdner, *Henry the Seventh* (London, 1909), p. 46.

diversion without tiring eight or ten horses, which he causes to be stationed beforehand along the line of country he means to take, and when one is tired he mounts another, and before he gets home they are all exhausted. He is extremely fond of tennis. . . . He is affable and gracious, harms no one, does not covet his neighbor's goods, and is satisfied with his own dominions, having often said to me, 'Sir Ambassador, we want all potentates to content themselves with their own territories; we are satisfied with this island of ours.' He seems extremely desirous of peace.

"He is very rich. His father left him ten millions of ready money in gold, of which he is supposed to have spent one-half in the war against France . . . he is the best dressed sovereign in the world. His robes are very rich and superb, and he puts on new clothes every holiday."

Because of the controversial character of the changes wrought by the Reformation, it is inevitable that historical estimates of this prince include extremes of praise and blame.[9] For the theme of these studies, again it is the legal historian who offers the best cue. While admitting Henry's "cruelty, his caprice, his selfishness, his ingratitude," Professor Holdsworth insists: "It was only a consummate statesman with a true understanding of the needs of his age, of his own position as king, and of the character of his people, their laws, and their institutions, who could have planned, and induced the nation to accept, the policy of making a Reformation in religion by way of evolution and not by way of revolution, who could have created a modern state upon the basis of medieval institutions and the common law, and not upon the basis of new institutions and Roman law."[10]

The two short reigns of Edward VI and Mary (1547–1558) constituted a strange interlude, for neither was typically Tudor in character. Under Edward, the boy king, only ten years old when his father died, England experienced again some of the evils of a minority. The Council of Regency, wisely established by Henry VIII, was replaced by the young king's uncle, Edward Seymour, Duke of Somerset, as Lord Protector, and a new council subject to his control. After three years Somerset was replaced by the ambitious John Dudley, Duke of Northumberland.

[9] For an extremely hostile view it is not surprising to find the following from a Catholic biographer of Sir Thomas More: "Henry VIII destroyed more things of beauty and more things of promise, than any other man in European history. And many of his contemporaries admire him for it." R. W. Chambers, *Thomas More* (London, 1935), p. 107.

[10] Holdsworth, IV, 32.

Both regents were inclined to Protestantism, and with the help of Archbishop Cranmer carried the Reformation further in respect to services and doctrine.

Mary Tudor, the daughter of Henry and Catherine of Aragon, was well received as the proper successor of her brother (both by inheritance and her father's will). She has been called "the most honorable and conscientious of all the Tudors." It was inevitable that she follow a Spanish-Hapsburg policy, but her marriage with Philip of Spain offended the growing national spirit and mercantile interests. Public opinion was still divided enough to secure temporarily the restoration of Catholic creed and worship (though not the restoration of the monastic lands). This was accomplished within six months of her accession. Before another year had passed, England had been formally received back into the Catholic fold. Yet in the persecution of Protestants the queen's zeal exceeded the advice even of her Catholic clergy and strengthened opposition — "the blood of the martyrs is the seed of the Church."

Doctrine and ritual were formulated by the clergy in Convocation, but in both these reigns the principal changes — forward or backward, radical or conservative — were carried through by acts of parliament. Henry VIII had set a precedent which did more than anyone at the time suspected to establish the omnicompetence of the "King in his Parliament." Thus, when in Elizabeth's reign the Puritans were warned to leave matters of the Church to the bishops, it was possible for the opposition to quote the words of "old parliament men" — how the Church of England came not from the clergy but from the parliament.

Elizabeth was a Renaissance princess. Fortunate in sharing her brother's tutors, she had some such training in languages and literature, music and manners, as the Italian princesses of the House of Este and others. Her uncertain status in the reigns of Edward and Mary had made her, like her grandfather, canny and cautious. A Protestant by force of circumstances, she yet liked dignity and ceremonial in Church as well as State. Her kingdom was to be Protestant, but she preferred to be tolerant: "she wanted," in Neale's words, "no inquisitorial practices, opening windows into men's souls. Outward conformity was enough; a man's conscience should be his own, not the State's concern."

Sir Thomas Smith, writing his *Commonwealth of England* early in the reign (1565), was not alarmed at the phenomenon of a *queen regnant*: "The sexe not accustomed (otherwise) to intermeddle with publicke affaires," would not lack "the counsell of such grave and discreete men as be able to supplie all other defectes." He was probably correct in assuming much tutelage by the Council in the early years of the queen's reign. Her first Privy Council consisted of eleven experienced members who had sat in Mary's Council. Seven of these had also sat in the councils of Henry VIII and Edward VI. Only six were new men, including the able Sir William Cecil as Secretary.

As time went on Elizabeth assumed more independence and initiative. Like her father she was a good actor and sometimes achieved her ends by staging a scene, but tact and finesse were more effective. "Harrington tells how she would covertly search out the minds of her councillors, talking to Burghley till late at night, and then calling in another councillor, and so on; and afterwards compare their real thoughts with their utterances in council." More significant was the quality expressed by Neale in the Tudor phrase, "the affability of their prince." "No prince has been a greater courtier of the people, nor any actress known better how to move her audience to transports of love and admiration."

Opportunities were afforded by the annual royal progresses from one palace or manor to another. Occasionally queen and courtiers were lavishly entertained by a noble host such as "the Princely Pleasures" at Kenilworth, immortalized by Sir Walter Scott. More important was the appeal to the less exalted elements of the political nation — the gentry, the universities, London, and other towns.

"Whenever a town was visited, there were great preparations . . . Rubbish was cleared, streets cleaned, houses gaily decked, speeches memorized, perhaps pageants prepared, and last, but not least, a silver-gilt cup purchased to present to the Queen, usually with money inside, varying from twenty to a hundred pounds according to the wealth of the town. . . . Coventry put a hundred pounds in its cup, and Elizabeth was pleased to say to her Lords, 'It was a good gift, £100 in gold; I have but few such gifts.' To which the Mayor answered boldly, 'If it please your Grace, there is a great deal more in it.' 'What is that?' said she. 'It is,' said he, 'the hearts of all your loving subjects.' 'We thank you, Mr. Mayor,' said she, 'it is a great deal more indeed.'"

VIII

Continuity Plus Progress

✿✿✿

THE *most high and absolute power of the realme of Englande, consisteth in the Parliament. [Whatever is done in Parliament] is the Princes
and whole realmes deede: whereupon justlie no man can complaine,
but must accommodate himselfe to find it good and obey it.* SIR THOMAS
SMITH, 1565

COULD a knight who had sat in one of Henry IV's parliaments, Sir
Arnold Savage, for instance, have returned in ghostly guise to a parliament of Henry VII, he would have found much that was familiar. There
were the Lords, a group of hereditary peers, with bishops and abbots;
and the Commons, still numbering a little under three hundred, knights
and burgesses, chosen under the same electoral laws and processes. It
was still the unquestioned authority of the ruler to summon parliament,
set the length of the session, prorogue or dissolve, accept or reject bills.
There was the customary formal opening with the speech on "the causes
of the summons," the election and presentation of the speaker, the same
clerks and *Rolls*, the same powers and duties, varying in importance
from session to session as circumstances warranted. As to the distribution of power, Sir Arnold might well have sensed a difference in the
effective leadership of King and Council, and the inclination of this
first Tudor to favor his Commons.

In the Tudor period, as in the fifteenth century, continuous parliamentary government was neither expected nor desired. Henry VII
prided himself on the infrequency of his parliaments. The medieval

142

plea for yearly parliaments was abandoned, though sessions were longer and interest in them was increasing. Though a Tudor ruler was still expected to "live of his own," this proved inadequate not only in times of crisis, but because governments paid more officials and undertook more enterprises than their medieval predecessors. Besides needing subsidies, each of the five rulers was faced with special problems calling for parliamentary support and cooperation. One historian does relate how in 1566 Elizabeth told the French ambassador that the three parliaments she had held were enough for any reign and that she would summon no more, but calls it an empty threat "oddly reminiscent of the intention attributed to her grandfather in 1498 of dispensing with parliament and ruling 'in the French fashion.' " [1] There were occasional long intervals, as in the last half of Henry VIII's reign and during Wolsey's ascendancy under Henry VIII, but never any plan to abolish this well established and useful institution.[2]

On the whole the Tudors were possessed of a strong sense of legality. Francis Bacon remarks of Henry VII that "he was a great observer of formality in all his proceedings." Though Henry VIII committed some rather high-handed deeds, usually he preferred to work through legal means, and was advised so to do by Secretary Cromwell. Elizabeth won practical victories at the expense of recognizing theoretical powers and privileges of her parliaments.

Although some essential features of parliament remained the same, as the sixteenth century wore on, changes and adaptations there were, for the most part of a gradual evolutionary character. These include: (1) changes in membership — the reduction of the number of spiritual lords in the upper House, and in the Commons an increase in numbers and "quality"; (2) a change in the relative importance of the two Houses; (3) effective leadership by King and Council; (4) elaboration of the rules of procedure and debate, with *Journals* for both Houses; and (5) more "modern" theories as to parliament's powers and privileges, supplied in part by the lawyers and writers of treatises, in part by Puritan zeal.

[1] Bindoff, pp. 213, 214.
[2] The number by reigns are: for Henry VII, 7 parliaments in 24 years (10 sessions); for Henry VIII, 9 in 38 years (including the remarkable Reformation Parliament with 8 sessions in 7 years); for Edward VI, 2 (one with 5 sessions); for Mary, 5; for Elizabeth's reign of 44 years, 10 parliaments (one with 3 sessions), an average of about one every 3 years, the shortest 35 days, the longest 145, a total of 35 months.

This chapter will be concerned with personnel, some aspects of procedure, and the influence of King and Council in parliament, with emphasis on the first half of the century. Other features may be best dealt with as characteristic of Elizabeth's reign, the time of their origin or fuller development, with a wealth of sources to inform us thereon.

The Two Houses: Lords and Commons

In early days *House* had only a locative sense; that is, the *place* where parliament — Lords or Commons — was meeting — not a unit of government. By the end of the fifteenth century it had "acquired its definite institutional sense."[3] Examples of the first include an early instance from *Hardyng's Chronicle* — "in the common house amonge the knyghtes chosyn for the comons"; Young's petition, 1455, citing freedom of the Commons to speak "in the Hous of their assemble"; and in 1483 the chancellor's charge to the Commons to assemble in their "common and accustomed house."

Approaching the institutional sense, as early as 1440 Gloucester's protest declares "where in dede I have herd full notable men of the Lower Hous saye . . ." A letter of 1454 comments on "the disposicion of the Comons House agayn their [Lords'] billes . . ." More clearly, in 1485, in the parliamentary diary of the burgesses for Colchester, they report that "it pleased the Kyng and all his lords for to sende for Maister Speker and all the house in to the parliament chamber."

With rare exceptions the Great Hall of Westminster Palace continued to be the scene of the opening and closing sessions of parliament. The Lords, as heretofore, used other smaller halls within the Palace for their deliberations. We hear little of the Commons' "house," but assume that it continued to be their "accustomed place," the chapter house of Westminster Abbey, until 1547. By the Chantries Act of that year St. Stephen's Chapel within the Palace fell to the king, who assigned it to the Commons. This then was their "house" for three hundred years until its destruction by fire in 1834. They were thus under the same roof as the Lords, and no longer had to "appear in parliament" by crossing the street between the Abbey and the parliament with the Speaker at their head.

As a collegiate church the plan of St. Stephen's was a rectangle with

---

[3] Chrimes (pp. 126–130) assembles an interesting variety of expressions, locative at first, variable or ambiguous as the century wears on, more clearly institutional in the last two decades.

rows of benches facing each other on opposite sides of a central aisle. This arrangement, originally designed to facilitate antiphonal singing, may, it is believed, have had some influence on the development of the two-party system. It served to accentuate the physical separation and unity of parties, and was advantageous for real debate. The form was preserved in the House of Commons built after 1834 and in the new structure formally opened in 1950. At the south end in front of the great window sat the Speaker. On the table before him was placed the mace — the symbol of parliamentary authority — and here, too, was a place for the Clerk with his papers. The Chapel afforded little accommodation for committees, which met elsewhere — at the Guildhall, the Temple Church, or most likely in halls and lodgings of the Inns of Court.

Of course, no provision was made for visitors. The House of Commons has always claimed and enjoyed the right to exclude strangers and to debate with closed doors. No outsider was allowed on the floor of the House. Even the fact of his being a gentleman and a member of the Inner Temple did not excuse one Charles Johnson, "confessing himself to be no member of this House," from being examined at the bar and temporarily committed to the Serjeant's ward (1576). The business of parliament, like that of the King's Council, was supposed to be secret. The oath taken by the Clerk of the Parliament contained the same secrecy clause as that of the councillors.

The Commons' House built after the fire of 1834 had a small gallery for the press and dignitaries at the Speaker's end and one for visitors opposite. According to custom, the exclusion of unqualified persons from voting, or on occasion, of visitors from the galleries, was effected by a member's uttering the picturesque ejaculation, "I spy strangers." Thus informed, the Speaker was obliged to order withdrawal without putting a question. In recent years the more routine "Mr. Speaker, I beg to call your attention to the fact that strangers are present" suffices, or as recorded in Hansard (*Parliamentary Debates*), "Notice taken, that strangers were present." The new House built since the War is commended for its larger public and press galleries.

The lay lords, now definitely a group of hereditary peers, normally fluctuated around fifty.[4] There were a few new creations by *letters*

---

[4] They were temporarily reduced to twenty-nine at the beginning of Henry VII's reign because of attainders, suspension, and minorities. In the parliaments preceding

patent, but on a modest scale. Henry VII created only five, Henry VIII about twenty in the first thirty years of his reign. The chief change was the reduction in the number of spiritual lords, due of course to the dissolution of the monasteries (1536–1539) — no monastery, no abbot. This left the two archbishops and nineteen bishops, raised to twenty-four by the creation of new bishoprics. Henceforth they were outnumbered by the lay lords, and were virtually nominees of the Crown. The second Act of Annates established a rule whereby members of a cathedral chapter directed by a royal missive — *congé d'élire* (permission to elect) — were expected to follow the Crown's nomination. Still, a bishop had considerable authority throughout his see. Amongst them were always men of ability, learning, and distinction — an asset in the House.

The judges, of course, continued to be summoned to give counsel, but they had no vote. Pollard finds evidence that Henry VII's laws were formulated in principle by the judges before submission to parliament. Under Henry VIII "it was the custom of the lords in parliament to secure copies of bills introduced in the house of commons and take the opinion of the judges upon them before they were sent up from the lower house."

In the Commons, changes were twofold: (1) a great increase in numbers, and (2) in the type of member a virtual reversal in the proportion of true burgesses to country gentlemen. Henry VIII's first House of Commons numbered 298 members; Elizabeth's first, 398; and at the accession of James I the number was 467. Twenty-seven of the newcomers are accounted for by Henry VIII's grant of representation to Wales (twelve knights and eleven burgesses) and to the border shires of Monmouth and Chester their two knights each. The rest came from the newly created parliamentary boroughs.[5] While a few of these may have been designed by the rulers themselves as a means of packing parliament, recent research reveals that the impetus came from the boroughs themselves, but more often from the neighboring lords and gentry.

the dissolution there were present in person or by proxy twenty-eight mitred abbots; three more had been included by Henry VIII in the earlier years of the reign. The abbots were naturally inclined to be independent, with foreign connections and loyal to the papacy.

[5] "Henry VIII added 14 borough seats (besides the Welsh ones), Edward VI's advisers 34, Mary 25 and Elizabeth 62. Thus the 224 borough members of Henry VIII's first parliament became the 308 of Elizabeth's first and the 372 of her last, and by the close of the century the House was half as large again as it had been at the beginning." Bindoff, p. 215.

Motives and methods may be best revealed by examples from Elizabeth's reign described below.[6]

The Tudors rarely packed their parliaments, nor did they bribe.[7] They did not need to, because of the common interests and harmony usually prevailing between Crown and people. They did not so much seek a numerical majority, says Neale, as leadership — a core of leaders to prepare and organize a program of official legislation. To this end they made recommendations which were usually received with respect and even approval.

Henry VIII occasionally sent letters to constituencies inviting support for suggested candidates. Apparently the opening session of the Reformation Parliament was not "packed," but in by-elections for the parliaments of 1536 and 1539 Thomas Cromwell interfered to secure support for policies, his master's and his own. Extant correspondence indicates that Cromwell even abandoned the gracious approach which often availed the monarch. When the sheriff of Canterbury, reporting the election of two burgesses, expressed regrets "that he was not made aware of the King's pleasure in time," Cromwell insisted on and secured a new election returning the preferred candidates. More typically Tudoresque was the scolding sent by the Council to the sheriff of Kent for making their lordship's *request* into a *commandment*!

Edward VI's councillors sent out some letters of recommendation, more in Northumberland's regency than Somerset's. Elections were relatively free for Queen Mary's first two parliaments. Only in the third and succeeding elections did writs to the sheriffs include the admonition to choose men "of the wise, grave, and Catholic sort." Under Elizabeth, in 1584, a crisis year, there were some admonitions, and in 1586 electors were urged to re-elect those of the previous parliament.

Circular letters like those of 1571 and 1597[8] were merely a more modern version of the medieval command to send up "good and lawful men," conversant with their districts. They contained sound advice which even a present-day electorate might well heed. The letters of 1571 from the Lords of the Council to certain notables complain of abuses in previous elections, in which persons were named "some for private respects and favour upon their own suits, some to enjoy some immunities from arrests upon actions during the time of Parliaments . . ."

---

[6] See below, pp. 156–161.
[7] The first recorded case of bribery is that by a candidate, not the Crown.
[8] Quoted in full in Tanner, *Tudor Constitutional Documents*, pp. 523–524, 525–526.

Letters of 1597 to all the sheriffs set forth that "Her Majesty meaning to have this her intended Parliament to be served with men of understanding and knowledge for the particular estate of the places whereunto they ought to be chosen, and of discretion also requisite in consultation for causes concerning the public weal of the realm, hath commanded us of her Privy Council to admonish you to whom her Majesty's writs of summons are now directed to have good regard how this her Majesty's good meaning may be observed and fulfilled."

Official Records: Procedure

The first extant *Lords Journal* dates from 1509,[9] the first *Commons Journal* from 1547. It is the *Lords Journal* that best replaces the old *Parliament Rolls* in describing the formal opening and closing sessions, complete with texts of the speeches. Both *Journals* do more for us than the old *Rolls* in recording day-to-day procedure in either House.

John Seymour, Clerk for twenty years from the first parliament of Edward VI in 1547, is credited with keeping the first record for the Commons. As time goes on Seymour's record increases in length and scope. He notes not merely the reading of bills (as in his earliest entries) but roll calls, orders of the House concerning privilege, and in 1553–1554 the first division figures. He also gives us an account of the election of the Speaker and his three requests for privilege.

His successor, Fulk Onslow (Clerk 1567–1602) in 1571 introduces a "new technique in compiling his Journal, writing a second or fair copy from the rough notes scribbled in the House." As time goes on he even attempts to include the substance of some speeches. In 1572 "comes the first recorded instance of the House ordering an entry to be made in the Journal. The Journal was no longer the private diary or *aide-mem-oire* of the Clerk. It had become the official record of the proceedings of the House."[10]

The classification of bills remained unchanged. There were public bills, those general in application and "serving the commonwealth as a whole"; subsidy bills (called *indentures* or *indentured schedules*); and general pardons. Private bills were, as in earlier days, concerned with

---

[9] Fragments of *Lords Journals* survive from earlier times.

[10] Neale, *Elizabethan House of Commons*, p. 369. The *Commons Journals* from 1580 to 1603 were lost, but fortunately much material from them was incorporated by the noted antiquarian Sir Simonds D'Ewes in his *The Journals of all the Parliaments during the Reign of Queen Elizabeth*. There were two or three private diaries which D'Ewes used to "enlarge and beautify" the *Journals*.

individual or sectional interests — the bills of singular persons, guilds and companies, cities and boroughs.

Public bills could originate with the government, with individual members, or with committees appointed by the House as the result of a motion. Private bills were not yet dealt with in committee by the quasi-judicial process of hearing counsel and witnesses for and against in use today. They were handled as were public bills and consumed much time. Lobbying was already an art.[11] The Crown, of course, could still assent to or refuse bills at will, but could no longer add provisoes. On occasion some use might be made of the dispensing power, exempting an individual or small group from the force of a statute.

Legislative procedure was becoming more precise. An ordinary public bill, written on paper, might be presented to the Commons either by the member sponsoring it or the Clerk. The Speaker determined the order in which bills were read. The practice of three readings, established in the course of Elizabeth's reign, worked as follows. There was usually no debate on the first reading; it was the means by which the contents of the bill were disclosed to the House. Two or three days elapsed to permit time to digest and reflect. The second reading, followed by debate, might lead to immediate acceptance or rejection, or more likely reference to a committee. The report from committee, together with amendments, was brought back to the House for the second reading, and if passed, engrossment. Final passage followed two or three days later on the third reading. Toward the end of the reign committees came to be used not only for amendment, but to transfer debate, in part, at least, from the floor of the House to the committee chamber.

Committees of the Commons were formed by members calling out names which the Clerk jotted down until he had a "convenient number." As Council members of the House usually sat near the Speaker and Clerk, their nominations were most likely to be heard and recorded!

Bills originating in the Lords passed through the same process. The differences between the Houses were compromised in joint conferences. Early in Elizabeth's reign Sir Thomas Smith was able to describe rules of debate as well established, but of these we shall hear more in another chapter.

Chancery continued to be the abiding place of the official *Statute*

[11] See p. 169.

Roll, but the new art of the printing press was now drawn into government service. In 1508 one Richard Pynson was appointed to the office of King's Printer. In this post he published Henry VIII's tract against Luther and the *Session Laws.* From the first year of the reign on it was the practice to publish in one volume all the acts of a given session of Parliament — hence the title *Session Laws.*[12] Thomas Berthelet, King's Printer 1530–1547, gratified his royal patron's taste for the magnificent by producing books of poetry or romances in luxury editions, with gilt-tooled bindings in the Venetian manner, and is believed to have brought Italian workmen to England for this purpose. The statutes, of course, required a more subdued and dignified format. Berthelet's volumes of the *Session Laws* (in what the bookmen call quarto size) are printed on a good quality of paper in large, clear black-letter type. The volume for 1534 has the following title page:

"Actes made in the Session of this Present Parliament holden upon prorogation at Westminster, the xxv daye of Januarye, in the xxv yere of the reygne of our moste dradde soverayne lorde kynge Henry the VIII and there contynued and kepte tylle the xxx. daye of Marche then next ensuying: to the honour of God and holy Church, and for the common weale and profyte of this his realme."

The table lists twenty-two acts, ranging from some of the major Reformation measures, such as those on restraint of annates and the determining of the succession, to one for "avoiding the destruction of wild fowl" and one for the paving of Holborn and other areas. At the end are a small engraving of the royal coat of arms and the words "God Save the Kyng."

"The King in His Parliament"

To those who have followed the evolution of government through the Middle Ages there is nothing new in the importance of the role of the Council. What is novel is that Tudor councils were better staffed and organized, and engaged in more activities — figuratively they had a finger in every pie. Tudor monarchs had greater freedom in their choice of councillors. They were able to ignore some of the old nobility; to find educated clerks and even chancellors who were laymen, not ecclesiastics; and to rely increasingly on the middle class. It was one of the

[12] Sets of the *Session Laws* are preserved not only in the British Museum and other English Libraries but in law libraries in the United States.

Parliament in the reign of Elizabeth I (1584)

The House of Commons in the reign of James I (1624)

complaints of the insurgents from the conservative north in the rising of 1536 (*Pilgrimage of Grace*) that the king "takes of his Council and has about him persons of low birth and small reputation." Councillors, of course, had ceased to be members of parliament per se, but there were always some peers in the Council and it was not difficult to secure the election of a few to the Commons.

"The King in his Parliament" was not yet merely a legal fiction. The ruler was still present on occasions other than the formal ceremonial opening and closing. The reigns of two queens, Mary and Elizabeth, may have helped to reduce the occasions for the royal presence in parliament, just as later the rule of two "foreign" princes, George I and George II, contributed to the absence of the ruler from cabinet meetings.

Henry VII was not as great a parliamentarian as his son, but he did appear and play an active role on occasion. In his first parliament, 1485, the king "with his own mouth" explained to the Commons the justice of his title. On December 10 he in person "graciously received" the welcome request made by the Speaker that he should marry the Princess Elizabeth of York. In the parliament of 1497 he "with his own hand delivered in a bill of trade then read." [13]

It was natural in view of the personalities of the Tudors, their competent councils, and the novel problems they faced, that most important bills should emanate from the government. Francis Bacon commends Henry VII in this wise: "Certainly his times for good commonwealths' laws did excel. So as he may justly be celebrated for the best lawgiver to this nation after King Edward the first: for his laws, whoso marks them well, are deep, and not vulgar; not made upon the spur of a particular occasion for the present, but out of providence of the future, to make the estate of his people still more and more happy; after the manner of the legislators in ancient and heroical times."

His first parliament, which met within ten weeks of the accession, helped to establish the dynasty: it recognized him as king, proscribed his vanquished rivals, and voted funds necessary to carry on. Later parliaments helped to re-establish the rule of law by the Star Chamber Act and measures regulating the powers and duties of justices of the peace. "Incomparably the best business man to sit upon the English throne," in the opinion of Bindoff, Henry sponsored several important economic measures. These included trade regulations designed to en-

[13] *Cottoni Posthuma*, quoted by Pollard, p. 264.

courage the English cloth industry and the new Company of Merchant Adventurers; an act giving the government control over the guilds; others dealing with weights and measures, prices and wages; well-intentioned but less successful acts to check enclosures and usury (the taking of interest), and to handle the problem of vagabondage.

Odd as it may seem at first thought, it is the most despotic and domineering of the Tudors, Henry VIII, who has been characterized by Pollard as the "great architect of Parliament." "Under his rule its privileges were consolidated, its *personnel* was improved, its constituency enlarged, its political weight enhanced in foreign eyes, its authority increased, its sessions made more frequent and prolonged."

The Reformation Parliament, with its eight sessions in the years 1529–1536, has been characterized as the first *modern* parliament — "something which has a life instead of being an occasion." Only by sweeping and unprecedented legislation was the break with Rome accomplished. The two sessions of 1532 lasted for over a hundred days. All told there were 137 statutes, "32 of them directly concerned with the great national issue."

It is Pollard again who effectively pictures the tactics of the royal parliamentarian:

"No one was ever a greater adept in the management of the House of Commons which is easy to humour but hard to drive. . . . Henry VIII was very assiduous in the attentions he paid to his lay Lords and Commons. From 1529 he suffered no intermediary to come between Parliament and himself. He constantly visited the Houses and remained within their precincts for hours at a time, watching every move in the game and taking note of every symptom of parliamentary feeling.

"He sent no royal commands to his faithful Commons; in this respect he was less arbitrary than his daughter, Queen Elizabeth. He submitted points for their consideration, argued with them, and frankly gave his reasons. It was always done, of course, with a magnificent air of royal condescension, but with such grace as to carry the conviction that he was really pleased to condescend and to take counsel with his subjects . . ." Pollard concludes: "He trusted his Parliament and expected his Parliament to place equal confidence in him." [14]

Some of the major acts of the Reformation Parliament are notable for their propaganda-like preambles, designed to make out a case. They

[14] *Henry VIII* (London, 1905), pp. 262–264.

have been compared to a leading editorial in a government-supporting newspaper in modern times. In the act transferring revenue from the papal to the royal treasury [15] the emphasis is on the duty and inclination of "faithful, loving and obedient subjects . . . to desire to provide not only for the public weal of their native country but also for the supportation, maintenance, and defence of the royal estate of their most dread, benign, and gracious Sovereign Lord, . . . calling to their remembrance not only the manifold and innumerable benefits daily administered by his Highness to them all."

Others, such as the Act in Restraint of Appeals, rise to higher levels in effectively advancing the new concepts of nationalism and sovereignty: "Where by divers sundry old authentic histories and chronicles, it is manifestly declared and expressed that this realm of England is an empire, and so hath been accepted in the world, governed by one Supreme Head and King having the dignity and royal estate of the imperial Crown of the same, unto whom a body politic, compact of all sorts and degrees of people divided in terms and by names of Spiritualty and Temporalty, be bounden and owe to bear next to God a natural and humble obedience; he being also institute and furnished by the goodness and sufferance of Almighty God with plenary, whole, and entire power, preeminence, authority, prerogative, and jurisdiction to render and yield justice and final determination to all manner of folk resiants or subjects within this his realm . . ."

It was in the parliament of 1543 that the king backed the Commons in vindicating their privilege. As we have seen, freedom from arrest in civil actions had long been recognized for members of both Houses. Release for a member of the Commons or his servant was effected by a petition of his fellow members, for a *writ of privilege* issued out of Chancery. The novelty in Ferrers' Case was the direct action by the House itself in securing its privilege.

George Ferrers is not unworthy to be the hero of the tale. He is one of those lesser lights rather eclipsed by the galaxy of more brilliant stars in which the Tudor era abounds. To students of English literature he is the poet, writer of masques, and inventor of the *Mirror of Magistrates*. To the legal historian he is the translator and publisher of the first printed volume of the *Statutes* in English (1534). He was a lawyer, a member of Lincoln's Inn, whose "oratory gained him a high reputation

[15] An Act Annexing First Fruits and Tenths to the Crown, 1534.

at the bar." According to the chronicler, Holinshed, who describes so vividly the episode of 1543, he was also "gentleman" and "servant to the King." In the parliament of that year he sat as burgess for the important Devonshire port of Plymouth.

It was "in the Lent season, whilst the Parliament yet continued," as he was going to the Parliament House that Ferrers was arrested as a surety for debt by deputies of the London sheriffs and detained in the Counter (local city jail) in Bread Street. Fortunately the Houses were sitting. The response was prompt and vigorous. On the arrest being reported to the Speaker and members present, order was given the Serjeant to "repair to the Counter in Bread Street . . . and there demand delivery of the prisoner." But resistance by city officials led to a fray, "not without hurt of either part," and the rueful Serjeant returned with a broken mace and no prisoner!

Fortunately for the vindication of privilege the Houses were still sitting. The Serjeant, "finding the Speaker and all the burgesses set in their places, declared unto them the whole case as it fell, who took the same in so ill part that they all together (of whom there were not a few as well of the King's Council as also of his Privy Chamber) would sit no longer without their burgess, but rose up wholly and repaired to the Upper House, where the whole case was declared by the mouth of the Speaker before Sir Thomas Audley, knight, then Lord Chancellor of England, and all the Lords and Judges there assembled, who, judging the contempt to be very great, referred the punishment thereof to the order of the Common House."

The chancellor readily offered to issue the customary writ of privilege "which they of the Common House refused, being in a clear opinion that all commandments and other acts of proceeding from the Nether House were to be done and executed by their Serjeant without writ, only by show of his mace, which was his warrant."

With this backing the Serjeant's second demand was successful. Ferrers was released, and next day the sheriffs with their deputies appeared at the bar of the House to answer for the contempt.[16]

[16] "The said Sheriffs and the same White were committed to the Tower of London, and the said clerk (which was the occasion of the affray) to a place there called 'Little Ease', and the officer of London which did the arrest . . . with four other officers to Newgate, where they remained from the 28th until the 30th of March, and then they were delivered, not without humble suit made by the Mayor of London and other their friends." — The quotations in this account of Ferrers' Case are from Holinshed's *Chronicles*, as per Tanner, *Tudor Constitutional Documents*, pp. 580–583.

But the best was yet to come. The king, calling before him the chancellor, judges, Speaker, and others of the "gravest persons of the Nether House," commended their wisdom in maintaining the privileges of their House. Further, "he alleged that he, being head of the Parliament and attending in his own person upon the business thereof, ought in reason to have privilege for him and all his servants attending there upon him. So that if the said Ferrers had been no burgess, but only his servant, yet in respect thereof he was to have the privilege as well as any other. 'For I understand,' quoth he, 'that you not only for your own persons but also for your necessary servants, even to your cooks and horsekeepers, enjoy the same privilege.'"

Following this assurance his Majesty expounded a theory of "the King in his Parliament" not to be surpassed by Sir Thomas Smith or any of the other learned "treatisours" of the age: "And further we be informed by our Judges that we at no time stand so highly in our estate royal as in the time of Parliament, wherein we as head and you as members are conjoined and knit together into one body politic, so as whatsoever offence or injury (during that time) is offered to the meanest member of the House is to be judged as done against our person and the whole Court of Parliament. Which prerogative of the Court is so great . . . as all acts and processes coming out of any other inferior courts must for the time cease and give place to the highest. . . . And this may be a good example to other to learn good manners, and not to attempt anything against the privilege of this Court, but to take their time better."

IX

Parliament in the Reign of Elizabeth I

✿✿

IN TUDOR England it was still true that the shire, or the county as it was now more commonly called, was the unit of local government. There was one new official, the Lord Lieutenant, usually the chief nobleman of the county, whose main duty was to hold annual musters of the militia and to act as military leader of the shire. It was still those "good and lawful men," gentlemen and freeholders, who served as sheriffs, coroners, and justices of the peace.

Local patriotism tied in with the new cult of antiquities (not classical lore but England's own past) to produce county histories, with descriptions of notable natural and architectural features, local legends and heroes. John Leland, named King's Antiquary by Henry VIII, did not live to complete his projected history of all the counties. Most notable was William Lambarde's *Perambulation of Kent*, 1576. The Preface, by a contemporary, extols the "studie of histories" and the lessons thereof, and insists that there is "no Historie so meete as the Historie of England" for the gentlemen upon whose good judgment and service the "good estate" of England rests. Lambarde's description served Lord Burghley as a guidebook with which to regale Queen Elizabeth on one of her progresses into Kent.

Electors, Elected, and Elections

The "country-gentleman's world was the county," says Neale.[1] Hence

---

[1] The account of electors, elected and elections in this section is based primarily on the admirable volume by J. E. Neale, *The Elizabethan House of Commons.* Any passages from Neale used in the following sections are so indicated.

an important factor in political and social life was his prestige within his county. Prestige might depend on his family's standing, his own ability, wealth, and hospitality, and even the favor of a great lord of whose retinue he was a member. Yes, for although the Court of Star Chamber may be credited with eliminating livery in its disturbing fifteenth-century form, a milder and less objectionable variant, clientage, had taken its place. Clientage, while it led to rivalry and faction, was also evidence of pride in ability and achievement, prestige based on worth. "It assumed the part played by politics in our modern society, and in the county is the main clue to parliamentary elections. A county election was in fact a mustering of the community."

Participants in elections displayed the same remarkable energy that characterized men in other activities: buccaneers or burgesses, pirates or politicians, it was all the same! Professor Neale has worked out in amazing detail all aspects of these elections. He finds for each county an electoral pattern of its own. For the purpose of these studies, a brief summary with a few selected illustrations must suffice.

These electoral patterns include the following:

(1) Occasionally a single family monopolized both county seats for a period of years. Such was Oxfordshire throughout much of Elizabeth's reign, for the Knollys, father and sons. Sir Francis, whose wife was first cousin to the queen, was vice-chamberlain and privy councillor, one of the most notable courtiers at Elizabeth's accession, and "a man without rival among the commoners in his county."

(2) In some counties one, in others two, families were so superior socially that no one could hope or dare compete. In Northamptonshire it was said to be "the ancient course to have a knight on each side," that is from the west and east. In 1597 and 1601 this arrangement served to divide the honors between the two greats — Sir Walter Mildmay and Christopher Hatton.

(3) Some counties had their senior and junior seats: "custom had come to assign much additional prestige to the 'first' of the two knightships of the shire." Surrey divided the honors between two families — one noble, the Howards of Effingham, the other gentle — the Mores of Losely. William, the first Lord Howard of Effingham, was father of the great Lord Admiral of Spanish Armada fame.

(4) Some counties present a more liberal pattern. One without men of noble rank was Huntingdonshire, where even the Lord Lieutenant

was a commoner. Here there were three families of gentry with large estates who for some time determined elections. Still more liberal was Warwickshire, where with one exception, the gentry inclined to share the honor of their county seats as widely as possible. Still more striking, as we might expect, was the situation in the western counties of Cornwall, Devon, and Dorset, where "a sustained monopoly was apparently out of the question; and, with few exceptions, twice was as often as the more influential gentry could hope to represent the county."

County elections present little that is new, but we know more about them and sense the increasing interest on the part of electors and elected. As in earlier days, the election was normally held at the county seat. In a big area like Yorkshire this meant a long journey on horseback or, for some of the freeholders, on foot; for those not equal to the occasion absence and thus disfranchisement resulted. The actual place within the county town was set by custom — the town hall or guild hall, a nearby castle, or even a church.

By statute the sheriff must hold an election at the first county court after receipt of the parliamentary writ. Proceedings were supposed to begin between 8 and 9 A.M. On the opening day formalities included these steps: the court was "set" — i.e., opened; the election writ read; nominations made; then the actual election by "voices." If competition proved close there followed the "view" or the "poll." [2] The final step rested with the sheriff, who drew up the indenture, sealed by a selection of freeholders, and made the official return to Chancery.

Although it is impossible to ascertain the proportion of contested to uncontested elections, Neale concludes that in Elizabeth's reign, at least, the majority went uncontested. If no contest was anticipated but rather an election with "no repugnant voices," "there was probably little canvassing of the ordinary freeholders and nothing like a full muster of voters. . . . Thus we should picture the average Elizabethan county election as a tame affair; a small and friendly gathering of the gentry, a somewhat formal meeting." If a contest was expected, canvass-

[2] "The view was a device to avoid the time-consuming procedure of the poll. It was taken by separating candidates' supporters into distinct companies, which the Sheriff or a party of gentlemen could survey, and guess at the relative size of each." When a poll was conceded, the freeholders had to pass before the Sheriff or his officer, "assisted by the representatives of the competing candidates. . . . Each side had the right to challenge a man's qualifications, and when challenged he had to declare on corporal oath that he possessed the statutory value of freehold and perhaps that he was a resident of the county."

ing was practiced, although sometimes frowned upon as conspiracy. The initiative might be taken by the would-be candidates, the leading gentlemen of the county, one or more groups. Canvassers compiled lists of freeholders, embryonic poll-lists.

In all this the key man was the sheriff, himself usually one of the leading gentlemen of the shire and apt to have partisan connections. There were many devices — tricks of the trade — by which an election might be manipulated. Now one, now another, served the turn. That we know most about the contests in which force or chicanery was employed is perhaps misleading. It was now realized that more effective than a suit against the sheriff (authorized by the Act of 1445) [3] was prosecution by a bill in Star Chamber. Here the aggrieved candidate could take action, not only against the sheriff, but his supporters, and might charge conspiracy or force, typical Star Chamber offenses. "And what a stroke of fortune for the historian!" exclaims Neale, for "all the proceedings, prior to the final hearing and judgment, were in writing," including the plaintiff's *bill* and the defendants' *answers*.

Remembering that most elections were uncontested, it is still interesting, indeed amusing, to note some of the tricks known to have been used by one or other of the sheriffs or candidates on occasion. There was the matter of time. An unscrupulous sheriff might conceal his receipt of the writ either to give his side further time for preparation or to inveigle opponents into assembling their voters in vain. Occasionally a change of place was effected, as in a Monmouth election staged in St. Thomas Church on the outskirts of the town instead of the customary hall of Monmouth Castle. Candidates might pre-empt inns and houses for their own supporters, and thus exclude opponents. If he dared defy the rules and face the consequences, a sheriff might conclude the election after the initial acclamation (voice vote) or refuse to proceed beyond "the view," or break off the poll, or falsify its verdict.

For the cities and boroughs two interrelated developments already noted need further comment: (1) the increase in the number of urban constituencies entitled to send representatives to parliament; (2) the new type of borough member, a result of the process whereby the landed

[3] A successful action in accordance with this statute is recorded in Plowden's *Reports* for the second year of Mary's reign. But upon occasion candidates and their supporters went so far as to agree with a compliant sheriff " 'to save him harmless,' as the phrase went, from the legal consequences of his trickery — in other words, to pay his fine."

gentry captured the boroughs and with them the House of Commons. The geographical distribution of the new constituencies in certain reigns seems to lend color to the assumption that there was a deliberate design of the Crown to pack the Commons. For instance, the Duke of Northumberland, regent for Edward VI, awarded twelve new seats to progressive Cornwall, while Mary Tudor assigned ten to conservative Yorkshire. But recent studies seem to prove that on the whole initiative came from the boroughs themselves, or more often from their lord or patron.[4]

Such a lordly patron was the powerful Earl of Huntingdon. It seems likely that the borough of Christchurch was enfranchised (1571) at his instance. In 1584, the borough's third parliamentary election, "we find the Mayor writing that the Earl 'hath and of ancient right ought to have the nomination of one of our burgesses.' " In the records of the borough of Newton in the Isle of Wight, enfranchised in 1584, it is noted that " 'at the special instance of Sir George Carey (Governor of the Isle) — two burgesses were admitted into the High Court of Parliament.' " Carey was granted for life the right to nominate one of the burgesses. Other patrons include a peer like the Earl of Leicester, and an eminent commoner like Sir Robert Cecil. One or both seats might be secured for an outsider; that is, a gentleman of the clientage. Some boroughs gave up both seats to such; others preserved a happy medium by electing one local member, so that " 'the law should be in force for the one burgess and at liberty for the other.' "

For the boroughs themselves, a gentleman M.P. might prove more influential in advancing their interests than a mere burgess. These interests were much like those of earlier days — municipal liberties to safeguard or augment, rivals to compete with, economy (for the gentry were glad to serve gratis), as well as broader interests of industry and commerce. Then, too, we are reminded that the medieval theory of the members as *attorneys* for their constituencies was still alive. It was not unusual to employ a stranger as attorney.

According to the letter of the law, about 1600 we should come out with a House of Commons composed of 90 country gentlemen repre-

[4] There were three methods of enfranchisement. (1) A few were "restored" boroughs — towns which once sent representatives, discontinued the practice, and now sought to resume it. (2) In a few instances a clause of enfranchisement was inserted in letters patent of incorporation. (3) Others, the greater number, merely received for the first time a writ from the sheriff, authorized by the Crown through Chancery.

senting the counties and 372 resident citizens and burgesses — four townsmen for every gentleman. Instead, we have the reverse! Some cities and boroughs preserved complete independence. Among these it is interesting to find the notable parliamentary boroughs of early days described above. London's four members were always citizens, as were those of several other large towns which could easily afford wages or find candidates ready to serve gratis. This was true (with one exception each) of the cathedral cities of York and Salisbury.[5] The latter, as of old, restricted choice of members to the city council and its Recorder. Bristol consistently returned its Recorder and one of its aldermen, although its High Steward was of the great patron type. Coventry usually returned its own local citizens.

Competition bore fruit in producing a House literally of all the talents, attractive, efficient, and assertive. There were country gentlemen, royal officials, lawyers, merchants, and financiers. Famous men who sat in Parliament include the Cecils, Sir Philip Sidney, Sir Walter Raleigh, Francis Bacon, and Edward Coke, scholars like Sir Henry Spelman and Sir Robert Cotton, and even such adventurers as Sir Humphrey Gilbert and Sir Francis Drake. As the reign wore on, there were an increasing number who had attended the universities or the Inns of Court, or both. As a rule, about half the members of an Elizabethan House of Commons had sat before.[6] "The 'Old Parliament Man,' as he was called — the habitué of the House of Commons — was already a conspicuous figure." It was such an authority, well versed in precedents, that we shall see the Puritan Peter Wentworth quoting to good effect: "I am told by old parliament men . . ."

Pageantry and Privilege

The opening of parliament followed much the line established in the fourteenth century, but with more emphasis on ceremonial. The procession to the Parliament House was virtually the full court in motion, including the sovereign, the courtiers, all the Lords led by the peers holding grand serjeanties and carrying the royal insignia — the cap royal

---

[5] Others were Bath, Ludlow, Newcastle-on-Tyne, and Worcester. The ports were more cosmopolitan. Both "Portsmouth and Southampton had impressive numbers of noblemen, courtiers, officials and gentry on their burgess-rolls . . . They were in consequence more exposed and susceptible to the intrusion of outsiders into their parliamentary seats."

[6] "Though only four Elizabethans seem to have sat in twelve or more parliaments, there were a few who managed to get ten into their lives. One even managed eleven."

and the sword of state — with heralds, and serjeants-at-arms. The queen usually rode in an open chariot or horse litter, resplendent in robes and jewels, just the type of performance in which she delighted.

As is true today, the Commons were not a part of the procession. After being sworn in, they assembled in their own House to await summons to join the queen and Lords. With their increase in numbers, the space allotted them at the bar must have been even more inadequate than in earlier days. The old phrase, "as many as could conveniently get in," still applied.

The eloquence of fifteenth-century chancellors in "showing the causes of the parliament" must have been somewhat obscured by being couched in Latin. A Tudor chancellor (or in this reign, the Lord Keeper) spoke in English, virtually the English of Shakespeare, and must have reached a wider audience. There was now little in the way of text or sermon, but a rather long oration with praise of the queen and a survey of the religious and political state of the country, sometimes including foreign affairs. "In 1589, after the defeat of the Armada, Sir Christopher Hatton used the occasion for a spirited, eloquent, and patriotic oration, not unworthy of comparison with Mr. Winston Churchill's great war-speeches" (Neale).

After the Speech from the Throne, as was long customary, the Commons returned to their House to elect their Speaker. There was no change in their officers, the same three described above — Speaker, Clerk, and Serjeant-at-Arms. Long service was characteristic of the Clerk at this time. As we have seen, there were only two in the whole of Elizabeth's reign: John Seymour, credited with instituting the *Commons Journal,* and Fulk Onslow, who completed its evolution.[7] For this period we know more about the Serjeant-at-Arms and his duties. Ordinarily he was one of the twenty-five serjeants-at-arms of the queen's Household. An esquire or gentleman by birth, he held office for life by letters patent. In parliament time he was to be attendant upon the Speaker and carry the mace before him. More particularly he was doorkeeper of the Commons' House, permitting entry of actual members, an occasional messenger from the Lords, or someone "willed by the House to come in." As the Commons assumed the right to enforce privileges and rules of order, the Serjeant served as policeman. To his

[7] See above, p. 148.

custody the House might commit anyone infringing its dignity or privileges.

As to the Speaker, the form of election was preserved, but nomination was apt to come from one of the privy-councillor members of the House, and was based on a preference already expressed by the queen and Council before Parliament met.[8] As we have seen in earlier days, it was an advantage to the House to have a Speaker acceptable to the monarch, and not impossible to secure one like Sir Arnold Savage, *persona grata* to both Crown and Commons. With true Tudor tact, no attempt was made to have a privy councillor chosen. Further, that would have prevented him from having a voice in the House and serving on committees. A lawyer was preferred, and in fact in Elizabeth's reign all the Speakers were eminent lawyers. The House voted by calling the nominated member's name or merely, "Aye, aye, aye."

When, in medieval parliaments, a Speaker-elect tried to "beg off," it may well have indicated real reluctance to serve in a difficult role. It is hard to believe that any eminent Tudor lawyer really felt inadequate, but as parliament met in term time (the sitting of the courts), the office did interfere with his private practice. Convention still required disabling speeches, one first to fellow members in the House and a second when presented to the queen, yet his "very ability in decrying himself proved his fitness." These ornate orations, carefully prepared beforehand, would have delighted Speaker Savage. Some were routine, but there was considerable originality, one drawing more heavily on classics and philosophy, another on history and the law. His oration concluded, the Speaker now made the formal request for the privileges, which were conceded by the Lord Keeper in the queen's name.

The request of the Speaker in the first parliament of Henry VII (virtually the form used throughout the reign) has a familiar ring.[9] It is

---

[8] "In 1593 Edward Coke, the famous lawyer, was 'named to be Speaker . . . at Hampton Court' by the Queen and Lords of the Council on January 28th; he was elected by the House of Commons on February 19th. Little wonder that in his *Institutes* he declared that 'the use is (as in the congé d'élire of a bishop) that the King doth name a discreet and learned man whom the Commons elect.'" (Neale, p. 355.)

[9] ". . . that everything to be proffered and declared in the aforesaid Parliament in the name of the said Commons, he might proffer and declare under such Protestation, that if he should have declared anything enjoined on him by his Fellows, otherwise than they had agreed, or with any addition or omission, that then what he had so declared might be corrected and emended by his fellows; and that his protestation to this effect be entered on the roll of the aforesaid Parliament."

merely a variant of the *protestation* we have seen voiced repeatedly in medieval parliaments. Sir Thomas More, Speaker in 1523, is credited with the first recorded plea for freedom of speech in parliament.[10] The petition for the privileges presented by Sir Thomas Gargrave in Elizabeth's first parliament (January, 1559) is typical for the future:

"And lastly [Sir Thomas Gargrave] came, according to the usual form, first, to desire liberty of access for the House of Commons to the Queen's Majesty's presence upon all urgent and necessary occasions. Secondly, that if in anything himself should mistake or misreport or overslip that which should be committed unto him to declare, that it might without prejudice to the House be better declared, and that his unwilling miscarriage therein might be pardoned. Thirdly, that they might have liberty and freedom of speech in whatsoever they treated of or had occasion to propound and debate in the House. The fourth and last, that all the members of the House, with their servants and necessary attendants, might be exempted from all manner of arrests and suits during the continuance of the Parliament, and the usual space both before the beginning and after the ending thereof, as in former times hath always been accustomed."[11]

These privileges were henceforth to be requested at the beginning of every parliament, though not always in the same order. Freedom of speech was soon to be accorded first place. The Lord Keeper's response on the queen's behalf in 1559 concedes the four claims but with characteristic Tudor cautions for moderation and "reverence and obedience to their Sovereign."

Practice accorded well with theory as to freedom from arrest on civil process. In spite of the royal backing in Ferrers' Case, custom was strong, and release by writ of privilege continued for some years. Only in 1593 (Fitzherbert's Case)[12] was direct action by the Commons themselves

---

[10] In substance, as to his fellow Commons, More points out: "Since among so many wise men every man is not equally wise; and amongst many, equally wise, every man is not equally well spoken, and as many 'boisterous and rude in language, see deep indeed, and give right substantial counsel' . . ." Matters of weight and importance concerning the realm, the royal estate, common affairs, could not be well handled unless "every of your Commons were utterly discharged of all doubt and fear."

[11] Tanner, *Tudor Constitutional Documents*, p. 551. — The first recorded formal request in the *Lords Journal*, I, 167, is in Latin and rather cryptic, noting only the request for freedom of speech and access.

[12] It was "in regard of the ancient liberties and privileges of this House" that this burgess was brought up from prison by the Serjeant-at-Arms to appear before the House, though in this instance it was decided that the member was not entitled to privilege. — Tanner, *Tudor Constitutional Documents*, p. 588.

successfully revived and established. Exemption from serving on juries during parliament time was also established, and members were even protected from being impleaded in civil suits. This last was handled by the issue of a writ of *supersedeas* to the judge, commanding a stay of legal proceedings during the time of privilege. Exemption from being summoned as a witness in a court of law was also claimed but not fully established.

The right of the House of Commons to decide the qualifications of members was assumed in this period. Doubtful points were no longer referred to the Lords and judges, but determined by the House as they arose. The right to determine contested elections was also asserted. In 1581 and 1584 the Commons appointed committees to examine returns. In 1586, however, in connection with an irregularity in a Norfolk election, the queen, through the Speaker, informed the House that "the returns belonged 'to the charge and office of the Lord Chancellor', whom she had instructed to confer with the Judges and to take such action as justice might require." Nevertheless the Commons appointed a committee which reported independently. It was in the parliament of 1593 that they entrusted the task of examining returns to their standing committee on privileges. This was first created in 1589, but was now enlarged to include all the privy councillors in the House and thirty other members.

There were two aspects of freedom of speech. The first, that which the phrase most readily brings to mind, freedom of debate, including criticism and dissent, was conceded. The queen recognized the right to vote freely and to speak on bills in moderation. This was well put in the Lord Keeper's reply to the Speaker's request in 1593: "For liberty of speech, her Majesty commandeth me to tell you, that to saye yea or no to bills, God forbid that any man should be restrained, or afraid to answer according to his liking, with some short declaracion of his reason therein, and therein to have a free voice, which is the very true liberty of the House." [13]

It was assumed that if speech went beyond the bounds of reason and decency, the House itself would punish offenders. No one was imprisoned for what he *said* in the House. A few bold spirits were summoned before the Council for warning and reproof, or were "sequestered" — that is, advised to keep to their lodgings for a few days and abstain from

[13] Quoted in full in Tanner, *Tudor Constitutional Documents*, pp. 552–553.

attendance in the House. Usually such offenders had been guilty of touching on the prerogative (a term of which we shall hear much).

More controversial was the other aspect — the freedom to initiate subjects for discussion and to introduce bills.[14] In the name of freedom of speech the Commons were virtually claiming an equal right of initiative with the Crown and its ministers. The Puritans were motivated by intense religious zeal. Others were concerned over national security and prosperity. With all the energy and talent in the House, no wonder "winning of the initiative" was to become an end in itself. The Commons were no longer content to be mere junior partners.

In particular the queen warned them off such matters of state as her marriage and the succession, the Church, and certain mercantile policies. In that critical era any of these might involve and incite foreign powers, with dangerous consequences. In 1566, for instance, Lords and Commons cooperated in a joint petition asking the queen to name her successor. The Lords accepted her evasive answer, but the Commons pressed their request. The queen's "express inhibition" led to Paul Wentworth's raising the issue of privilege by a series of questions. "Those two businesses," observes D'Ewes, "of her Majesty's marriage and declaring a successor, coming into agitation at this time . . . Mr. Paul Wentworth and others used so great liberty of speech as (I conceive) was never used in any Parliament or session of Parliament before or since."[15]

When in the parliament of 1571 Mr. Strickland was sequestered for bringing in a bill for reformation of the *Book of Common Prayer,* the House took issue so effectively that Strickland was shortly allowed to return to his place in the House. The debate had produced some speeches of real constitutional significance in defining the position of the Commons in the government. Mr. Carleton in calling attention of his fellow members to Strickland's detention argued: "But forasmuch as he was not now a private person, but to supply the room, person, and

[14] Neale makes clear a point often overlooked — why it was important to forestall objectionable bills: "By Elizabeth's reign not a word of an act could be altered without the assent of the Lords and Commons; the Crown's power had thus been limited to a veto." The queen did make vigorous use of the veto, quashing twelve bills in a single session.

[15] The queen's "inhibition" on November 9 was modified on the 12th by permission to any dissatisfied member to show his reasons before the Council, and finally on the 25th, Mr. Speaker's declaration from the queen, "that for her good will to the House she did revoke her two former commandments."

place of a multitude, specially chosen and therefor sent, he thought neither in regard of the country which was not to be wronged, nor for the liberty of the House, which was not to be infringed, we should permit him to be detained from us."

Another, Yelverton too "remembered how that men are not there for themselves but for their countries [i.e., counties]." He also warned against establishing a precedent, tolerable "in this happy time of lenity . . . under so gracious a Prince," yet dangerous should times be altered. He even dared to conclude that "it was fit for princes to have their prerogatives; but yet the same to be straitened within reasonable limits." As to the bolder approach of such as Peter Wentworth in 1576, we shall see more in the next chapter.

Rules of Order; the Lawyers in the House

Only for the reign of Elizabeth and after, not before, do we have the wealth of evidence for a true picture of the House of Commons at work, and the formulation of the "rules of the game," a field in which the Englishman has excelled, whether in politics or sports. Some though not all, of these rules and conventions were transferred by the American colonists to their councils and assemblies, and thus may be called the ancestors, indirectly, of what Americans know as *Robert's Rules of Order*. The following account is admittedly oversimplified.

"Much of the quality and success of our English parliament," says Neale, "depends upon decorum — upon rules and conventions, some obviously essential to any large debating assembly, some archaic but pleasing little ceremonies or courtesies that maintain the dignity of the House and eventually cast the spell of ritual over even the most combative and sceptical of new-comers."

Rules, of course, had existed from early days, but now old ones were being recorded in the *Journals* and new ones framed. In 1576 a motion was adopted for the orderly departing at the rising of the House, "in comely and civil sort for the reverence of the House." In 1601 the Speaker reminded members of "the ancient order" for putting off their spurs before they entered the House. Voting on bills, as in elections, was oral — *ayes* and *noes*. Divisions were apparently rare before Elizabeth's reign, but for 1593 we read: "Mr. Speaker [Coke] said, the order of the House is, that the Aye being for the bill must go out, and the No against the bill doth always sit. The reason is that the inventor that will have a new law is to go out and bring it in; and they that are for the law in possession must keep the House, for they sit to continue it." [16] In practice this method tended to weigh the scales against the *ayes*, for the timid or indifferent kept their seats!

Rules of debate are described with assurance and satisfaction by Sir Thomas Smith in his *Commonwealth* as early as 1565:

"In the disputing is a marvellous good order used in the Lower House. He that standeth up bareheaded is understood that he will speak to the bill. If more stand up, who that first is judged to arise is first heard; though the one do praise the law, the other dissuade it, yet there is no altercation. For every man speaketh as to the Speaker, not as one to another, for that is against the order of the House. It is also taken against the order to name him whom ye do confute but by circumlocution, as 'He that speaketh with the bill,' or 'He that spake against the bill and gave this and this reason.' And so with perpetual oration, not with altercation, he goeth through till he do make an end. He that once hath spoken in a bill, though he be confuted straight, that day may not reply; no, though he would change his opinion. So that to one bill in one day one may not in that House speak twice, for else one or two with altercation would spend all the time. The next day he may, but then also but once.

"No reviling or nipping words must be used. For then all the House will cry, 'It is against the order': and if any speak irreverently or seditiously against the Prince or the Privy Council, I have seen them not only interrupted but it hath been moved after to the House and they have sent them to the Tower. So that in such a multitude, and in such diversity of minds and opinions there is the greatest modesty and temperance of speech that can be used. Nevertheless, with much doulce and gentle terms they make their reasons as violent and as vehement the one against the other as they may ordinarily, except it be for urgent causes and hasting of time."

Parliamentary oratory from the floor was on a high plane, in keeping with the example set by the Lord Keeper and Speaker at the opening of the session. The audience (of fellow members only, of course) — "an audience of connoisseurs" — expected and enjoyed what they got. Some speeches were thought worthy to be preserved in literary collections.

[16] This and the following quotation are from Tanner, *Tudor Constitutional Documents*, pp. 547–548.

There were great speeches from the privy councillors in the House in times of crises such as those of the 1580's involving the problem of Mary Queen of Scots, the Jesuit Mission, the pope, or Philip of Spain. Neale singles out for honorable mention "the incomparable Francis Bacon, so wise, so sententious"; Sir Walter Raleigh, "incalculable, superb"; and Robert Cecil, "the embodiment of efficiency." Of the lawyers we shall hear more presently.

Private bills occupied much of parliament's time. Although these were not yet handled in committee by the quasi-judicial procedure of modern times, interested parties might ask to be heard in person or by counsel in the House or a committee. Thus did the art of lobbying take form with London as arch lobbyist. Citizens or city crafts and companies were required to secure the approval of the Lord Mayor and aldermen before introducing a bill. There was also organized opposition against measures thought detrimental to the city's interests. For instance, in 1572 a bill was introduced "against injuries offered by corporations in the City of London to divers foreign artificers." This bill was opposed by London's Recorder, and did not reach a second reading. In 1593 a contest arose over a bill promoted by the city to defend its privilege of excluding alien strangers from selling at retail foreign commodities. "For the last three parliaments of the reign, the Court of Aldermen appointed a committee 'to consider what bills are fit to be preferred at this next parliament for the good and benefit of this city'; in short, to prepare a legislative programme." [17] London naturally made much use of its able Recorder, William Fleetwood.

The presence of lawyer members in parliament was no novelty, as we have seen above, but their numbers and influence were increasing, even to the extent of evoking some hostile criticism. Since the House sat during the same hours as the law courts, the lawyer members were divided in their loyalties. It was tempting to slip out of the House and across to the courts in Westminster Hall. The Speaker was generous enough to forego practice during the session. Membership also had advantages, affording publicity and thus securing new clients and favorable notice from persons in high places, even the queen. Twenty of the lawyers sitting in the parliament of 1597 were eventually promoted to legal office.

It was in this period that some of the rules and practices which Holds-

[17] Neale, Chapter 20, *passim*.

worth assumes were transferred from the courts to the Houses were effectively established.[18] Minute attention was paid to matters of form: "The absence of the proper form of endorsement on a bill sent to the Lords, . . . the use by the Lords of paper instead of parchment for their amendments, were serious matters to be gravely discussed."

We may assume that the lawyers had a share in formulating the rules for passing bills and for debate described above. Their presence was considered essential for the proper scrutiny of bills. They served on committees, and were assigned to certain extraordinary committees used by the House in the last three parliaments of the reign. For instance, a committee of 1593 was composed of all the privy councillors in the House, all *serjeants-at-law,* and sixty others. In 1597 bills relating to the relief of the poor and punishment of "sturdy beggars" were assigned to a large committee including *all readers at the Inns of Court* and all *serjeants-at-law.* For the drafting and sponsoring of private bills outsiders might be employed, but probably much of this business went to lawyer members.

A nice bit of by-play which must have originated in some barrister's brain was the custom of the Commons, on returning to their House after presenting their Speaker to the queen, to have one bill read "to give the Speaker seisin of his chair before they rose for the day."

Holdsworth, our legal historian, insists that "the whole idea of Parliamentary privilege . . . springs from the notion that it is a court which like other courts must have its peculiar and appropriate privileges; and to the end many of these privileges — notably the power to imprison for contempt — retain a strong analogy to the privileges of other courts." The Speaker himself, in 1589, noting the disorder in the House, reminded them "that every member of this House is a Judge of this Court, being the highest Court of all other courts, and the Great Council of this realm," and urged that "they would hereafter forbear to attempt the like disorders, as the honour and gravity of this House justly requireth" (Tanner, pp. 548–549). In Fitzherbert's Case the House claimed to be a court of record.

It was the lawyer M.P. who was most likely to rise to a point of order. We have already seen Fleetwood lobbying for London and Sir Edward Coke ruling on a division, but each is worthy of further attention.

Sir William Fleetwood was not originally a Londoner, but of Lan-

---

[18] See pp. 123–126.

cashire descent. He began his parliamentary career as burgess for Lancaster in 1559. It was through the influence of the Earl of Leicester that he was elected Recorder of London (April 26, 1571).[19] He was returned to parliament for the city in 1572, 1586, and 1588. He had another indirect connection as "freeman by patrimony" of the Merchant Taylors' Company and had served as counsel for the company in a suit against the clothworkers.

Fleetwood was a barrister of the Middle Temple, which could boast many distinguished Elizabethans among its members. He served his Inn as Reader in 1563 and 1568. In 1580 he became a Serjeant-at-Law, but never attained the office of Baron of the Exchequer, which had been promised him in 1586.[20] This disappointment, attributed to Leicester's enemies, happily prolonged his connection with London and the Commons.

In parliament the Recorder proved a most able proponent of the city's interests, a lobbyist par excellence. He was noted for his fluent and witty speeches. "An incorrigible raconteur," Neale dubs him. "With his wit and fund of legal and historical lore he held a privileged position, playing on his audience as a skilled musician on his instrument." Yet there was usually some point to what he said, witness the many instances in which our parliamentary historian uses Fleetwood to illustrate a point of parliamentary theory or practice.

For instance, it is to some notes made by the Recorder that Neale turns for an account of the initial ceremony of roll call and administering the oath of supremacy to the members of the Commons. The lack of precise distinction between public and private bills is illustrated by a debate in which Fleetwood says, "I did advise him to make [it] a private bill but he would not, and therefore he shall see what will come of it." Again in a great debate on an important government bill, he warned against haste: "the sudden commitment of bills . . . very often is the cause that bills be never heard of again."

He was ready to appreciate and praise eloquence in others. In debate members were not supposed to read their speeches, but even the fluent

---

[19] As Recorder he was famous for his zeal in enforcing the laws against the so-called "vagrants, mass-priests and papists," and was even committed for a short time to the Fleet prison when an excess of zeal led to his breaking into the Portuguese ambassador's chapel.

[20] He was made Queen's Serjeant in 1592. He had resigned his office as Recorder in 1591, when the Common Council voted him a pension of £100, and he died in 1594.

Recorder reminded the House that one might jog one's memory: "I will be bold to look in my tables [notes]; I see other men do it." Naturally he was well versed in statutes and precedents. "Criticizing a bill with retrospective provisions, he cited a number of old statutes, then smugly said: 'Ye would think I had studied this year, I am so ready and perfect . . . I could keep you here till two a clock with like cases, for I had a collection of them till my book was picked from me. But I have said thus much of old statutes that young men may note it in their tables.' " Again a law precedent served to support the right of the House to reverse a previous decision — "namely, that since parliament was one day in law it could do as the courts of justice, where, the term being theoretically one day, the same judges might reform any error, during the same term." [21]

Sir Edward Coke was only one of a succession of able lawyers who served as Speaker. The choice of a "man of law" was not mere chance. It was felt that the Speaker would handle his task more efficiently if he was skilled in the common law.

Coke is best known as leader of the opposition to Stuart absolutism, first in the courts, and then the parliaments of the 1620's. In Elizabeth's reign it was still possible for him to see the *rule of law* operating through the Crown in parliament and in the courts. He writes: "If in other kingdomes, the Lawes seeme to governe, but the Judges had rather misconster [misconstrue] Law, and do injustice than displease the king's humour . . . Blesse God for Queene Elizabeth, whose continuall charge to her Justices agreeable with her auncient Lawes, is, that for no commaundement under the great or privie Seale, writtes or letters, common right be disturbed or delayed." [22]

In presiding over the Commons, Coke proved a strict disciplinarian, painstaking, and efficient. He it was who defined the procedure in a *division* described above. Neale relates how, on an occasion, desiring leave to speak on a troublesome privilege question, "Coke explained that since the beginning of the parliament he had 'thought upon and searched . . . this point of the privileges of the House, for I judged it would come in question upon many occasions.' "

He was skillful in guiding debate and directing it along lines desired by the privy councillors. When a bill was up to which Cecil, Heneage,

[21] Neale, Chapters 19–21, *passim*.
[22] Preface to *Second Report*, published 1601.

and Bacon were opposed, his "subtlety in propounding the question thus gained the casting away of the bill." To please the queen he pocketed the bills introduced by the Puritan James Morice, one restricting procedure of the Court of High Commission against nonconformists, the other confirming Magna Carta as a guarantee of "liberty of the subject." As Morice tells the story: "This my speech ended, I delivered my two Bills unto the Speaker, who then was Mr. Edwarde Cooke her Majesty's Solicitor. . . . The Speaker promised the House to bring those Bills again the next day, and in the meantime safely to keep them from the view of any man. But as I have heard, he was in the meantime commanded to come with the Bills to the Court, which accordingly he did. What became of them after, he best knoweth."

As to oratory, Sir Edward was equal to the best, and like his colleagues quoted on occasion from Scripture and the classics, but naturally drew most heavily on history and legal precedents. But of these we shall hear more in the next reign.

X

Parliament at Work: Actual Sessions

✿✿✿

1563. Pageantry and Progress

THE second parliament of the reign was formally opened January 12, 1563, and prorogued April 10, a rather long session of almost three months. Although some details are lacking (such as information on debates and committees), it is possible to reconstruct a fairly complete picture as to ceremonial, subsidy, legislation, and the general spirit of harmony which prevailed. It was a session in which the leadership of the queen, and perhaps even more that of her councillors, was dominant, though Lords and Commons did express themselves emphatically in respect to the problems of the queen's marriage and the succession.

We are fortunate in having a detailed description of the opening ceremonies, replete with "trumpeteers sounding," costumes described, and notables listed by name. For instance, in the procession to the Parliament House, there were thirty barons, "their mantles, hoods and surcoat furred and two rows of miniver on their right shoulder"; twenty-two bishops, "their robes of scarlet lined, and a hood down their back of miniver," and nineteen earls, "their robes of scarlet with three rows of miniver." [1] Privy councillors and judges included Sir William Cecil, "chief secretary," Sir Nicholas Bacon, Lord Keeper of the Great Seal,

[1] "*The Lords Journals* for 15 January, 1563, three days later, records the attendance of 39 barons. There also attended 1 duke, 2 marquises, 13 earls, and 3 viscounts — 58 temporal peers in all. The number of bishops attending on April 3 was 24, so 22 was not a full attendance for so important a ceremonial occasion." Tanner, *Tudor Constitutional Documents*, p. 542n.

and Sir James Dyer, Chief Justice of Common Pleas. Immediately preceding the queen rode the Duke of Norfolk with the gilt rod as Marshal, the Lord Treasurer with the Cap of Estate, and the Earl of Worcester with the Sword.

It was on Tuesday, the 12th of January, "about eleven of the clock in the forenoon, the Queen's Majesty took her horse at the Hall door and proceeded in manner as followeth: . . . her Grace apparelled in her mantle, opened before, furred with ermines, and her kirtle of crimson velvet, close before, and close sleeves, but the bands turned up with ermines, and a hood hanging low round about her neck of ermines. Over all a rich collar, set with stones and other jewels, and on her head a rich caul [close-fitting cap]. And the next after her the Lord Robert Dudley, Master of the Horse, leading the spare horse. And after all other ladies, two and two, in their ordinary apparel. Beside the Queen went her footmen, and along on either side of her went the Pensioners with their axes; after the ladies followed the Captain of the Guard, Sir William St. Loe, and after him the Guard."

Following a short religious service at Westminster, "her Majesty and the rest orderly on foot proceeded out of the south door, where she delivered the Dean the sceptre, and so proceeded into the Parliament Chamber . . ." After queen, councillors, peers and bishops, judges and clerks had assumed their places, the Commons were notified. Knights, citizens, and burgesses, "being, as many as conveniently could, let in" (the old routine phrase!), the queen commanded Sir Nicholas Bacon, the Lord Keeper, to set forth the cause of calling the parliament.[2]

His speech emphasized two problems. "Religion for the setting forth of God's Honour and Glory, and the other concerning Policy, for the Common-Wealth, as well for provision at home as to provide for the Foreign Enemy abroad." With typical Tudor tact, he contrasted the queen with those princes who delight to spend treasure for their own pleasure — "the relieving of the Realm's necessities is our Prince's whole delight" — and emphasized the reluctance of her Majesty to request any financial aid of her parliament "if by any other means it might have been holpen."

As soon as the Commons had returned to their House, "Mr. Comptroller" (one of the councillors in the House) "rehearsed the Lord Keeper's oration, for the Election of a Speaker, and said, that in his Opinion,

[2] Tanner, pp. 542–545.

Mr. Thomas Williams Esq., one of the Fellows of the *Inner Temple,* being grave, learned and wise, was very meet to that Office; whereupon the whole House with one entire Voice, cried *Mr. Williams, Mr. Williams*; and then *Mr. Williams* standing up, and reverently disabling himself, required the House to proceed to a new Election; unto whom Mr. Secretary *Cecill* answering that the House had greatly considered of him; and therefore required him to take his place; and he approaching was led and set in the Chair by Mr. Comptroller." [3]

Everything proceeded according to form. Williams' second disabling speech before the Lords was promptly rebutted by the Lord Keeper, since "her Majesty is credibly informed, as well of your knowledge and experience in other Parliaments, as in other great and weighty matters . . ." Then followed the new Speaker's oration (which fills over four folio columns in the printed *Journals*) on the orderly government of a Commonwealth, enriched with Biblical and classical examples. The now customary request for the privileges was conceded, but with characteristic cautions on the *use,* not *abuse,* of each.

As to matters of public weal, most important to the queen and councillors, besides the subsidy, was the success of the Church settlement. To Lords and Commons most vital was the problem of the queen's marriage and the succession. The first parliament of the reign, 1559, had restored the new Anglican Church, with slight modifications, to its status at the end of Henry VIII's rule. But effective enforcement of the new Acts of Supremacy and Uniformity had proved difficult. Not satisfied with the progress of settlement, the privy councillors now secured the passage of two supplementary acts. The first and most important had the impressive title "An Act for the Assurance of the Queens Majesties Royal Power over all States and Subjects, within her Highness's Dominions." [4]

Prompted partly by the anxiety aroused by the queen's recent illness (October 1562), when for several days she "seemed to hover between life and death," Lords and Commons both presented petitions. The Lords urged the queen to marry and to designate a successor; "thereby she shall strike a terror into her adversaries and replenish her subjects

[3] D'Ewes, *Journals,* p. 61a. — Thomas Williams was a west-country lawyer, a member of the Inner Temple, who had sat in three previous parliaments, and was now one of the members for Exeter.

[4] The other, An Act for the Better Execution of the Writ *de excommunicato capiendo,* was designed to support the censure of the English Church in its use of excommunication.

with immortal joy." The Commons emphasized delimiting the succession. The queen sent an evasive answer, skillfully suggesting the advantage of delay: she could not "wade into so deep a matter" without deliberation, but hinted that she might marry. Modern historians commend her caution, even suggesting that to name a successor at that critical time might well have endangered the life of the nominee, a dubious honor. The Houses were disappointed, but still hopeful, and were to revert to the problem repeatedly in later sessions. There was no lack of suitors, princely or merely noble, but the queen's indecision really amounted to playing the game of the balance of power by matrimonial diplomacy.

The *Journals* do little with debates or committees, but do reveal considerable legislative activity. Day after day there is recorded for both Houses the bills read and the action thereon. For instance, in the Commons: "On Monday, the 8th day of March, three bills had each of them one reading; of which the first, being the bill that St. Katherine's Church shall be a parish church, and the second for the repairing and mending of highways, were read the third time and passed the House, and were sent up to the Lords by Mr. Comptroller. Mr. Attorney brought from the Lords three bills, of which one was the bill for denizens' children. The bill also against the unlawful taking of fish, deer, or hawks was read the third time and passed. *Post Meridiem.* In the afternoon eight bills had each of them one reading; of which one was the bill for the subsidy of the clergy. Richard Parrott, gentleman, burgess for Sandwich, for his sickness was licensed to be absent." [5]

Our antiquarian, D'Ewes, repeatedly calls them "bills of no moment," but the outcome was impressive. At the close of the session, April 10, "Then were the several Titles of the Acts read, and thirty-one publick Statutes and seventeen private, were made Laws by her Majesty's Royal Assent." All told, its work, Bindoff says, included "a greater output of economic legislation than had ever been passed in a single session, and one which bears comparison with those of our own day."

For instance, there was an act intended to check enclosures and encourage husbandry. A forerunner of the notable Poor Law of 1601, an Acte for the Reliefe of the Poore, made the local collection of rates for the same compulsory. The importing of luxuries (apparel, ornaments, weapons) was discouraged by the exclusion of "dyvers foreyne Wares

[5] Stephenson and Marcham, p. 363.

made by Handye Craftsmen beyonde the Seas." An act for the encouragement of native shipping, including compulsory fish-days ("political Lent") was aptly entitled, "Politic Constitutions for the maintenance of the Navy." Best known and longest in force was the Statute of Artificers, designed to distribute labor adequately in country and town.

A few episodes are high-lighted in the *Journals* — for instance, the importance placed on the problem of the succession. As early as Saturday, January 16, "A motion was this day made by a Burgess at length, for the Succession of the Crown . . ." [6] On the Monday following, "Certain Arguments were this day had in the House, by divers wise Personages, for motion to be made for the Queens Marriage, and Succession of the Crown." On Tuesday, the 19th, "Mr. Speaker with the Counsel, and twenty-four more of the House, were appointed to meet this Afternoon, to draw Articles of Petition for the Queens Marriage and Succession. . . . Mr. Comptroller is nominated one of them." Then the climax came on Thursday, January 28: "In the afternoon Mr. Speaker, with the whole House (with a Notable Oration) did exhibit their Petition to the Queen's Majesty, in the Gallery at the Palace, touching Marriage and Succession; which her Highness thankfully accepted (with an Excellent Oration) deferring the Answer to further time, for the gravity of the Cases."

The new interest in parliament as evidenced by the eagerness of certain boroughs to renew their representation (long since discontinued) appears in such entries as the following. For January 19 we read, "it seemed to the House, being very full, that they were a greater number than were returned. . . ." More specifically for Thursday, the 22d: "For that Burgesses be returned of divers Boroughs, not lately returned in the Chancery, viz., the Burgess of [six towns listed], Mr. Speaker declared to the House, that the Lord Steward agreed they should resort into the House, and with convenient speed to shew Letters Patents, why they be returned into this Parliament." On Thursday, March 11th: "Long Arguments were had upon the Bill for increase of the Navy, whether the *Wednesday* shall be a Fish-Day, and upon the Question the House was divided; and to have it a Fish-Day were a hundred fifty-nine, and not to have it a Fish-Day were ninety-six; and immediately after, upon the qualification of that day, the great number agreed to the qualification."

[6] This and the subsequent quotations in this section are from D'Ewes, *Journals*.

The closing session, on April 10, at 3:00 P.M., like the opening, required the presence of the queen and of the Commons, more speeches, and some important business. "Mr. Speaker made an Excellent Oration, rehearsing divers Lawes made by divers Queens of this Realm, and requiring the Queen to assent to the Acts passed by both Houses, and presented to her Majesty the Book of Subsidy, and the Book of the general Pardon, with most humble thanks for the same. And the Lord Keeper, by the Queen's Commandment, gave great thanks unto the Nobility and Commons, and earnestly required them severally in their Countries, to look that the Lawes might be executed. And touching the Succession . . ." [7]

When Lord Keeper Bacon commanded the Clerk of the Crown to read the acts, there ensued the regular procedure determining whether a bill was to become law. As each was read, the Clerk of the Parliament, consulting a paper signed by the queen, gave the royal answer. The ceremony would have seemed familiar to Speaker Savage, for it was still customary to use the set Norman-French phrases natural enough in the old days, when the *Parliament Rolls* were couched in French. The French ambassador, DeMaisse, says Neale, "was very surprised to find his language used in these responses."

Special forms were reserved for the subsidy and the pardon — the queen's thanks to the Houses for the first, the Lords' and Commons' thanks to her Majesty for the second.[8] For public bills accepted by the queen, as one clerk read the title, the other replied, "La Royne le veult" (the queen wills it). For private bills it was, "Soit faict comme il est désiré" (be it done as it is desired). For a veto, or as contemporaries would have preferred to state it, "to such Acts as her Majesty did forbear to allow," the reply was still the polite and evasive, "La Royne s'advisera" (the queen will consider, will be advised).

1576. Puritans and Privileges

The parliament of 1576 was unique in several respects. Strictly speaking, it was not a *parliament* but merely a *session*, the second of three

---

[7] Thus the *Commons Journals*. The *Lords Journals* has a fuller account with text of the speeches, including a written statement from the queen on the succession, read by the Lord Keeper to insure accuracy.

[8] "La Royne remercie ses loyaulx subiects, accepte leur benevolence, & aussi le veult." For the pardon: "Les Prelates, Seigneurs et Communes en ceste presente Parlement remercient tres humblement votre Majestie et prient a Dieu vous donne, en santé, bonne vie et longue."

(1572, 1576, and 1581). It was the only parliament of the reign to have three sessions, spanning the longest interval, eleven years, without a new election. The Houses sat for about five weeks, from Wednesday, February 8, to Thursday, March 15. Because it was not new, there were none of the opening ceremonies, and the queen did not appear. It was the last occasion on which Sir Nicholas Bacon officiated, for the great Lord Keeper died in 1579. Even now, because of age and infirmities, he was assisted by the Lord Treasurer acting in his place. The Speaker was the less well known but capable lawyer Robert Bell, a member of the Middle Temple. As a private member in the parliament of 1571, Bell was rebuked by the Council for a bold speech criticizing abuses in high places, involving licenses and promoters. This evidently did not disqualify him as Speaker. He was rewarded with a judgeship in 1577.

The queen's presence was necessary at the closing of the session, March 14, and there were the customary formalities. Speaker Robert Bell's "oration to her Majesty" ran true to form. Carrying with him the bill of one subsidy, and two *fifteenths and tenths,* he was placed at the rail or bar at the lower end of the upper House. "First, He spoke touching sundry kinds of Government which had been in this Kingdom, and so drew his Discourse to the present time. Then he made a large enumeration of her Majesties many Vertues, and of the many benefits which the Kingdom received by her gracious Government. After which he proceeded humbly to Petition her Majesty to make the Kingdom further happy in her Marriage, that so they might hope for a continuous succession of those benefits in her Posterity. To which having added a compendious relation of such Acts as had passed the House of Commons, he concluded with the Presentation of the Bill of Subsidy in their names unto her Majesty." [9]

The Lord Keeper's response in the queen's name was remarkably gracious and commendatory. To select only a brief passage: "And besides this I may and dare certainly affirm unto you by her Majesties own Mouth, that if the Vertues of all the Princes in Europe were united within her Highness' Breast, she should gladly imploy the same to the best of her Power about the good Governance of you, that be so good and loving unto her; so great is her Highness' good will and inward

[9] This and the subsequent quotations in this section are from D'Ewes, *Journals,* pp. 232–251 *passim,* unless otherwise indicated. Tanner has some passages on Charles Johnson, Walter Williams, and Peter Wentworth, *Tudor Constitutional Documents,* pp. 591, 537–538.

affection toward you. . . ." The crowning compliment was the assurance that "of the great good liking her Majesty hath conceived of you that be of this Parliament, her Highness meaneth not to determine [dissolve] the same, but to prorogue it until the next Winter."

More specifically, the queen commended the Houses for their "travail and pains" taken in the passing of laws. Actually she gave her assent to twenty-three public and thirteen private acts. There was little of major importance or novelty, but much in the way of practical improvement in existing laws and their administration.[10] Most effective was her warning that all these efforts would be lost "except you look better to the Execution of Laws than heretofore you have done. . . . Laws without Execution, be nothing else but Pen, Ink and Parchment, a Countenance of things, and nothing in Deed, a cause without an effect, and serve as much to the good Governance of the Common-weal, as the Rudder of a Ship doth serve to the good Governance if it be without a Governour; . . . as Torches do to direct mens goings in the dark, when their Lights be put out. . . . [Not to execute the laws] is to breed a contempt of Laws and Lawmakers and of all Magistrates, which is the Mother and Nurse of Disobedience . . ."

The modern student of parliamentary history may agree with our antiquarian D'Ewes in his enthusiasm over other aspects of this session: "This present Journal of the House of Commons containeth in it, not only many good Passages touching the ordinary usages and privileges of the House, but is plentifully stored also with divers extraordinary and rare Occurences touching the maintenance of the Liberties of the House, not only *from the indignity of private Persons,* but also against the pressures of the Lords of the Upper House; in which also there wanted not the zealous endeavour of the House for the reformation of divers Ecclesiastical matters, and *the remarkable Imprisonment of a member of the same by* themselves . . ." (italics added).

As to the "indignities of private persons," there was the intruder whose rank and position afforded no excuse for the presence of a non-member amongst the Commons. For February 13 we read: "Charles

[10] For instance: An Acte against the deminisheing and empayringe of the Queenes Majesties Coigne and other Coignes lawfullye curraunt within this Realme; An Acte for the setting of the Poore on worke and for the avoyding of Ydlenes; An Acte of addicion unto the former Acts for the amending and repayring of Highe Wayes; An Acte to redresse Disorders in comon Infourmers upon penall Lawes; An Acte for Reformacion of Abuses in Goldsmythes; An Acte for the perpetuall Maintenance of Rochester Bridge. *(Statutes of the Realm.)*

Johnson, of the Inner Temple, gentleman, being examined at the Bar for coming into this House this present day (the House sitting) confessing himself to be no member of this House, is ordered that Mr. Wilson Master of the Requests, Mr. Recorder of London, and Mr. Cromwell to examine him (wherein he feigned to excuse himself by ignorance); he was committed to the Serjeant's ward till further order should be taken by this House."

Indignities were not confined to private persons. As in medieval parliaments, tempers still flared on occasion. For February 29 we read that "Walter Williams, being brought to the Bar, confessed that he did strike Mr. Bainbrigge, and that he offered to strike at him with his dagger. Whereupon it was ordered that he remain in the Serjeant's ward till the order of this House be further known."

More flagrant was the deliberate abuse of privilege by Edward Smalley, "yeoman, servant unto Arthur Hall, esquire, one of the burgesses for Grantham." In its early stages Smalley's Case offered an opportunity for the Commons to reassert their authority, assumed in Ferrers' Case (albeit now for a mere member's servant). Although a committee had reported that Hall must secure his servant's release by applying for a writ of privilege "by divers precedents," the House, after some argument, resolved "that Edward Smalley, servant unto Arthur Hall, esquire, shall be brought hither tomorrow by the Serjeant, and set at liberty by warrant of the mace, and not by writ." But further investigation revealed that Smalley had fraudulently procured his own arrest in order to avoid paying a debt.[11] On March 10 he was brought to the Bar and sentenced by the Speaker in the name of the House to a month's imprisonment in the Tower, and longer if necessary to secure "good and sufficient assurance" for payment of £100 to his creditor and 40s. for the Serjeant's fees.

As to the "remarkable imprisonment" of a member of the House by themselves, D'Ewes was doubtless referring to the episode of the Puritan, Peter Wentworth. The name Puritan was applied in the sixteenth century, like the name Lollard in the late fourteenth, to various nonconformists. Peter and his brother Paul, Walter Strickland, and others who shared their views, were not extremists (like the Separatists and Presbyterians). They were literally *puritans* who wanted to remain

---

[11] "And this illustrates the degree of abuse which led to the omission of members' servants from the Act of 1770 to confirm the privileges of members themselves." Tanner, *Tudor Constitutional Documents*, pp. 580, 584–585.

within the State Church but to *purify* it of what they called "popish forms and ceremonies." The emphasis at first was on the elimination of clerical vestments and liturgical ceremonies. But it was easy to move on to criticism of the ignorance and inefficiency of the clergy, lack of good preaching, and so on, even to changes in doctrine and organization. "From refusing to wear a surplice," says Bindoff, "it was not far to denying the power of a bishop to enforce such a thing, and from that to denying his authority altogether; and to deny the authority of a bishop was really to deny the authority of the Crown which appointed him and gave him his orders."

Leaders of this group in the Commons might have found considerable support for procedure by petitions of moderate tenor, but they preferred the bolder method of introducing in the House "a bill and a book" — that is, a revised Book of Common Prayer and a new Act of Uniformity to enforce it. It was the introduction of such a bill that had led to Strickland's being sequestered in 1571, and this in turn to the stern warning in the first session (1572) of this very fourth parliament. In warning the Houses against intrusion in this sphere, the queen was asserting her authority as "Supreme Governor of the Church of England." In matters of doctrine and discipline, she deferred to the bishops and advised the Commons to do the same. The Commons were informed, through the Speaker, that "her Highness' pleasure is that from henceforth no bills concerning religion shall be preferred or received into this House, unless the same should be first considered and liked by the clergy."

On the whole these admonitions were observed in 1576. Agitation for ecclesiastical reform was restrained in both scope and method. The striking exception was Peter Wentworth. It was the government's policy whereby, as he put it, "God's cause was shut out of doors" that aroused him to his notable defense of free speech at the beginning of the session.

Peter Wentworth came of an Oxfordshire family, but sat for the borough of Tregony in Cornwall, a region noted for its independent spirits. His brother Paul was in parliament in 1563 and 1566, and he himself had sat in the two sessions, 1571 and 1572. Thus he had seen Robert Bell subdued, Strickland sequestered, members intimidated by rumors, and warned against introducing bills on religion. Though like his fellow Puritans he was impelled mainly by religious zeal, he is also credited with eloquence, courage, and fervid political zeal, one who had the qualities of a great parliament man. But his procedure was too bold, his theories on parliamentary freedom of speech and action too advanced for his day.

Only one bill had been read in the new session when he rose to astonish the House with his famous speech. As Wentworth explained presently before a committee, he had composed it some three years before, after most careful consideration, but even sympathetic colleagues were shocked by its boldness. It was at the point where his aspersions extended from the bishops to the queen — "So certain it is, Mr. Speaker, that none is without fault, no, not our noble Queen, since then her Majesty had committed great fault, yea, dangerous faults to herself" — that the Commons stopped the zealot. "Upon this speech the House, out of a reverend regard of her Majesty's honour, stopped his further proceeding before he had fully finished his speech."

He was committed to the Serjeant's ward, to be examined the same afternoon by a committee of the House composed mainly of privy councillors. On its report Wentworth was sent to the Tower by a resolution of the House itself, and remained prisoner there until March 12, when he was "by the Queen's special favour restored again to his liberty and place in the House."

There is extant an account of the examination in committee made by Wentworth himself, a verbatim report of questions and answers. Even here he was undaunted. Parliamentary privilege was emphasized by his nice distinction that if the committee questioned him as privy councillors he could not be compelled to answer them; if as members of the Commons, he would reply. Although the committee were eager to extenuate his fault by taking note only of what was actually said in the House, he wanted the whole speech showed to the queen! The report leads one to agree with the statement credited to one of the committee, Mr. Seckford: "Mr. Wentworth will never acknowledge himself to make a fault, nor say that he is sorry for anything that he doth speak."

His famous speech in the House was long. It fills over eight folio columns in D'Ewes's *Journals*. Only key passages can be quoted here.

It was the *Puritan* Wentworth who complained of the ill effects of rumors and messages commanding or inhibiting. Most deplorable, of course, was "the Message Mr. Speaker brought the last Sessions into the House, that we should not deal in any matters of Religion but first to receive from the Bishops. Surely this was a doleful Message. . . . God of his justice could not prosper the Session; . . . God . . . was the last Session shut out of doors." He further reminded fellow members, "I have heard of old Parliament men, that the Banishment of the Pope and Popery, and the restoring of true Religion had their beginning from this House, and not from the Bishops . . ."

It was the *parliamentarian* Wentworth who eulogized liberty itself in words inspiring both to fellow members and those of later generations:

"Mr. Speaker, I find written in a little Volume these words in effect: 'Sweet is the name of Liberty, but the thing itself a value beyond all inestimable Treasure.' So much the more it behoveth us to take care lest we, contenting ourselves with the sweetness of the name, lose and forego the thing, being of the greatest value that can come unto this noble Realm. The inestimable treasure is the use of it in this House. . . .

"I was never of Parliament but the last and the last Session, at both which times I saw the Liberty of free Speech, the which is the only Salve to heal all the Sores of this Common-Wealth, so much and so many ways infringed and so many abuses offered to this Honourable Council, as hath much grieved me even of very Conscience and love to my Prince and State. . . .

"Sometime it happeneth that a good man will in this place (for Argument sake) prefer an evil cause, both for that he would have a doubtful truth to be opened and manifested, and also the evil prevented; so that to this point I conclude, that in this House, which is termed a place of free speech, there is nothing so necessary for the preservation of the Prince and State as free Speech, and without, it is a scorn and mockery to call it a Parliament House, for in truth it is none, but a very School of Flattery and Dissimulation." [12]

The speech made a deep impression not only in the House, but beyond its walls. It was even reported in diplomatic dispatches sent abroad. Although ahead of his times, Wentworth was a prophet.

Undaunted by this experience, in the parliament of 1587 Wentworth attempted to raise the question of freedom of speech by a series of questions which he handed to the Speaker. Again he was sent to the Tower and his questions were not moved in the House. In 1593, when he and

[12] The first lines quoted above constitute the beginning of the speech; the others come fairly early, the last as the seventh of the "commodities that grow to the Prince and whole state by free speech." Hence it seems safe to assume that all this was heard by the House.

others urged settlement of the succession, they were suspended from parliament and committed to prison by order of the Council. Apparently he remained in the Tower until his death in November 1596, a martyr to the causes of puritanism and parliamentary privilege.

1601. Opposition Prophetic of the Days to Come

BY *these degrees came the House of Commons to raise that head which since has been so high and formidable to their princes that they have looked pale upon these assemblies.* JAMES HARRINGTON, 1656.

IN THE later parliaments of Elizabeth's reign, after the key year 1588, a new spirit appears. For the modern student, well aware that England was successfully to defeat the Armada, it is hard to realize the feeling of insecurity that had prevailed. The English had long felt themselves virtually in a state of siege, and consequently were willing to accept strong-arm government, secret diplomacy, and powers exercised under the guise of prerogative. After 1588 there was a new spirit of freedom and self confidence, an eager desire for independence and initiative, which even respect for the old queen could not restrain. Besides the checkmating of Spain, there were other favorable factors — the accession of the tolerant Henry of Navarre to the French throne and the coming of age of the young Protestant prince, James VI, of Scotland. There were changes in the Council and in parliament. Elder statesmen like Walsingham (d. 1590) and Burghley (d. 1598) passed away. New men, young and ambitious, took their places. Puritanism, too, was growing in strength and numbers.

Heretofore discussion of public affairs outside the Council Chamber or the Parliament House had been frowned on. Parties and party conferences, the modern caucus, were unknown.[13] Still, it is hard to believe that the purlieus of the Inns of Court had not been the scene of informal discussions among lawyer members and their friends. In Henry VIII's time some members were known to have discussed parliamentary business over dinner at an inn — a dangerous practice! In the session of 1589 the Speaker admonished the House, on the motion of Sir Edward Hobby, "that speeches used in this House by the members of the same be not any of them made or used as table-talk, or in any wise delivered

[13] Mackenzie credits the Puritans with "initiating the principle on which government by party rests. As an organized party they sought admission to the House of Commons, obtained a majority there and successfully resisted the queen's policies" (p. 108).

in notes of writing to any person or persons whatsoever not being members of this House . . ."

Within the House of Commons the new spirit showed itself in disrespect shown to privy councillors, bold opposition to the requests for subsidies, "levity and disorder." Yet with it all emerged constructive leadership and parliamentary oratory as a power. The Lord Keeper's answer to the Speaker at the conclusion of the session of 1593 voiced the queen's dislike "that such irreverence was shewed towards privy councillors, who were not to be accounted as common knights and burgesses of the House that are counsellors but during the Parliament, whereas the other are standing counsellors, and for their wisdom and great service are called to the Council of the State." It was doubtless the boldness and volubility of the Commons in this session and the next (1597) that led to the Speaker's warning in 1601 against "time spent in idle and vain matter, pointing the same out with froth and volubility of words, . . . long and vain orations to hinder the proceeding in matters of greater and more weighty importance." A suggestion of party alignment appeared when the radical section of the Commons took to sitting at one end of the House. This, says Neale, "must have given physical solidarity to their group, and since courage assorts with numbers, must have made considerable difference to the voting upon measures that privy councillors, courtiers, and staid lawyers condemned."

This, the last parliament of the reign, sat from October to December, 1601. It has been called the most turbulent of all. The advice of the privy councillors was ignored; speakers were interrupted, cried, or coughed down; voting was interfered with. On one occasion members were even pulled back into the House or pulled out into the lobby against their will.

The parliament was summoned largely from financial necessity. Generous tax grants were needed to handle the deficit created by the war with Spain and the costly rebellion in Ireland (£140,000), and new outlays estimated at £300,000. The Commons were asked to grant twice the amount reluctantly approved in 1589. Only after protracted debate did the Houses agree to four subsidies and eight *tenths and fifteenths*.

In the course of the debate there were practical suggestions for a more equitable assessment and concern over the burden on the little man of small means. It was on November 9 that Serjeant Heyle, speaking for the Council, went so far as to say that " 'all we have is her Majesty's, and she may lawfully at her pleasure take it from us.' " At this "all the House hemmed and laughed and talked." " 'Well,' quoth Serjeant Heyle, 'all your hemming shall not put me out of countenance.' " Even the Speaker's rebuke against such "a great disorder" was disregarded. When the Serjeant "had spoken a little while, the House hemmed again, and so he sat down." [14]

Besides the subsidy, the chief matter of dispute was the problem of monopolies. As defined by one of the members, a monopoly "is a restraint of any thing public in a city or commonwealth to a private use, and the user called a monopolitan." The monopolies of the Tudor period were manufacturing, rather than commercial, privileges and were not controlled by the Crown. The patentee applied for the grant, and then was left free to act under the powers conferred by it. Abuses appeared when persons who had introduced no new product or process into the country were granted all kinds of commercial privileges, oppressive powers to enforce these privileges, and dispensations from the existing law.

In the next reign the power of patentees to proceed against "interlopers" was to constitute an additional grievance, an infringement on common law procedure and its safeguards, but the issue in Elizabeth's parliaments was rather the economic one of freedom of occupation.

Opposition to monopolies had been voiced with little result in 1597. Now in 1601 the Commons were determined but uncertain how to proceed. Some favored a bill, others that all patents be brought before the House and canceled, while still others, including the councillors, assumed that the only proper way was to petition the queen. A bill was introduced and hotly debated. Francis Bacon, son of the great Lord Keeper, as the queen's Solicitor General, urged petition, defending the grant of monopolies as a part of the Queen's prerogative power: "For the prerogative royal of the Prince, for my own part I ever allowed of it, and it is such as I hope shall never be discussed. The Queen, as she is our Sovereign hath both an enlarging and restraining power. For by her prerogative she may first set at liberty things restrained by statute law or otherwise; and secondly, she may restrain things which be at liberty."

Bacon explained that the queen had withdrawn several of the less desirable monopolies, and defended others, including those which the

<hr>

[14] Tanner, *Tudor Constitutional Documents*, pp. 549–550. For the debate on monopolies, Tanner, pp. 573–576.

reader may recognize as the ancestors of our modern patents: ". . . if any man out of his own wit, industry, or endeavour finds out anything beneficial for the commonwealth, or brings in any new invention which every subject of this kingdom may use . . ."

Nevertheless, member after member rose to voice, not so much any personal complaint, as the real grievances of his constituents in town or county. For instance, in the debate of November 20, to one, Doctor Bennet, "the grievance out of the city for which I come," is a monopoly of salt; "fire and water are not more necessary." "Mr. Martin said, I do speak for a town that grieves and pines, for a country that groaneth and languisheth under the burden of monstrous and unconscionable substitutes to the monopolitans of starch, tin, fish, cloth, oil, vinegar, salt, and I know not what, nay, what not? The principalest commodities both of my town and country are engrossed into the hand of those bloodsuckers of the commonwealth."

Sir Robert Wroth read off such a list as to lead Mr. Hakewell of Lincoln's Inn to ask, "Is not bread there? . . . If order be not taken for these, bread will be there before the next Parliament."

It was accounted a triumph for the queen that she secured withdrawal of the bill on her promise that she herself would handle the matter: some monopolies would be repealed, some suspended, for the rest "to leave the validity of the patent to the judgment of the common law." [15] "Her Majesty's most gracious message" to this effect was reported to the Commons by the Speaker on November 25. The House promptly voted to "yield her most humble and hearty thanks," and to crave pardon for "divers speeches . . . made extravagantly in this House."

On November 30 the Council Chamber in Whitehall was the scene of the final act in the drama. The queen, sitting under the cloth of state at the upper end of the hall, received the Speaker accompanied by "some seven score" of the Commons (this large number at the queen's own suggestion). Her speech was gracious and conciliatory, even expressing thanks and approval that she had been set right by her Commons on a matter of moment, bespoken "out of zeal for their countries."

[15] A memorandum in the *State Papers* directed to "your Lordship" (Robert Cecil?), perhaps submitted about this time, asks: "To leave to the judgment of the Common Lawe disarmed of her Majesties protection all such Monopolies, privileges and grants as are already put in practice to the prejudice of every particular subject of this Lande; being of no better strength then her Majesties prerogative and that contrarie to the Greate Charter of England."

The opportunity for the judgment of the common law, that is, a test case, came shortly when Darcy, patentee for the sole importation and sale of playing cards, sued Allen, a haberdasher of London, for infringing his patent. Chief Justice Popham and the whole court resolved in line with counsel for the defendant "that the said grant to the plaintiff of the sole making of cards within the Realm, was utterly void, and this for two reasons: (1) That this is a monopoly, and against common law; (2) that it is against various acts of Parliament."

This, the last parliament of the reign, then, evidenced less of harmony between Crown and parliament. There was loyalty to the old queen but less enthusiasm. Yet in the following years, in the reigns of the first Stuart king and his son, Englishmen looked back with increasing fondness to the good old days, the golden age of Elizabethan England. Old parliament men with their memories or young lawyers with their books could produce many a useful precedent to uphold parliamentary privilege and the rule of law.

PART III. PARLIAMENT IN THE EARLY STUART PERIOD

XI

The England of the Early Stuarts

✿✿✿

THE land to which King James came in 1603 was, on the whole, the England of Elizabethan days and ways. Naturally many a notable Elizabethan lived well into the Stuart era — Shakespeare to 1616, Sir Walter Raleigh to 1618, Francis Bacon to 1626, and Sir Edward Coke from 1552 to 1634! Even so, some new features deserve attention. The changes evolved in the century of transition described above were nearing completion. Other more "modern" novelties were soon to appear.

Although three fourths of the population still lived in rural areas, cities were growing and constituting a market for agricultural products. London, as usual, exceeded all the rest, increasing from 60,000 consumers in 1540 to more than 300,000 in 1640. Mineral deposits — iron, zinc, copper, lead, and tin ore — were being exploited as never before. There was a gun-casting industry in some old monastic buildings in the Weald of Sussex. The domestic, or "putting out," system was well established, with increasing exports of English-made woolens. Means of transportation were still primitive. "The old wool-pack inns of England," Trevelyan writes, "recall the time when it was common to meet, round the turning of a country lane, a train of horses laden with sacks of wool hanging to the ground on either side; or a clothier riding into market with pieces of cloth upon his saddle-bow." In the areas of arable farming probably about half the acreage under grain was enclosed, half still in the old open-field system.

Commerce ranged over a much wider area. Most striking and appealing to the imagination were the reports of the explorers, about which the Englishman of James's reign could read in the printed volumes of Hakluyt's *Voyages*. English fishing-boats had long occupied a position of major importance in Newfoundland waters. The successful establishment of colonies at Jamestown and Plymouth was soon to take place. Tobacco had been introduced by Hawkins, and popularized by Raleigh. The first shipment from Virginia arrived in London in 1613. The new chartered companies, such as the East India Company and their interests, would command the attention of parliament.

Villeinage had finally disappeared. The common lawyers could boast that every Englishman was of free status. The "political nation" was increasing, not by the inclusion of lower classes of society, but numerically within classes. It was possible to cross the line. There were such additions as "descendants of the clothiers, who purchased old lands with new money, or of the richer yeomen who 'gentleised' their sons" (Trevelyan). The yeomen were prospering, and many could qualify as 40s. freeholders, i.e., voters for their county representatives in parliament. "The yeomanry is an estate of people almost peculiar to England. . . . The yeoman wears russet clothes, but makes golden payment, having tin in his buttons and silver in his pocket. . . . In his own country he is a main man in Juries. He seldom goes far abroad, and his credit stretches further than his travel." So were they aptly described by a contemporary, Fuller, writing in the reign of Charles I.

The sixteenth century witnessed a rise of prices. Landlords whose tenants paid fixed rents saw the purchasing power of their incomes fall while the cost of maintaining their households rose. Some peers and great landholders managed to carry on by substituting leaseholders for customary tenants. Others expanded and exploited their domains. Some were lucky enough to tap deposits of iron ore, coal, and stone. Others were forced to sell land. The Crown too, sold ex-monastic lands to help balance its budget. "Between 1558 and 1640 English rulers parted with land worth over £4,000,000, and most of it was bought by the local gentry. Of more than 3,000 manors examined by Professor Tawney, squires owned 80 per cent in 1640, peers had less than 7 per cent, and the crown had only 2 per cent. The king of England now owned very little of England, and the squire had become the backbone of English rural life." [1]

[1] Herbert Heaton, *Economic History of Europe* (New York, 1948), pp. 310–311, 316–317.

Though wealthy young noblemen finished their education with the grand tour — to Italy, France, and now even to Spain — England no longer relied on Italy for its cultural inspiration. It was in the full flower of its own literary renaissance with Ben Jonson, Shakespeare, and others. The theater was popular. The Chamberlain's Company, of which Shakespeare was a member, was established in its new building, the Globe, by 1598.[2] It had given performances before the queen at the Christmas season, 1594. On February 2, 1602, a special production of *Twelfth Night* was put on for the young gentlemen of the Middle Temple in their new hall. The Chamberlain's Company under a new title, the King's Men, continued under the direct patronage of James.

A play, to be successful, as Shakespeare's were, had to please diverse elements in the audience; officials, lords, and gentlemen of the court, some of refined tastes; the commercial population of London, including "a keen-witted but ill-educated popular audience" who delighted in slapstick comedy, and the lawyers and students of the Inns of Court. In an era of increasing interest in legal knowledge and principles, Notestein reminds us, "even the plays were packed with law, and very good law." It was a period when the lines spoken by the actors were more important than the stage effects. People spoke of *hearing* a play rather than of *seeing* it.

By and large it was not a scientific age. The common people still believed in goblins and fairies. Before leaving Scotland King James had written a tract condemning those who *dis*believed in witches! The King's English subjects, too, became affected by the witch mania already prevalent in northern Europe and Scotland, and hundreds of "witches" were put to death. Even educated persons in Church and State, while perceiving that mistakes had been made in certain cases, believed in witchcraft. Still, England could boast of such savants as Francis Bacon and William Harvey and of the College of Physicians in London. Bible-reading was to be stimulated by the production of the revised or King James version which appeared in 1611, a happy combination of scholarship and literary charm never to be excelled.

The reading of history had become a popular pastime in Tudor England. To scholar and amateur alike its value was believed to be in

[2] From 1594 there were two companies, the Admiral's Company, so called because its patron was Charles, Lord Howard of Effingham, Lord Admiral, and the Chamberlain's Company, whose patron was Hunsdon, Lord Chamberlain. It was he who, with the aid of the Master of the Revels, arranged festivities at court.

examples to be imitated or shunned. Some chroniclers catered to bourgeois readers, thus gratifying civic pride. Others played up recent and
contemporary events. Still another group attempted to cover the whole
known history of England, such as Holinshed in the *Chronicles of England, Scotland, and Ireland* and Stow in his *Annals*. The motive was to
glorify the ruling monarch by an account of his "illustrious ancestors,"
reign by reign. But inevitably there were some royal ancestors not so
illustrious, "evil" ministers, and instances of opposition to the same,
which furnished useful precedents for seventeenth-century parliamentarians.

Even before the end of Elizabeth's reign old chronicles like *Matthew
Paris* were being rediscovered and read with interest. A few brave scholars delved into the mystery of Anglo-Saxon manuscripts, long a closed
book. The lawyer scholar, William Lambarde, translated some of the
old laws into Latin, thereby unwittingly reading modern ideas into
ancient words like *witan,* and furnishing precedents, though faulty ones,
as to the antiquity of parliament.

John Stow, author of the *Annals* mentioned above, was a tailor by
profession, a member of the Merchant Taylors Company. From 1560 on
he was more and more concerned, as he put it, "with the search of our
famous antiquities." His great work was to the glorification of his native
city, the comprehensive *Survey of London* (published 1598, 1603).

In the reigns of James I and his son the most learned and accurate
of legal historians was John Selden, a lawyer of Lincoln's Inn. The
"Prince of Antiquaries" was Sir Robert Cotton (a descendant of Robert
Bruce, and hence a cousin of James), one of the founders of the Society
of Antiquaries. This was a gentlemen's literary club. The members
dined together, probably at Sir Robert's. Then one, so assigned, read a
paper on some subject drawn from England's antiquities. Some of those
read by Cotton himself deal with such subjects as castles and towns,
heraldry, the offices of high steward and constable, the ceremonies of
lawful combat, and the introduction of Christianity into Britain. Sir
Robert's house in Old Palace Yard by Thames-side, Westminster, became the rendezvous of members of the society and others, including
scholars, poets, lawyers, and parliament men — Lambarde, Camden,
Ben Jonson, Selden, John Eliot, and many others.

Cotton was elected to the Commons in the parliaments of 1604, 1624,
1625, and 1628. He was indefatigable in serving on committees when a

search for precedents was involved. He was a diffident speaker, and his collections served to furnish materials to his friends for their speeches rather than his own. On the whole, contributions from his library seem to have come from the chronicles rather than the law books — historical episodes (rather than legal precedents) such as figured in the speeches of his friend John Eliot and others in the sessions of 1625 and 1626 or in his own little history of Henry III.

James's hereditary right to the throne was not questioned in England. Elizabeth's councillors had long looked upon the king of the Scots as her successor. Robert Cecil, son of the great William, Lord Burghley, had carried on a secret correspondence with James, assuring him of his ultimate accession. Immediately on the old queen's death he was proclaimed king by the Privy Council. Under Cecil's able direction all worked out according to plans. The first parliament of the new reign (in contrast to parliamentary recognition of Henry VII as a *de facto* king) passed an act recognizing his lawful right: "A most joyful and just recognition of the immediate, lawful, and undoubted succession, descent, and right of the crown." [3]

The new monarch was well received at first. It was not yet apparent how the personality of James Stuart was to jar the nice balance of Crown and parliament, prerogative and common law. In spite of their loyalty to the old queen, the English people were glad and rather relieved to have a king to rule over them. "For a month of spring weather James rode south. The land seemed bursting into bud to welcome him, growing greener each day as the ever increasing train of courtiers wound slowly down out of the north country into the midland valleys; through shouting market-places where the masque of welcome and the corporation with its address were lost in the press of men; by ancient steeples rocking with the clash of bells; along open roads hedged with countrymen who had come on pilgrimage across whole counties." [4]

Popular anticipation was rewarded. At this time the king was in the

[3] It reads in part: ". . . we, being bounden thereunto, both by the laws of God and man, do recognize and acknowledge . . . that immediately upon the dissolution and decease of Elizabeth, late queen of England, the imperial crown of the realm of England . . . did, by inherent birthright and lawful and undoubted succession, descend and come to your most excellent majesty, as being lineally, justly, and lawfully next and sole heir of the blood royal of this realm as is aforesaid." Stephenson and Marcham, pp. 431–432.

[4] Trevelyan, *England under the Stuarts*, p. 74.

prime of life, a good horseman, and over middle height, devoted to the chase, with pleasant though not strong features. England's royal line has produced a variety of talents: the troubadour and crusader Richard I; warrior knights, like Edward III and Henry V; a veritable man of law, Edward I; a dilettante of the arts, Richard II; the businessman, Henry VII; and much later, "Farmer George" III and sailor James IV. Never before or since, perhaps, has there been such a scholar-king as this first Stuart. Educated under George Buchanan, the first Latin scholar of the day, James not only read and spoke Latin with ease but wrote learned treatises and polemical tracts. Most notable of these was his *True Law of Free Monarchies,* which set forth his theory of the divine right of kings.[5] As he put it pointedly to his first parliament (1610): "The state of monarchy is the supremest thing upon earth: for Kings are not only God's lieutenants upon earth and sit upon God's throne, but even by God himself they are called Gods. . . . I conclude then this point touching the power of kings with this axiom of Divinity, that as to dispute what God may do is blasphemy, . . . so is it seditious in subjects to dispute what a king may do in the height of his power; but just kings will ever be willing to declare what they will do, if they will not incur the curse of God. I will not be content that my power be disputed upon, but I shall ever be willing to make the reason appear of all my doings, and rule my actions according to my laws."

This power was summed up in the word *prerogative.* In the thirteenth and fourteenth centuries this term was used in the plural. "Prerogatives" were those rights of the king as suzerain — lord of lords — which mesne lords did not possess. In the Tudor period, as we have seen, *prerogative* covered the handling of matters of state and national crises, as well as the newly acquired headship of the Church. Even in modern times and popular governments it has a place. "In every State there must be some ultimate power to deal with emergencies, and exceptional situations — the power which modern jurists speak of as 'sovereignty.' This also was prerogative, and in the seventeenth century the emergency power was unquestionably vested in the Crown. . . . It only required a few touches to convert the Tudor doctrine of 'royal prerogative' into the Stuart doctrine of 'absolute power'." [6]

[5] Others included *Basilicon Doran* (1599), a royal gift for his son Prince Henry, and *Demonologie* (1597), to counteract the "damnable opinions" of those "who deny there can be such a thing as witchcraft."

[6] Tanner, *Constitutional Documents of the Reign of James I,* p. 5.

A trait of the new ruler which was to prove significant was his love of learned conversation and argument, especially at the dinner table. "As a boy in Scotland he was accustomed to the reading and discussion of the Scriptures during his meals; and later in England he loved to gather round him at table his favorite divines and a few selected laymen whose learning and dispositions were such as he could appreciate. . . . 'That King's Table was a trial of wits,' wrote Hacket. 'The reading of some books before him was very frequent while he was at his repast. . . . He was ever in chase about some disputable doubts which he would wind and turn about with the most stabbing objections that ever I heard. And was as pleasant and fellow-like in all those discourses as with his huntsmen in the field.' " [7]

Naturally such a scholar-king was not averse to presiding in person over formal debates such as the Hampton Court Conference and the later disputations between the civilians and the common lawyers over High Commission. He was ready to argue with committees of the Commons or to answer their petitions and protests. All this helped to make possible the defining of positions on both sides — the veritable war of words, precedents, and documents, which in the end was to be more lasting in establishing parliament's role than the actual civil wars of the 1640's.

Less admirable traits of the new ruler soon appeared. He took a deep interest in parliament, but interfered too much. He lacked both dignity and tact. He told the Commons, as an argument in favor of union with Scotland, that England had often been conquered in the past, but Scotland never. His struggle with the fanatical Presbyterian clergy in Scotland made him suspicious of puritanism; in fact, incapable of understanding the moderate Puritans in the House of Commons. He admired the Spanish monarchy as an embodiment of his own conceptions. Coming from a land poor in resources and backward in economic development, he found his new realm rich indeed and its wealth something to tap at will, whether for personal desires or rewards to royal favorites. As to finance, there is something to be said on behalf of the government. This was a prosperous age as was evidenced in the building of manor houses, the collections of plate, Jacobean furniture and works of art, and the increase in foreign trade. The crown did not share in

[7] D. H. Willson, "James I and His Literary Assistants," *Huntington Library Quarterly*, Vol. viii, No. 1, p. 35.

this prosperity, but legitimate expenses increased, such as the salaries of diplomats abroad, more expensive equipment for the army and navy, and the protection of new colonies.

James's Privy Council carried on fairly well as long as it contained some of the members inherited from the previous reign, such as Robert Cecil, Earl of Salisbury. As time went on the Council increased in size and declined in quality. There was the administrator type, the capable clerk, efficient in his department but lacking in statesmanship. The courtier type included such royal favorites as the Howards, Robert Carr, Earl of Somerset, and after his fall George Villiers, Duke of Buckingham. There were a few able men, such as Chancellor Ellesmere and Francis Bacon. The king was apt to prefer the courtier to the statesman and even to reject the sound advice of the majority. Trevelyan gives us a vivid word picture of what probably happened on many an occasion: "At some country seat within a day's ride of London, under the trees after the deer had been pulled down, or at the table after the last bottle had been emptied, James arranged the outline of high policy in familiar discourse with a single favourite, whose claim to advancement was neither birth nor wisdom, but beauty of face, and graceful though discourteous manners."

Even before parliament met, James revealed the directions in which prerogative and kingcraft were to lead. He made peace with Spain, was on friendly terms with the pope, relaxed penal laws against the Catholics, and at the Hampton Court Conference rejected the points of the Puritans' petition which would have enabled them to remain within the fold. Yet with the check imposed by the bond of loyalty to the old queen removed, and the spirit of independence in nation and parliament, "a wiser King than James would have found England difficult to govern in 1603." The result virtually poses the old dilemma as to what happens when an irresistible force meets an immovable body!

James's son and heir, Charles I, who succeeded him in 1625, had some of the qualities of a popular sovereign. By this time, in the hands of Flemish artists like Van Dyke, portrait-painting had become a fine art. First as prince, then as king, Charles is pictured as rather handsome, with refined features and a dignity and princely mien which his father lacked. He was appreciative of belles-lettres and the arts, and at the same time deeply religious. John Eliot tells us that already as a prince he was in good repute for "his exact government in the economy and order of his house, in the rule of his affairs, and in the disposition of his servants; whereby his honour had been maintained, yet no thrift neglected." By attendance at Council meetings and parliament he seemed to be preparing for his future role in kingcraft.

On becoming king he improved the personnel and decorum of the court. His prompt calling of a parliament was taken as a good omen. But as time went on, it became apparent that he lacked insight in reading the temper of the times, and the skill and tact essential for leadership. To him opposition was error, and its advocates his enemies. Thoroughly imbued from childhood with his father's belief in the divine right of kings, the prerogative of the Crown was not merely a matter of personal power and satisfaction but a sacred trust, which must be preserved and passed on intact to his heir. This explains why he made promises which he did not keep, and entered into engagements with mental reservations which would enable him to resume true kingly authority when opportunity offered. Indeed, he eventually suffered martyrdom in the cause of kingship. In 1645, when the civil war was going against him, he wrote to his son Charles that if he should at any time be taken prisoner, not to yield to any conditions ("though it were for the saving of my life"), "that are dishonourable, unsafe for your person, or derogatory to *regal authority*."

It was in 1614 that certain courtiers, personal and political enemies of the Scottish favorite, the Earl of Somerset, introduced at court one whom they hoped to use as a rival. This was young George Villiers, son of an obscure Leicestershire knight. He was just the type to attract King James — handsome, charming, audacious, and ambitious. He was not much of a scholar, "being by nature little contemplative," in the words of a contemporary, but was apt at dancing and fencing, and a pleasant hunting companion. His rise was phenomenal, and indeed soon raised him out of the reach of his sponsors. Beginning as cup-bearer, in sixteen months he was elevated from a commoner to a marquess, and was made Lord High Admiral. He was created Duke in May 1623. He thus took precedence over and aroused the jealousy of the older nobility. He was deep in the secrets of state and increasingly the medium through which "the world at large approached the sovereign." He was High Church and pro-Spanish, and his wife was a daughter of the Catholic Earl of Rutland. Although he was not guilty of all the charges brought against him later, there was certainly truth in the charge of "utter inefficiency" and the practices of patronage, nepotism, and sale of honors. In early years he was the companion and friend of Prince Charles, and was to dominate the first few years of his reign. From 1624 to 1628, says Gardiner, he was "virtually King of England."

At first approach it is hard perhaps for the student to realize that the twenty-five years from 1604 to 1629 represented an era of notable parliamentary progress. The negative side appears the more striking: unsolved grievances, short sessions and sudden dissolutions, intervals of no parliaments, and judgments from the courts upholding features of the prerogative. Yet it can be demonstrated that parliament in general and the Commons in particular gained in independence and initiative. *While in session* it was no longer controlled by King and Council.

But first, briefly as to grievances. These included unpopular financial methods of King and Exchequer. *Impositions* meant, not taxes in general, but the raising of the rates of customs duties above those required for a protective tariff, expressly to increase the royal revenue. In the interval of no parliaments, 1614–1621, and again in the 1620's, there were forced loans and benevolences and on occasion the sale of offices and honors, including the new title Baronet. Monopolies increased in number, were controlled by favorites, had little of the character of true patents, and conceded to the patentees the dangerous right of arresting unlicensed competitors.

There were no concessions to the Puritans; on the contrary, there was a tendency within the Anglican Church to move back to more ritualistic services and ceremonial.

After 1613 foreign policy was complicated by the presence at court of the Spanish ambassador, Gondomar, "one of the most astute diplomats of the age." Closeted alone with the king, he was able to exert more influence than the privy councillors. His aims were to win England away from the German Protestant alliance and restore it to the Catholic fold. This was to be effected in part by the marriage of Prince Charles to a Spanish princess.

It was the refusal of the Protestants of Bohemia, on the death of the childless Emperor Matthias in 1619, to accept as their king his cousin the Hapsburg Catholic Emperor Ferdinand, that precipitated the Thirty Years War on the Continent. They invited Frederick, Elector Palatine, ruler of a small Protestant state in the upper Rhine Valley, to be their ruler. Frederick's wife was King James's daughter, the Princess Eliza-beth. Frederick accepted the offered crown, but Spain supported Aus-tria, and other powers were drawn in on one side or the other. The "winter King" was not only driven from Bohemia, but a Spanish army invaded the Palatinate and he was obliged to flee to Holland. As to how England was involved, we shall hear in the account of the 1621 parliament described below.

To return to early Stuart parliaments in general, most sessions pro-duced some useful legislation, including private acts. Committees worked on repeal or amendment of existing laws, though with no plan for codification such as Francis Bacon proposed.

A search of the *Statute Roll* and Court Records for the years 1604–1629 would reveal some measures that could be called parliamentary or popular victories, but the list would be a short one. There were the acts in Shirley's Case described below, a decision of the judges in 1610 defin-ing and limiting the royal power to issue proclamations, a significant act on monopolies in 1624, and the unique Petition of Right in 1628. This last assured parliamentary control of direct taxation. Its other clauses were vital indeed, but dealt with "liberty of the subject" outside of parliament. The Apology (1604) and the Protestation (1621) were, as we shall see, significant as *claims* of powers and privileges by the Com-mons, but had not the force of statutes. In the *Lords Journals* would be found a record of the revival and successful use of impeachment in 1621 against the monopolists and Chancellor Francis Bacon, and in 1624 against the Lord Treasurer.

The very life of parliaments was in the king's hands. His it was to decide on a summons, set the date, prolong or cut, prorogue or dissolve. Only in the early days of the Long Parliament, 1641, did the Commons force through an act assuring them of regular meetings and a reasonably long session. Three of James's four parliaments were dissolved by the king in fits of anger. Charles's first was dissolved under pretense of threat of the plague, but actually for its failure to vote subsidies. The second was abruptly terminated to prevent impeachment of the favorite, Buckingham. The third was prorogued. Dramatic and even ominous was the dissolution of its second session in 1629, effected by the royal speech reading in part: "We shall account it presumption for any to prescribe any time unto us for Parliaments, the calling and continuing of which is always in our own power, and we shall be more inclinable to meet in Parliament again, when our people shall see more clearly into our intents and actions."

Nevertheless, progress there was. This will be described in the next chapter, but first a word about the sources, for we are fortunate in having fuller reports, both official and unofficial, about what went on in Stuart parliaments.

The *Lords Journals* contain effective statements of the charges against the patentees and those against Bacon and Cranfield, and of course, record the judgments pronounced in the High Court of Parliament. As was customary, no official speeches were recorded but the king's. The peers allowed their Journals to record their official acts and to list the bills read, the messages sent to the Commons, and the reports brought from committees. Nothing said by a peer in his individual capacity was set down.

The *Commons Journals* are now more complete. They give us the sequence of events and speeches, the readings of bills, lists of members appointed to committees. The clerk does more in attempting to include the substance of some of the speeches, but in compressed and discreet form. They lose the character and variety of the speakers, modify statements critical of the government, and reflect less of the tension and excitement that characterized some debates.

Luckily the present-day student has a new source in the remarkable collections of diaries that have been discovered hidden in museums and libraries and in the chests of castles and country houses, and now carefully edited and printed. Though customarily called *diaries,* most of them are notes taken in the House or committee chamber. As Professor Notestein describes them: "The note-takers of early Stuart days jotted down the various speeches in little tablets upon their knees, in very bad scrawls, occasionally in shorthand, often with almost verbal completeness."

Some of the diarists succeeded in catching the flavor and idiom of speeches, and included quotations, illustrations, "precedents," and stories, all of which the clerk ignored. They also recorded at length what went on in the committees on which they served, sometimes summaries, sometimes *verbatim* reports of the debates and arguments. On occasion they even "tell us what men said as they left the Commons and came together at a tavern. One note-book tells of an early-morning caucus of the Opposition."

The Venetian ambassador was still the top news-reporter of the day, and includes in his letters to his government items on parliament along with those on affairs at court. In addition there were now professional news-writers. Persons living in the country remote from the court or someone abroad, such as the English ambassador at Paris, could subscribe for these newsletters. Some came to be devoted particularly to parliament, including copies of speeches. "Parliamentary business," wrote a courtier in 1614, "is the greatest entertainment that we have."

XII

The Winning of the Initiative

❀❀

[THE *Commons of this realm*] *contain not only the citizens, burgesses and yeomanry, but also the whole inferior nobility of the kingdom, and knights, esquires, and gentlemen; many of which are come immediately out of the most noble families, and some other of their worth advanced to high honour of your majesty's privy council, and otherwise have been employed in very honourable service. In sum, the sole persons of the higher nobility excepted, they contain the whole flower and power of your kingdom; with their bodies your wars, with their purses your treasures, are upheld and supplied. Their hearts are the strength and stability of your royal seat. All these, amounting to many millions of people, are representatively present in us of the house of commons.* —
THE APOLOGY

AN ASSEMBLY such as the English parliament had become was a novelty to the new ruler, for the Scottish Estates were differently organized and still played a minor role in government. Parliamentary elections were held four times in James's reign of twenty-two years. The first parliament, by the device of proroguing, met in five sessions, 1604–1611. The second was the futile assembly of 1614, aptly named the Addled Parliament. Then followed six years of no parliaments in which James tried his preference for one-man government and kingcraft. The third parliament met in two sessions, 1621, and the last in 1624.

The progress made in the role of the Commons in parliament during a period of less than two generations (1604–1629) has been summed up by Notestein in the phrase "the winning of the initiative." "Almost without observation, Privy Councillors ceased to guide the Commons. And, quite as much unobserved, with no document or charter to serve as a mile-stone, there came into power in the Commons a group of leaders, who had no official connection with the Government, who had no common tie, except those of the opinions and feelings that bound English country gentlemen together. These men without purpose or intent but to do the next thing that came to hand, created a new leadership. With the establishment of that leadership the Commons gained the real initiative in legislation." With the sources now available, it has been possible for historians to work this story out in amazing detail.[1] For our purpose here the advances may be highlighted as follows: a "visit" to the first session, 1604, for the keynote; then in succeeding parliaments evidence of the changes in the relation of the Commons and the Privy Council, the Commons and the Lords; a new and effective committee system; and last, but not least, new leaders armed with an effective array of legal and parliamentary precedents.

The First Session, 1604

The opening session in 1604 gives us the keynote for the reign and is striking in two respects. It reveals (1) how promptly and efficiently the Commons got down to business on their own initiative, and (2) how early in the reign positive assertions on political powers and theory were made from both sides — King and Commons.

No sooner had the Speaker "with all submissive reverence to his Majesty" taken leave and led the Commons to assemble in their own House than matters of moment were introduced on the motion of private members.[2] Sir William Fleetwood spoke on behalf of his fellow knight from Buckinghamshire, Sir Francis Goodwin: "the return of his election being made, it was refused by the clerk of the crown, *quia utlagatus* (because he was outlawed), and because Sir John Fortescue, upon a second writ, was elected and entered in that place." This raised the question of the right of the House itself to determine disputed elections.

It was promptly followed by another motion also "tending to matter of privilege," designed to effect by action of the House the release of Sir Thomas Shirley, arrested for debt, an arrest made "just four days

---

[1] Notably D. W. Willson, *The Privy Councillors in the House of Commons*.

[2] For extracts from the *Commons Journals* on these debates, including Goodwin's and Shirley's cases and the Apology, see Stephenson and Marcham, pp. 407–424.

before the sitting of the parliament." On the motion of Sir George Moore, a select committee was appointed, as was now customary, to consider all questions of returns and privileges during the time of parliament.

The next day, March 23, "after prayers ended and the house settled with expectation of what should be propounded for the weal of the common subject, Sir Robert Wroth . . . moved that matters of most importance might first be handled; and to that purpose offered to the consideration of the house these particulars," that is, seven grievances, including wardship, abuses of purveyance and monopolies. Sir Edward Montague followed, naming three grievances currently vexatious in his own county of Northamptonshire, but readily recognized as common to others too. The first and second affected Puritans everywhere in the realm, and the third some of the small farmers. These were (1) the burden, vexation, and charge of Church courts; (2) "the suspension of some learned and grave ministers for matters of ceremony and for preaching against popish doctrine; (3) depopulations by enclosure." Two committees were appointed to consider these and report on possible action.

The case of Sir Thomas Shirley was successfully handled by the Commons with no interference from the king. Shirley was arrested for debt at the suit of a city alderman and detained in the Fleet Prison. This, the reader may be reminded, is arrest as a regular judicial process, and does not necessarily involve any political ill-will or desire to exclude a member. In securing Shirley's release by direct action the House was following the precedent set in Ferrers' Case, 1543, and reaffirmed in Fitzherbert's Case late in Elizabeth's reign. In the present instance they had recourse to stronger measures than before, but in the long run solved a crucial problem.

When the warden of the Fleet, summoned to the bar of the House, refused to release his prisoner on the grounds that he would thereby become liable for the debt, the Commons proceeded to commit to the Tower for breach of privilege both the creditor and the bailiff who made the arrest. Even the warden was detained for some days in the Tower cell aptly dubbed "Little Ease," as he stubbornly held out until some legal protection was forthcoming.

Thus impelled, the House passed a private act to protect the individuals involved — creditor and warden [3] — and constructively a public act determining practice in the future. The second enabled creditors whose prisoners should be set at liberty by privilege of parliament to sue out new writs against them as soon as the time of privilege expired. It protected the officials who arrested them from the legal consequences of releasing them in response to a claim of privilege.

The case of Sir Francis Goodwin raised the question of authority to determine disputed elections. There were Elizabethan precedents on both sides. In 1593 the Commons had assumed the right to entrust the task to their standing committee on privileges. Now in 1604 it was Chancery which declared Goodwin disqualified,[4] ordered a new election, and seated his rival Fortescue, a privy councillor. In the end the king secured the Commons' assent as a personal favor. While he never actually acknowledged their right to determine disputed elections, they continued to act on this assumption throughout the reign.

Before this compromise was arrived at, some vigorous debate and exchange of views had taken place between King and Commons, and no wonder. James's answer to the first report of the House on the case was highly provocative. It reads in part: ". . . he was indifferent which of them were chosen, Sir John or Sir Francis; that they could suspect no special affection in him, because this was a counsellor not brought in by himself. That he had no purpose to impeach their privilege; but since *they derived all matters of privilege from him, and by his grant,* he expected they should not be turned against him" (italics added).

As to precedents, his Majesty adroitly shelved whole batches of them by ruling out the reigns of certain English predecessors not up to his standards: He said "that there was no precedent did suit this case fully; precedents in the times of minors, of tyrants, of women, of simple kings, [were] not to be credited, because such were for some private ends." The reader may like to check with the royal historian as to which rulers may be properly included in each of these categories!

The royal challenge was met by the Apology (June 20, 1604), "To the

[3] "An Act to secure the debt of Simpson and others, and save harmless the Warden of the Fleet in Sir Thomas Shirley's case." Tanner, *Constitutional Documents of the Reign of James I*, p. 302, and sources, pp. 303–317.

[4] As this was merely outlawry as a feature of civil process, the Commons maintained that it did not disqualify. Besides, process had not been carried through. "The outlawry remained in the Hustings [local court], so the law could not take notice of it." For Elizabethan precedents, see above, p. 165.

King's most excellent Majesty: from the House of Commons assembled in Parliament." This was *apology* in the sense of vindication, not excuse or admission of error. Carefully framed by a select committee, it was couched in respectful, even flattering terms, but was striking in its candor and assurance. It contained an impressive description of the political nation with which his Majesty had now to deal (quoted above). There were such striking assertions as these: "The prerogatives of princes may easily and do daily grow; the privileges of the subject are for the most part at an everlasting stand." "The voice of the people in things of their knowledge is said to be as the voice of God."

The Commons "with great thankfulness to God acknowledge that He hath given us a king of such understanding and wisdom as is rare to find in any prince of the world," yet point out that "no human wisdom, how great soever, can pierce into the particularities of the rights and customs of people." His Majesty has been gravely misinformed as to his new land. The widespread effects of these errors is then contrasted with the happier regime of Queen Elizabeth, "in the latter times" of whose reign merely some *one* privilege now and then was by "some particular act attempted against."

More particularly as to the privileges of the Commons, his Majesty is mistaken in assuming ". . . first that we hold not our privileges of right, but of grace only, renewed every parliament by way of donative [gift] upon petition, and so to be limited; secondly that we are no court of record, nor yet a court that can command view of records, . . . and lastly, that the examination of the returns of writs for knights and burgesses is without our compass, and due to the chancery."

The Apology denies the second and third as false assertions, and adroitly explains away the first: "that our making of request in the entrance of parliament to enjoy our privileges is an act only of manners and doth not weaken our right, no more than suing to the king for our lands by petition." Then follows an emphatic, positive assertion: "The right of the liberty of the commons of England in parliament consisteth chiefly in these three things: first, that the shires, cities, and boroughs of England . . . have free choice of such persons as they shall put in trust to represent them; secondly, that the persons chosen during the time of parliament, as also of their access and recess, be free from restraint, arrest, and imprisonment; thirdly, that in parliament they may speak freely their consciences without check or controlment, doing the same with due reverence to the sovereign court of parliament — that is, to your majesty and to both the houses, who all in this case make but one politic body, whereof your highness is the head."

The Commons and the Council

An old parliament man — and there were several sitting in these sessions — would have noticed that there were in the House few privy councillors or government-sponsored M.P.'s. James's conception of his kingly role made such measures of control seem unnecessary. There was less of the constructive planning for a parliament or of the practical leadership which had characterized the Tudors. Yet councillors in the House still had certain formal functions to perform: to nominate the Speaker, administer oaths, carry important bills and messages to the Upper House, bring letters, messages, and commands from the king. They had individual access to the sovereign and knew or were supposed to know secrets of state.

It was now assumed that councillors were to be treated just like ordinary members and that their presence was not essential even for important business. They were not favored in debate, sometimes even refused leave to speak. "In debate, wrote Eliot, 'the meanest burgess has as much favor as the best knight or counsellor, all sitting in one capacitie of Commoners.' Sir Edwin Sandys told Cranfield in 1621 that when he entered the House he must lay aside his greatness." [5]

As time wore on and differences between king and parliament became more acute, there was evidence of growing hostility towards councillors. This is reminiscent of the "hemming and hawing" of Elizabeth's last parliaments, but in a bolder tone. Debates reveal examples of "studied discourtesy." "When in 1621 Edmondes told Sir Edward Coke that a certain bill read 'Oxford and Cambridge' rather than 'Cambridge and Oxford,' Coke answered rudely that Edmondes need not trouble himself since he had attended neither university. . . . The Venetian ambassador wrote in 1621 that 'various signs of contempt and various ways of mortification had been shown in the assembly against the said secretary of state [Calvert] on various occasions when he has uttered many important particulars in the name of his Majesty.' . . . Carleton

[5] Willson, *The Privy Councillors in the House of Commons*, upon which this section and the two following (Commons and Council, Commons and Lords, Committees) are mainly based and from which, unless otherwise indicated, the quotations are taken.

was reminded quite unnecessarily, when he became a lord, that he had no property from which to take a title."

The Speaker of the House, as in Elizabethan days, was an able lawyer. Three of the four who served in James's parliaments were virtually servants of the Crown. In the first it was Sir Edward Philips, ablest of them all; in the second, 1614, Sir Robert Crew, and in 1621 Thomas Richardson, most disliked by the Commons.[6] The form of election by the House meant even less than in Tudor parliaments. For instance, a privy councillor (Edmondes) nominated Richardson as one "whome the King liked," and in 1624 said that the King had "ever used to interpose his Judgment, whom he thinketh to be the meetest person to be employed in that service." The Speaker continued to receive instructions from the court, so much so, in fact, that Philips was told that "he was the mouth of the House to the King, and not from the King to the House." Nevertheless, through able leaders and new rules of procedure or better enforcement of old rules, the House successfully checked the Speaker. He was losing the right to interrupt members, to determine who should speak, to arrange the order of business, and to frame messages to king and Council.

The one exception, a really impartial Speaker, was Serjeant Crewe (Sir Thomas, younger brother of the notable Chief Justice Randall Crewe), who served in the last parliament of James and the first of Charles. Crewe is praised by Sir John Eliot as one in whom nature and art "concurred to make him equal to his place"; a great master of the law, and also one in whose studies "religion had so shared, as to win him special name and reputation"; an orator who on all occasions could express himself *pulchre et ornate* (beautifully and elegantly). At the opening of the 1625 parliament, in the customary second speech to King and Lords requesting the privileges of the House, he advised the young sovereign "that in comparison of a parliamentary way he would find all other courses to be out of the way; told him that his imperial diadem shone all the brighter, in that it was enamelled and compassed with a beautiful border of the antient and fundamental laws; and gravely counselled him to have it in perpetual remembrance, that those fundamental laws were what held the body of the commonwealth together, and that, *being suitable to the nature of the people, they were safest for the sovereign.*"[7]

[6] In 1626 the Speaker was Sir Heneage Finch and in 1628 Sir John Finch.
[7] As paraphrased by Forster.

The Commons and the Lords

There was some increase in numbers in the Commons and considerable in the Lords. Many new men — Scotsmen, favorites, and upstarts — were raised to the peerage. The peers of older lineage were offended by this "affront to the dignity of birth." Many were staunchly Protestant and hostile to Spain. Memories of Elizabethan naval victories suggested a weapon more effective than James's kingcraft and diplomacy. "Grudges general and grudges individual figured with them," says Notestein. "Many an important family had seen its representative overlooked in matter of preferment at Court, while pushing northerners had fallen into offices and dignities." Thus many of the Lords were ready to cooperate with the Commons in opposition to the Crown.

Conference between the two Houses by means of committees was not new. We have seen measures framed by a group of Lords and Commons as early as 1340 and planning for concerted action in the Good Parliament of 1376. Only in the sixteenth and seventeenth centuries did such conferences become formal and set to rules. Though recognized as useful, there was the danger that the Lords would overawe the Commons. The committee men of the latter labored under several disadvantages. There was physical discomfort: the Lords *sat* "covered" (that is, with hats on), while the Commons *stood* "uncovered" (hats off), no matter how long the conference. One suspects that this matter of hats was not merely one of rank and dignity but climate — the cold, damp, foggy atmosphere penetrating council chambers and committee rooms! It was hard on "divers ancient gentlement of the House," able conference men, but not quite equal to such an endurance test. Sometimes the Lords demanded a conference on short notice. As one of the members put it in 1606, "This appointment of so Suddaine a tyme by the Lords, did, he feared, not proceed from their alacrity to confer, but to surprise us of a suddaine." In conference the Lords presumed to reject subjects the Commons wanted discussed, or they would insist on reopening matters already determined in the lower House. The Lords also had the expert legal opinion of the judges and the Attorney General, and even used them to argue points in conference. "In April, 1621, Alford objected to a conference on the ground 'that then the young Lawyers, Members of this House, should be put to debate with the learned Judges there, and with the King's Attorney, who are no Members of that House, but only Assistants there.' "

As time went on, the Lords treated the Commons with more respect and deference, a sign of the growing equality of the two Houses. The Commons protected themselves in two important ways. They learned to plan for the conference and to instruct their members, sometimes merely to hear what the Lords had to say and report back to their House, again with authority to agree or dissent or present alternatives. As Pym put it later (1640), "At a conference wee only bring our Eares, at a Free conference there is liberty to speake." Parts were assigned to individual conferees. Sometimes members rehearsed their speeches before the House, so that colleagues might approve or criticize.

Committees

Old parliament men would be impressed by the change in committees. Whereas in Elizabeth's reign committees were small, few, and dominated by councillors, they now tended to be numerous and large, with few or no councillors, sometimes but one or two in a committee of thirty or forty! The naming of members was no longer haphazard. The clerk was required to name individuals instead of using a word or phrase to indicate a group, or the old customary "all the privy councillors who are members of the house." The Commons nominated or approved those of special knowledge or interests appropriate to the work in hand, such as merchants, financial experts, those conversant with colonial problems, civilians, and "all the lawyers in the House." It was customary now to have large standing committees. In James's first parliament there were such for major subjects — religion, grievances, continuation and repeal of statutes, privileges and returns — and for conference with the Lords on the Act of Union with Scotland, debated in the 1607 session.

Members who had served in the last parliaments of Elizabeth's reign would recall the expedient of the large General Committee, that is, one which any member of the Commons not actually named to the committee might attend and "inform," though not vote. It was in the session of 1607 that this developed into the Committee of the Whole House, repeated in 1610, and used constantly in the 1620's. Its advantage lay in the fact that the Speaker left his chair, indeed, left the House, and was forced to sit in an adjoining room while the House elected a temporary chairman to preside in his place. "In 1621 a member moved that the house go into a committee of the whole 'that we might not be troubled this day with the Speaker; and that it might not be permitted him to speak, till the House call him up.' " [8]

Strict rules of debate were relaxed. Members could speak as often as they could catch the eye of the chairman. They need not rise, and could refer to each other by name. There was real debate with short pithy speeches, question and answer. " 'In committees,' said Sir Herbert Croft, 'by short Arguments many times truth is beaten out.' " In the 1620's the Committee of the Whole for grievances played a major role. With the help of subcommittees it collected grievances from various sources, sifted and stated them in concrete form as a basis for action. Thus "the whole membership of the House was engaged in gathering the case against the government." Committees of the Whole House, through subcommittees of expert lawyers, handled the task of legislation. The procedure has been described as something like this. One of the lawyer members might rise and say that a new law was needed to remedy a defect in a statute, to meet some economic problem, or to clarify a legal procedure. The matter would be referred to the appropriate Committee of the Whole House, such as for continuation and repeal of statutes, trade, or courts of justice. A subcommittee of three or four lawyers would draft a bill and report it back to the Committee of the Whole to be criticized and, if need be, amended. Then it would be reported to the House in formal session, where its passage would likely be a mere formality.

Popular Leaders

By 1610 the opposition party had grown in strength until it constituted a virtual majority in the Commons. Its leaders in that and succeeding sessions could hold their own both in debate in the House and in conference and committee. Naturally their abilities and talents varied and were utilized accordingly. By way of illustration here we may introduce Sandys for his business ability and acumen, Phelips for his dramatic qualities, Hakewill and Coke for their legal training and precedents.

Sir Edwin Sandys was active in the first two parliaments of the reign. "His wisdom and moderation," remarks Willson, "his powers of debate and wide experience of affairs marked him as the most outstanding of

[8] "Again in 1626, when the house was determined to do no business and the speaker was trying to carry on as usual, the house went into committee of the whole for the obvious purpose of being rid of him." Willson, p. 225.

all who opposed the king." He had studied at Oxford, where he received degrees of B.A. in 1579 and M.A. in 1583. He was for a time a student of the Middle Temple, but did not make law his profession.

While still a young man, about twenty-five years old, Sandys was elected to parliament as member for Andover (1586). From the first he took an active part in proceedings, serving repeatedly on committees. In succeeding years he had the breadth of view which comes from travel. In 1593, with a friend, he made a three-year tour of the Continent, visiting France, Italy, and Germany. In 1603 he was one of those who went to Scotland and accompanied the new king to England. He was rewarded with a knighthood in May 1603. Sir Edwin was returned to James's first parliament for a Hampshire borough and sat for other constituencies in 1614, 1621, and 1624, as well as in the first two parliaments of Charles I.

Sandys's experience in economic and colonial affairs was due in part to his connection with the East India Company and his active interest in the Virginia Company.[9] His election as Treasurer of the latter in 1619 has been heralded as "a date to be remembered in the history of English colonization" (Gardiner), for it was Sandys who was largely responsible for the establishment of the Virginia Assembly of Burgesses, modeled on the English House of Commons. Although in 1624 the Company's charter was annulled and its government was assumed by the Crown, "representative and other institutions established by Sandys remained to become a model for other American colonies."

His astonishingly active role in parliament, session after session, included motions on points of procedure and "liberty of the subject," [10] but he contributed most on matters of finance and trade, where his business ability and knowledge of practical economics came into play. In 1604 he headed a committee to investigate grievances against the great trading companies and to consider a bill for throwing trade open, a policy he continued to support. In 1606 he led the House in attacking purveyance, and in 1607 opposed the government on the union with Scotland. Most notable were his speeches on impositions in 1610 and 1614. In 1621 he made an able report from the Committee of Trade,

[9] He was a member in the council for Virginia as early as 1607, was chosen in 1617 to assist the Treasurer in the management of the Company, and in 1619 elected Treasurer.

[10] In the committee for the conference on naturalization he equated the Great Charter with the Englishman's heritage. In the same session (1607) he urged that all prisoners be allowed the benefit of counsel.

and was a member of the committee concerned with the monopolists and their arrests of competitors, more particularly to prepare a bill "for the better securing of the subjects from wrongful imprisonment."

In 1614 he was a moving spirit on a committee to consider impositions, and in bringing in its report, May 21, delivered a remarkable speech, striking in its divergence from the royal theory of kingship. He maintained that the origin of hereditary monarchy lay in election. Even if a new sovereign does not go through the formalities of election, he must remember that his authority came by "Consent of the People, and with reciprocal Conditions between King and People. That a King, by Conquest, may also (when Power) [when force permits?] be expelled." [11]

Sir Robert Phelips, like Sandys, was knighted by the new ruler in 1603. He entered James's first parliament as member for a borough in Cornwall; in later parliaments he sat for other boroughs, and finally for Somerset. He too had traveled — in France in 1613 and in 1615 to Spain on a diplomatic mission with Digby (afterward Earl of Bristol). He was active in the last two parliaments of James, in 1621, for instance, in the attack on the monopolists and as chairman of the committee to inquire into charges of bribery against Chancellor Bacon, and in supporting the Commons' petition against the Catholics and the Spanish marriage. He has been credited with being the key man among the opposition leaders in Charles's first parliament.

Besides all this, however, Phelips interests us as much for what he was as for what he did. He had a fearlessness, an impulsive dramatic quality that often carried the day. It was from the southwest counties of Cornwall, Somerset, and Devon that other bold spirits had come. A notable Cornish man in Stuart parliaments was, of course, the Puritan Sir John Eliot, who later died in the Tower, virtually a martyr to the cause of freedom of speech.

It is amusing and instructive to notice how the modern historian, describing in detail debates in the House, incidentally time and again pictures Phelips's readiness and "punch." For instance, following the account of a speech by Sir Edward Coke against Spain (1621) we read: "Never yet had been levelled so daring an assault on the darling project of the king [the Spanish marriage]; and in the temper excited by it, *Phelips rose and carried a proposal* to refer the whole subject of supply

[11] *Commons Journals*, I, 493; compare Gardiner, II, 240.

to committee, which should be instructed to include in their report as well religion as supply. *A general shout of assent arose.*" Following a speech by Alford, we are told, "Sir Robert Phelips spoke *altogether more decidedly.*" In 1625 in the debates on Richard Montague: " 'Send the serjeant for him,' cried Phelips, *speaking yet more strongly.*" The Serjeant was called!

In the debates of December 1621 on privilege (leading to the Great Protestation), Sir Francis Seymour urged "it was their duty to take at once some course to settle their privileges, so that they should leave them not worse than they found them when they entered these walls." *The suggestion was put in more distinct form by Phelips*: "Since, he remarked, his majesty hath said that we hold our privileges by the grace of princes, and not by a right descended to us, it was indeed rendered necessary that they should expressly declare their powers. And in so doing they would do no more than was disputed of in the first of his majesty, when the king said that they held their liberties by a toleration, not by right; whereupon there was entered a public declaration that they held them by inheritance from their ancestors. He would have that course taken now." [12]

We are fortunate in having in Sir John Eliot a member who has left in writing some astute estimates of his fellow members as speech-makers. He makes a dry comment upon "the break-down in the house of a crack orator from Cambridge, when the gentleman 'found that the cold rhetoric of the schools was not that moving eloquence which does affect a parliament.' " It was after Phelips's speech in the debate on supply, 1625, that Eliot comments on his style. He says (in part) that there was in him a natural grace of oratory. "A choice store he had, and elegance of words; a readiness and dexteritie in fancie and conception; a voice and pronunciation also of much sweetness . . . A redundancie and exuberance he had, and an affected cadence and deliverie: but upon all occasions, at all times, he spoke from the occasion, *ex re nata,* which made his arguments as more genuine and particular, so more acceptable and persuasive: For in that place, alwaies, premeditation is an error." This very "redundancie and exuberance" makes it impractical to quote Phelips's speeches verbatim here, but we shall see him in action in the parliament of 1621.

[12] These examples are drawn from John Forster's biography of John Eliot. The italics are mine.

"All the Lawyers in the House": Personalities and Precedents

We have seen something of the importance of the lawyers in Elizabethan parliaments. Their influence was certainly as great, if not greater, in early Stuart parliaments. "To the Common Law their deepest loyalty was engaged," says Notestein; "when James seemed to be undermining it they were ready to join the Opposition." A sympathizer with the Crown declared the lawyers "ready to 'second any complaint against both Church and King . . . with their cases, antiquities, records, statutes, presidents (precedents) and stories.' " They continued to contribute to decorum and procedure. They were useful in the revising of laws or the framing of new ones.

It was a lawyer, Whitelocke, in a speech in the Commons, 1610, who clearly raised the question, "Where the sovereigne power is in this kingdome?" It was still too early for a theory of parliamentary sovereignty. He finds the *jura majestatis* — that sovereign power which is *potestas suprema,* a power that can control all other powers and cannot be controlled by itself — in *the King in Parliament.* This was not new, but had not been so publicly and emphatically proclaimed.[13]

It was in the parliament of 1624, according to one of the diarists, that King James declared: "The lawyers of all the people in the world are the greatest grievance to my subjects, for when the cause is good for neither party, yet it proves good and beneficial himself [for themselves]." Yet the king had capable lawyers in his service, both common lawyers and civilians. The judges continued to sit in the Lords as advisory, not voting, members, as did the Attorney General in most sessions. The Commons opposed the influence of Crown counsel in their House, claiming that all alike, as members of the high court of parliament, were in a sense legal advisers of the king. They assumed that learned counsel could speak only as ordinary members, subject to the usual rules of debate and procedure.

A novel problem appeared in the fall session of 1606, since a member of the House, Sir Henry Hobart, had been appointed Attorney General

---

[13] "The sovereign power is agreed to be in the King: but in the King is a twofold power, — the one in Parliament, as he is assisted with the consent of the whole State; the other out of Parliament, as he is sole and singular, guided merely by his own will. And if of these two powers in the King, one is greater than the other and can direct and control the other, that is *suprema potestas*, the sovereign power and the other is *subordinata*. It will be easily proved that the power of the King in Parliament is greater than his power out of Parliament, and doth rule and control it." Tanner, *Constitutional Documents of the Reign of James I*, p. 260.

in the summer. The Committee of Privileges reported that there was no precedent for an attorney's serving in the Commons, but as the House could not agree on the issue, Hobart continued to attend for the rest of the session. In 1614, with Francis Bacon in the dual role of attorney and M.P., the House took a firmer line. In debate on the problem it became clear that if a vote was taken Bacon would be excluded. Finally the king suggested a compromise, which was accepted. Bacon was to remain, but in the future no attorney was to be permitted to serve in the Commons.

Personal ambition naturally played some part in the attitude of learned counsel. Serjeants hoped to become King's Serjeants and, ultimately, judges. Still, it was their duty to protect the interests of the Crown. They were often technically correct in the citing of precedents and in the defense of the prerogative.[14]

There were distinguished and sound scholars among the civilians.[15] Their services were valued not only in the ecclesiastical courts but in Chancery and Admiralty, and the Privy Council might employ them on nice points of diplomacy and international law. Some were elected to the Commons, where, as specialists in certain fields, they served on committees. The lists of committee members in the *Commons Journals* sometimes contain the item, "all the civilians in the House."

Doctor John Cowell was not actually one of these elected to parliament, but aroused the attention and interest of both king and Commons by his law dictionary entitled *Interpreter or Booke containing the signification of Words,* published in 1607.[16] His aim was in part to acquaint his fellow civilians and students of the civil law with terms current in the English common law. Students today are used to consulting law dictionaries in which old Latin and French terms are listed and Englished. For the readers he had in mind, Doctor Cowell did the reverse, listing terms to be found in the current English versions of statutes and treatises, followed by a brief definition or longer exposition. Eventually the book became a best seller and long remained the

[14] The learned counsel "passed upon the legality of many of the patents of monopoly. They drafted much of the legislation desired by the crown, including the bills of subsidy" (Willson).

[15] Specialists in Roman (i.e., Civil) and Canon Law trained at Oxford or Cambridge or universities on the Continent.

[16] At Cambridge University he was Regius Professor of Civil Law, Master of Trinity Hall and Vice-Chancellor. He was a member of Doctors' Commons and Vicar General to Archbishop Bancroft. His book was reissued in 1637 and had passed through seven editions by 1727.

standard dictionary of English law. The immediate effect was to alarm the Commons with its definitions of such terms as *king, parliament, prerogative, subsidy*. For instance:

King. He is above the Law by his absolute power . . . And though for the better and equal course in making laws he do admit the three estates, that is, Lords spiritual, Lords temporal, and the Commons unto counsel, yet this, in divers learned men's opinions, is not of constraint but of his own benignity, or by reason of his promise made upon oath at the time of his coronation . . .

Prerogative of the King. . . . Now for those regalities which are of the higher nature (all being within the compass of his prerogative, and justly to be comprised under that title,) there is not one that belonged to the most absolute prince in the world which doth not also belong to our King, except the custom of nations so differ (as indeed they do) that one thing be in the one accounted a regality that in another is none.[17]

It was also rumored that Doctor Cowell was encouraging the king to substitute the civil law for the English common law. In the session of 1610 conferences were held between Lords and Commons, but the Lord Treasurer announced that the king had condemned the book and would take action accordingly. It was withdrawn from circulation, not because his Majesty disagreed with the definitions, but because he felt it out of place for a mere subject, even so learned and loyal a subject as Doctor Cowell, to discuss the prerogative!

Among the "Common" lawyers, it is hard to choose. In the parliament of 1626 alone, for instance, there were such notable "men of law" as Glanvile, Noy, Selden, Bulstrode, and Sir Henry Martin. It was still customary and advantageous for cities and boroughs to return their legal adviser as one of their two representatives. Such was Glanvile, Recorder of Plymouth, one of the southwestern ports growing in importance in this era of "Westward ho." Eliot called him "that pregnant westerne lawier," while Coke said that he "carried a *bibliothecam in capite*" (a library in his head)! It was in conference with the Lords, arguing against their saving to the Petition of Right, 1628,[18] that he showed a knowledge of the history of parliament. In ruling out the particular historical "savings" cited by the Lords as precedents, Glanvile traces the evolution of parliamentary procedure. Up to 2 Henry V, he says, legislation was by petition. "To these Petitions the Kings made

[17] Tanner, *Constitutional Documents of the Reign of James I*, pp. 12–14.
[18] See below, pp. 247–250.

Answer as they pleased; sometimes to Part, sometimes to the Whole, sometimes by Denial, sometimes by Assent, sometimes absolutely, and sometimes by Qualifications." But in 2 Henry V, as established by parliament, "ever since then the Use hath been as the Right was before, that the King taketh the whole, or leaveth the Whole, of all Bills or Petitions exhibited for the obtaining of Laws."

In earlier parliaments William Hakewill (1574–1655) was outstanding. He was a barrister of Lincoln's Inn and served as one of its chief benchers for nearly thirty years. His coat of arms is set up in the west window of the chapel. Hakewill represented several Cornish constituencies in Parliament. The last of these, Amersham, after long disuse, had been newly awarded its right to send representatives, and this owing to Hakewill's findings in the old records. He was a member of the Society of Antiquaries, and became pre-eminent as a legal antiquarian and master of precedents. His writings, besides some on technical points of law, include a tract printed in London in 1641, actually the speech he made in the parliament of 1610,[19] and *The Manner how Statutes are enacted in Parliament by passing of Bills collected many Yeares past out of the Journals of the House of Commons* (also printed in 1641).

In the session of 1610 the debates on impositions furnished an occasion on which both the search for and the exposition of precedents were undertaken seriously and methodically. They were even justified by a precedent for searching precedents — a copy of an Act of Parliament in 46 Edward III, produced by Sir Roger Owen, "that a subiect may have free accesse to recordes uppon any occasion." These debates are also noteworthy as the first in which a chapter of Magna Carta figures as a major precedent, and the Charter's origin, history, and fundamental character are publicized. Most convincing and masterly was Hakewill's speech, the one chosen by the Long Parliament to be printed in 1641.

He admits that he accepted the judgment in Bate's Case at the time, 1606, but his recent search of records has led him to "stagger in his opinion." Some of the records urged then were "untruly vouched and many misapplied." He wisely grants his opponents' contention that custom did not originate through parliament but is due at common law. Even so, the common law leaves no doubt that it is a "duty certain," [fixed rate] not an absolute power in the king to demand more or less:

[19] *The Libertie of the Subject against the pretended Power of Imposition maintained by an Argument in Parliament anno 7° Jacobi regis.*

"That the common law of England, as also all other wise lawes in the world, delight in certainty, and abandon uncertainty, as the mother of all debate and confusion, than which nothing is more odious in law."

It is under his third head, "whether or no hee (the King) bee not bound to the contrary by acts of parliament," that Hakewill accords the Great Charter its first public eulogy and history in the Commons since 1593 (James Morice). The first statute, he says, is in Magna Carta, cap. 30:

"The statute, of which this is a branch, is the most ancient statute-law we have, wonne and sealed with the blood of our ancestors; so reverenced in former times, that it hath been by parliament provided, (25 E. 1, cap. 1, 2, 3, 4) that transcripts thereof should be sent to all the cathedrall churches of England there to remaine; that it should be twice every yeere publikely read before the people; that likewise twice every yeere there should be excommunication solemnly denounced to the breakers thereof; that all statutes and all judgments given against it shall be held as void; that it should be received and allowed as the common-law, by all such as have the administration of justice; and it hath been no lesse than 29 times solemnly confirmed in parliament. I will, therefore, with so much the more care, endeavor to free this law from all the objections that have been made against it." [20]

The most astonishing, in fact, quite unique, man of law in the parliaments of 1621–1622, 1624, 1625, and 1628–1629 was Sir Edward Coke, the same Sir Edward whom we met as Speaker of the Commons in Elizabeth's parliament of 1593. It was unusual to have in the Lowei House one who had served not only as Solicitor and Attorney General, but as Chief Justice of the Court of Common Pleas (1606–1613) and of King's Bench (1613–1616). As a judge he had been an advisory though not a voting member of the Upper House. Now in the Commons he was decidedly *persona grata* to the Lords, active in conferences, reporting back to the Commons, conveying bills and messages.

Parliamentary historians are not as enthusiastic as were contemporaries, feeling that Coke has been overrated at the expense of abler

[20] Though Hakewill presents arguments based merely on construction of the text of the Charter, he finds even more convincing fourteenth-century interpretations implied in the statutes of 2 and 14 Edward III. Like most of his contemporaries, he does not question that it is a *statute*, but does a nice bit of critical work in attempting to date it, comparing printed and manuscript copies, official records, and the testimony of chronicles.

parliamentarians like Sandys and Phelips, but in his own day his prestige was tremendous. His rich political and official career extended over forty years, under three sovereigns, in parliament, Privy Council, and courts. He could say, "When I was Speaker . . ." and, "Because I had served as attorney and so conversant in every court." Again, "He said he was once a Judge of the King's Bench, and did wonder how the Judges of those times did interpret that Statute."

Equally impressive were his recollections of actual historical events. Fellow members listened with respect to one who could ridicule Buckingham's inefficiency by comparison with the Lords Admiral of the Elizabethan age: "It was never heard that Queen Elizabeth's navy did dance a pavan." He could recall vividly the plots against the queen, such as that of William Parry: "I myself have seen him walking with the Queen when he had his stiletto in his pocket (as he confessed afterwards) and the Lord preserved her."

Certain episodes suggest that his age may have begun to tell upon him, though even in the 1628 session his activity and vigor were extraordinary, and his speeches still "packed a punch." Fortunately two of the diarists (for 1621–1622) were partial to recording his speeches. If these sometimes seem choppy and incoherent, we may suspect that he was just too much for the note-takers. While they were struggling with some learned Latin phrase or quotation — and many of his speeches began in this impressive but disconcerting fashion — he got away from them. One of the diarists caught not only the learned citations, but the pat phrases and anecdotes which had led Prince Charles to delight in listening to Sir Edward's speeches: "Commonly when you follow two hares you lose bothe." "I would never take breviate [brief] of one syde, unles I might have of bothe. Ile keepe my eares open for bothe parties, I love to come even." "Amongst the Locrenses he that propounds a new lawe was to come in with a halter about his neck, and if reiected to be hanged. A fitt Lawe for new proiectors." "[The Statute of Magna Carta] called *Magna* not for the Largeness, but for the Weight."

There were few subjects with which Coke did not deal. In the debates of 1625 he used historical precedents based on the *Parliament Rolls*. For instance, in his powerful speech at Oxford on August 5, insisting that redress of grievances precede supply, he used a petition of the Commons to Edward III,[21] and a whole series of instances (directed at Buck-

---

[21] 37 Edward III, a petition "that Edward should command his bishops and clergy to pray for three things: the state and happiness of his Majesty, the peace and good

ingham) of the replacing of incompetent and extravagant officials cited reign by reign — Edward III, Richard II, Henry IV, V, and VI, Edward IV, Henry VII, and Henry VIII.

Naturally the great lawyer was at his best in the legal field — the correction of faults in courts of justice, the misuse of informers, points of procedure and privilege. In these last respects he did much to help the House of Commons acquire something of the dignity and formalism of a court of law. Sir John Eliot once referred to Coke, "that great Father of the Lawe," as "having consulted with his memorie of the proceedings in like cases." It was he who was largely responsible for the linking of Magna Carta first to the grievances against the monopolists and then to the privileges of the House. It was he who suggested the happy device of adapting *a petition of right,* hitherto a mere routine procedure enabling an individual subject to secure redress against the Crown and its officials, as a liberty document — *the Petition of Right* for all Englishmen.[22] The great lawyer was not the equal of Cotton or Selden as an antiquarian. He gave to parliament and to the common law too ancient a lineage, but can we blame him? He took at face value the assertions of the *Modus Tenendi Parliamentum* as to the antiquity of parliaments and of Fortescue as to that of the common law.[23]

The citing of precedents was a game at which two could play. In 1621 King James himself had said to the Commons, "Reason is too large. Find me a precedent and I will accept it." By 1625 opposition precedents were proving inconveniently numerous and damaging. In the debates one of the councillors (May) warned, "Ill presidents are noe where so dangerous as in Parliaments." Again, "Let no man despise ancient president(s); no man adore them. Examples are powerful arguments, if they be proper, but tyme(s) alter; every parliament must be wise with his owne wisdome; hee valewes more a dram of wisdome fit for the present, then a mountaine of wisdome that was fitted for 500 years past." In the same debate Sir George More advised "Precedents have always changed with the Times."

Privy councillors were apt to adopt, for all unwelcome precedents, the view that the king had used as to the privileges of the Commons: a

government of the kingdom, and the preservation and continuance of unity and love between his subjects and himself. These had been put in hazard by the conduct of his officers; and till the doers of such wrong to the king, obscurers of his glory, were removed, no subvention would be possible." Forster, I, 374.

[22] See below, pp. 247–250.
[23] Described above, pp. 115–116, 127–128.

concession was a royal act of grace, temporary and revocable. Opposition leaders, and especially the lawyers, insisted on the force of custom and prescription. In many instances neither side was actually correct, because of lack of adequate knowledge of past times. Fortunately, the opposition clung to its course. As Phelips reminded the House, "We are the last monarchy in Christendome that retayne our originall rights and constitutions. . . . Hee added the safety of keepinge to our presidents." Precedents that, like Magna Carta, were equated with fundamental law inspired a stubborn confidence, a consciousness of authority and power.

XIII

The Opposition in Action, 1621

THE parliament which met in two sessions, 1621, January 30 to June 4, and November 20 to December 18, is striking both for its dramatic quality and for its constructive work. It reveals the new devices of procedure in use and the outstanding leaders in action. There are advances such as the revival of impeachment and a more comprehensive definition of powers and privileges. These are the sessions, too, for which the official Journals are so richly supplemented by the parliamentary diaries, or Commons Debates.[1]

After an interval of six years of no parliaments, indeed of ten years since a parliament had passed laws or granted a subsidy, there was summoned what has been termed a "parliament of necessity." The king was desperately in need of funds. The recent attempt to collect a benevolence had failed. A sum of £28,000 was received from London, but only £6,000 from the nation at large. But popular interest was also aroused, with expectations of action at last. "Strangers crowded up to London," says Forster, "the streets became thronged with people, and the belief everywhere prevailed that a blow was yet to be struck for the good cause."

This cause was the situation abroad. It is important to realize with what interest and concern both Anglican and Puritan watched the ebb and flow of Protestantism on the Continent. Success was attending the arms of the Catholic League. News had reached England that the "winter King" was not only driven from Bohemia, but his homeland, the

[1] *Commons Debates, 1621*, ed. by Notestein, Relf, and Simpson.

Palatinate, was overrun by Spanish troops. It was felt that England ought to come to the rescue, not only of their princess and her husband, but of Protestantism in general. Parliament was ready to rally in support of war, but the king still hoped to gain his ends through kingcraft and diplomacy. Only gradually did he realize that Spain through Gondomar was duping him.

Affairs at home, however, were not to be neglected. Although there was a willingness to proceed with caution, "to make his majesty in love with Parliaments," the Commons set themselves an ambitious program. As the editors of the *Commons Debates* put it: "A good many things which members of parliament had on their minds had been waiting since the later years of Elizabeth. Many of the bills introduced had long been on the Commons' schedule in one form or another and now seemed about to become laws."

There were abuses in the law, especially those that were "obnoxious to country gentlemen"; fees and new offices in the courts, abuses in the administration of wills as handled by ecclesiastical courts. It was hoped to define the jurisdiction of courts, especially to limit Chancery in favor of the common law courts. There were obsolete statutes which needed weeding out. There were economic problems to be discussed and remedies proposed — the decay of money and the decline of trade, and especially the abuse of monopolies.

The First Session: Monopolies, Impeachments

The parliament was opened on Tuesday, January 30. As described by Forster: "Simonds D'Ewes, a shrewd, observant, quick-eyed youth of eighteen, was among that 'greatest concourse and throng of people that hath been seen,' which . . . saw this parliament opened. He saw the king, amid magnificent attendance, ride down to the abbey, and observed him, as all the great ladies thronged the windows on his way, single out for recognition only the mother and wife of Buckingham. He saw him nodding particularly to the Spanish ambassador Gondomar; and heard him, contrary to his usual wont of bidding a 'pox' or a 'plague' seize such as flocked to see him, crying out a 'God bless ye! God bless ye!' to the crowds standing thick and threefold on all sides."

As the clerk of the *Lords Journals* records it, "The King's Majesty being placed on his seat of Estate, and the Lords in their Places, and the Commons in the Lower House assembled at the Bar," the king himself as was his custom declared the cause of the summons of the parliament in Latin. According to the clerk it was a suave and profound oration (*suavi et profunda oratione*). Happily it was shorter than James's usual loquacity, and not ungracious. It noted the need to reform errors in Commonwealth and Church, grievances of the subjects, the religious situation at home and abroad, and especially the need of a generous grant of subsidies. Typically, his Majesty did not explain how the money was to be used.

As to personnel, there were now ninety-two lay lords in the Upper House as compared to only fifty-four in Elizabeth's last parliament. There were a few liberal peers, notably the Earl of Southampton. On the whole, the government had a good following in the Lords, but on occasion the two Houses cooperated effectively. Francis Bacon, as chancellor, was presiding officer, but was soon to be removed by impeachment proceedings.

As to the Commons, the government had probably exercised some influence in elections, but so cautiously that it is hard to spot.[2] Normally the government communicated with the Commons through Secretary Calvert, but had no outstanding leader in the House.

The opposition in the Commons was well organized and operating along the lines described above. It included the men to whom the reader has just been introduced — Sandys, Phelips, Hakewill, and Coke — as well as others,[3] who supported each other in speeches and strategy. Some of them actually met outside of the parliament with the Earl of Southampton at his house in Holborn or at Dorset House in Fleet Street to lay their plans. Sir Edward Coke "assumed such a leading role in opposition," Willson says, "that James called him Captain Coke, the leader of the faction in parliament." As a member of the Council, he also clashed with his colleagues there and was zealous in the prosecution of his fellow councillor and judge, Francis Bacon.

As the king, in asking for funds, had not revealed plans for its use, the Commons granted a mere two subsidies as a token of good will. While awaiting further information, they turned to the solution of grievances and the introduction of reform measures. First came monop-

---

[2] "Bacon and the other judges associated with him in the work of preparation had considered 'what persons were fit to be of the House' and how they could be placed 'without novelty or much observation'." Willson, pp. 156–157.

[3] Such as Alford, Sir Dudley Digges, John Pym, and Francis Seymour.

olies, and this issue may serve as our main illustration here of how matters were handled.

In Elizabeth's reign the main complaint had been unlawful restraint on freedom of trade. Now after several years of experience with James's patentees the problem was aggravated by abuses committed by the monopolists and their connection with persons in high places. These included the Attorney General, Yelverton, and relatives and protegés of Buckingham. The Crown received little, but the favorites made a large profit from acting as figureheads in companies or selling their rights.

Some patents of long standing and value, such as that for the manufacture of glass, were not questioned. Exclusive rights of trading in a certain area, such as were accorded the East India Company, were justifiable because of the enormous risks involved. Most of the patents now objected to in parliament were new or reissued in the last ten years. They affected persons in many walks of life and social strata. For instance, two patentees backed by the Company of Fishmongers had a method of keeping salmon and lobsters alive in boats from Ireland to the London market, but in practice this deteriorated into plundering poor fishermen. The patents for licensing inns and alehouses offended justices of the peace by encroaching on their jurisdiction. Said Crewe, before the Lords, "justices are made servants to him (Mompesson). . . . He hath vexed ancient inns."

It was the grants empowering patentees to arrest and imprison infringers that aroused the greatest indignation and that were alleged to be contrary to Magna Carta. Conspicuous among these was the patent for gold and silver thread.[4] This was offensive to the London goldsmiths, long one of the most distinguished of the London craft guilds: "In the reign of Henry VII an Italian traveller wrote: 'in one single street, named the Strand, leading to St. Paul's, there are fifty-two goldsmiths' shops, so rich and full of silver vessels, great and small, that in all the shops in Milan, Rome, Venice and Florence put together, I do not think there would be found so many of the magnificence that are to be seen in London.' "[5]

It was these goldsmiths who were presently to give London its private

[4] In 1618 this manufacture had been taken into the king's hands; new commissioners, including Sir Giles Mompesson and Sir Francis Michell, had been added, and their powers had been increased.

[5] Quoted by Trevelyan, *English Social History*, p. 83n.

banks. By 1660 they were displacing the scriveners in handling money, and offered the advantage that their strong rooms served for the safe deposit of their clients' cash and other valuables.

Matters came to a crisis in the spring of 1619, with fresh imprisonments, houses broken into, tools and "engines" seized. One can imagine the indignation in London when bonds were forced on the goldsmiths and silkmen, obliging them not to sell their wares to unlicensed persons. It was alleged that the patentees had threatened five silkmakers that if they refused to seal bonds "all the prisons in London should be filled, and thousands should rot in prison." The city was in an uproar. Four aldermen offered to stand bail for the prisoners for £100,000. When a deputation protested to the king, he ordered the prisoners released, yet a fresh proclamation supported the patent!

Eventually the Commons presented the most obnoxious patents to the Lords and left it for them to take action. But it was in the preparation for this move, the speeches in debates and committees, that indignation was effectively voiced and charges of illegality were supported by Magna Carta and other precedents.

On March 3 the Commons took up the question of the patent for gold and silver thread. Two days later their committee which had examined Michell and Yelverton in the Tower (Mompesson had fled) reported to the House through Sir Robert Phelips. Immediately following the report, Sir Edward Coke set the key for what was to follow. His speech evidently impressed his hearers, for there are four versions of it recorded by the diarists. All of them include his reference to thirty-two confirmations of the Charter, and three include his explanation of the name: "The Statute of *Magna Charta* 29° *cap.* confirmed 32 Times: — None to be imprisoned, Ec. — Called *Magna Charta,* not for the Largeness, but for the Weight . . . All the old writers called *Magna Charta Chartam Libertatis* [Charter of Liberties]."

Next day Hakewill reported to the House plans for the conference with the Lords to be handled by a formidable array of legal talent. Following Digges's introduction, Crewe, Finch, and Hakewill, with able assistants, were to handle the body of the conference. Sir Edwin Sandys was "to aggravate the whole." "Lastly for matter of precedents to justify our proceedings for punishment for the offences and remedies to prevent the like in time to come and so to conclude, and this is referred to Sir Edward Coke, who hath been a father of the law." The conference took place March 8 "after dinner, the Lords being sat in the Painted Chamber (the prince [Charles] also being present and sitting at the end of the table)."

The king himself finally agreed to "damn the patent." He urged the Lords to "proceed judicially and spare none, where you find just cause to punish; but let your Proceedings be according to Law." Fitting the penalty to the crime, the Lords included in their sentence of Michell "that he shall be imprisoned during the King's pleasure in *Finsbury Gaol,* in the same Chamber there, where he provided for others, *The Tower* where he now remains, being a Prison too worthy of him."

In addition to presenting the most obnoxious patents to the Lords as grievances, the Commons introduced a bill "for renewing of Magna Carta," or more fully, "for the better securing of the Subjects from wrongful Imprisonment, and Deprivation of Trades and Occupations, contrary to the 29th Chapter of Magna Charta." Although the bill did not reach the Lords, it was much debated in committees, where concepts of "liberty of the subject" were defined and defended. It is significant as a true forerunner of the various measures introduced in 1628, culminating in the Petition of Right.

Impeachment had not been used since the trial of the Duke of Suffolk in 1450. Its revival in 1621 was incidental to the problem of dealing with the patentees and Chancellor Bacon, and served to define and limit the role of the Commons as a court. In planning how to proceed against Mompesson, they were made to realize that according to current practice they could proceed against an individual only for breach of privilege or "an indignity to the House." They appointed a committee to search for precedents "to shew how far and for what offences the power of this House doth extend to punish delinquents against the State as well as those who do offend against this House." The committee reported "that we must join with the Lords for punishing of Sir Giles Mompesson, it being no offence against our particular House or any member of it, but a general grievance."

Similarly in the case of Chancellor Bacon, the technical rules of impeachment were not strictly observed, but it was an important step in the revival of a practice long in disuse — an assertion that the king's ministers are responsible to the law. James proposed that Bacon be tried by a commission of his selection consisting of six Lords and twelve of the Commons, but the Lower House supported the claim of the Lords to act as judges in an impeachment.

Francis Bacon, a distinguished Renaissance scholar and man of letters, is best known for his scientific treatises and literary essays. He was also an active man of affairs. Trained in law at Gray's Inn, he had served as Solicitor and Attorney General, and had advocated revision and codification of the law. He was made Lord Keeper in 1617, Lord Chancellor and a peer in the following year. The charge brought against him was judicial corruption in the Chancellor's office, the accepting of gifts and money from suitors while their cases were pending in Chancery. Technically he was guilty, and so pleaded, but claimed, perhaps rightly, that he had not allowed his decisions to be influenced. It was not unusual in his day for public officials to receive pay for representing the interests of foreign countries. Judges sometimes accepted gifts from successful suitors. In Bacon's case, however, at bottom parliament was alarmed rather by his consistent support of the royal prerogative. His political philosophy envisaged a "philosopher king" — a strong monarch ruling for the popular good, merely *informed* and *advised* by parliament. Even if scholar James had matched up to Bacon's ideal, the Commons were not minded to tolerate even a benevolent despot. The sentence, designed as a warning to others, was not carried out in full.[6] Bacon retired from court to spend his last years with his beloved studies.

Still another episode brought home to the Commons the limitations on their judicial powers. Edward Floyd, a Catholic barrister, rejoiced, as was natural, over the battle of Prague and the resultant exile of Protestant Frederick and Elizabeth from Bohemia. It was Floyd's disrespectful allusion to their princess and her husband that angered the Commons: "Goodman Palgrave and Goodwife Palgrave were now turned out of doors." Again he argued that Frederick had no more right to the Bohemian crown that he had, and termed him "that poor lad." The Commons sentenced Floyd to fine and the pillory, but had to drop the case and leave it to the Lords.[7] After amicable conferences between the Houses, evidencing "love and good correspondency," the general ruling of the Upper House was accepted. "And their Lordships having

[6] The sentence imposed a fine of £40,000 and imprisonment in the Tower. He was, of course, to give up the great seal, and to be henceforth disqualified from holding any office of state or sitting in parliament. The fine and imprisonment were remitted.

[7] At the bar of the Lords Mr. Attorney charged Floyd with "notorious misdemeanors and high presumption." The sentence imposed was severe enough to satisfy even the Commons. Tanner, *Constitutional Documents of the Reign of James I*, pp. 274, 319ff.

determined that the question at this time is not whether that House be a Court of Record . . . nor whether they have right of judicature in matters concerning themselves; but the question is, whether that House may proceed to sentence any man who is not a member of that House, and for a matter which concerns not that House; for which the Commons alleged no proofs nor produced any precedent."

Almost the last act of the Commons in May was to draw up a bill against monopolies, but time did not permit going ahead with this. After parliament was prorogued, the king revoked by proclamation eighteen of the most objectionable. That the cause of religion at home and abroad was still uppermost in many minds is brought home by a dramatic scene in the House on the eve of adjournment. As recorded in abbreviated form by the Clerk, on June 4, "Sir *J. Perrott* moveth a public Declaration here, before our Departure (sithence his Majesty, at the Beginning of the Parliament, made his Protestation, about the *Palatinate,* to adventure himself, his Son, and all his Estate) that at our next Access, we will (if the King shall require it) adventure ourselves, and all our Estates, in Defence of Religion, etc., Which, he hopeth, known abroad, will facilitate his Majesty's Treaties abroad with foreign Princes."

True to form, Sir Robert Phelips rose to second the proposal in even bolder terms: "To declare, that, if his Majesty shall not, by Peace, obtain the [Settlement] of true Religion, which now shaken, and for the Recovery of the *Palatinate,* we all undertake for the several Shires and Places, for which we serve, we will adventure all our Fortunes, of Lives and Estates, for these Services." "Which," concludes the Clerk, "upon Mr. Speaker's Motion, by a general Acclamation, and Waving of Hats, [was] allowed." [8]

A final touch came just before the Speaker pronounced the adjournment: "Then Sir Edward Coke, standing up, desired the House to say [after] him; and he recited the Collect for the King and his Children, with some Alteration . . ." This was popularly known as the "Gunpowder thanksgiving."

The Second Session: Controversy, the Protestation

In the second session (November 20 to December 18) the differences over foreign policy led to a dispute between King and Commons which

[8] *Commons Journals,* I, 639.

raised in acute form the question of parliamentary initiative — its extension to foreign policy. James still sought to avert war and to recover the Palatinate for Frederick by diplomatic representations at the court of Spain, supported by a marriage of Prince Charles with a Spanish princess. He again asked for supply without adequate explanation. The Commons, impelled by a sense of danger, granted a small subsidy and prepared a petition (December 3). Couched in respectful language, it was none the less astonishing in its explicit and constructive recommendations for policies at home and abroad.

The Commons "humbly represent what we conceive to be the causes of so great and growing mischiefs, and what be the remedies." These "mischiefs" are then set forth, fourteen in number, followed by the four "very dangerous effects both to Church and State" which they foresee will follow. "The remedies against these growing evils, which in all humility we offer unto your most excellent Majesty," are ten in number. These include, of course, better enforcement of the penal laws, war with Spain, and that "our most noble Prince may be timely and happily married to one of our own religion." The petition concludes: "This is the sum and effect of our humble declaration, which we (no ways intending to press upon your Majesty's undoubted and regal prerogative) do with the fulness of our duty and obedience humbly submit to your most princely consideration."

There resulted a bitter controversy, an exchange of petitions and royal messages.[9] The king, as we might expect, forbade the Commons to meddle with matters of state, and reasserted his earlier assumption that their privileges were a matter of *grace,* though legitimate if kept within bounds. The Commons persisted in their recommendations, with more emphatic statements as to their right so to do, culminating in the famous Protestation just before the session was terminated.

There were some dramatic and picturesque episodes. Most astonishing, or so it would have seemed in Elizabethan days, was the fact that Gondomar saw a copy of the first petition before it was dispatched to the king. The ambassador wrote to James a letter "the like of which," says

[9] These were the Commons' petition and the king's answer of December 3; a second petition framed December 9 and delivered on the 11th; the king's reply through the Speaker (same date) in terms which particularly aroused the Commons; and a similar message on the 16th, sent through Secretary Calvert.

For these see Tanner, *Constitutional Documents of the Reign of James I,* pp. 276–289.

Gardiner, "had never before been placed in the hands of an English sovereign." Among other things, Gondomar said that did he not depend on the king to punish the House of Commons, he would have left England already! " 'This,' he added, 'it would have been my duty to do, as you would have ceased to be a King here, and as I have no army here at present to punish these people myself.' " The king did not order Gondomar to leave the country, but sent a tart reply as a command to the Speaker "to make known in our name unto the House . . . that none therein shall presume henceforth to meddle with anything concerning our Government or deep matters of State, and namely not to deal with our dearest son's match with the daughter of Spain, nor to touch the honour of that King or any other our friends and confederates."

It was in connection with the Commons' concern over Sandys's imprisonment that the king declared, ". . . we think ourself very free and able to punish any man's misdemeanors in Parliament, as well during their sitting as after."

It was on December 11, when the Commons presented their second petition to the King at Newmarket, that James made his famous quip, "Bring stools for the ambassadors," a thrust at their assumption of independence and authority. Even the weather played its part. The days when the Protestation was debated, Saturday, Monday, and Tuesday (December 15, 17, and 18) "were remarkable," according to Forster, "for one of the severest frosts ever known in London. 'Such heat within,' wrote an old courtier to Weston, 'and the Thames impassable without for frost and snow.' Yet was the heat tempered by a settled and solemn resolve."

In justice to his Majesty, however, some quotations from his replies are in order, annoying to the Commons but rather clever in their setting forth of the prerogative. On December 11, for instance, he says: ". . . we wish you to remember that we are an old and experienced King needing no such lessons, being in our conscience freest of any king alive from hearing or trusting idle reports . . . In the body of your petition you usurp upon our prerogative royal, and meddle with things far above your reach, and then in conclusion you protest the contrary; as if a robber would take a man's purse and then protest he meant not to rob him. . . . And to this vast generality of yours we can give no other answer, for it will trouble all the best lawyers in the House to make a good commentary upon it." [10]

The Commons determined to cease arguing with the king and instead to define their constitutional rights. The Great Protestation, framed in committee and reported back in late afternoon of Tuesday, December 18, was adopted and entered on the *Journals*: "The Speaker being in the chair, it is ordered, by question in the House, that this protestation shall be entered forthwith in the book of the House, and there to remain as of record. And accordingly it was here entered, sitting the House between five and six of the clock at night by candle-light."

The key clauses are these: "That the liberties, franchises, privileges and jurisdictions of Parliament are the ancient and undoubted birth-right and inheritance of the subjects of England; and that the arduous and urgent affairs concerning the king, state, and the defence of the realm, and of the Church of England, and the making and maintenance of laws, and redress of mischiefs and grievances which daily happen within this realm, are proper subjects and matter of counsel and debate in Parliament." Properly there is also an emphatic assertion on freedom of speech in handling these "proper subjects." [11]

In the margin of the *Commons Journals,* where the Protestation had been recorded, is the memorandum, "King James in council with his own hand rent out this protestation." Actually the king's action was not the sudden outburst of anger which the words "rent out" have suggested to historians, but according to a report in the Privy Council *Register* was a rather solemn and deliberate proceeding. At the end of December "the King came in person to the Council, 'the Prince his Highness and all the Lords and others of his Majesty's Privy Council sitting about him, and all the Judges then in London, which were six in number, there attending upon his Majesty,' and sent for the Journal which contained the Protestation. He declared himself 'justly offended' with it, but nevertheless 'in a most gracious manner' announced that he had never had any intention of depriving the House of Commons of privileges to which they were really entitled; but this Protestation of the

[10] At the end he reverts to their privileges as a matter of grace, and to be exercised within limits. In a message sent the House by Secretary Calvert, December 16, he says: "The plain truth is, that we cannot with patience endure our subjects to use such anti-monarchical words to us concerning their liberties, except they had subjoined that they were granted unto them by the grace and favour of our predecessors."

[11] For the full Protestation see Stephenson and Marcham, p. 429.

Commons' House, so contrived and carried as it was, his Majesty thought fit to be razed out of all memorials and utterly annihilated, both in respect of the manner by which it was gained and the matter therein contained.' He therefore, 'in the full assembly of his Council and in presence of the Judges,' declared the Protestation to be 'invalid, annulled, void, and of no effect, and did further, *manu sua propria,* take the said Protestation out of the Journal Book of the Clerk of the Commons' House of Parliament, and commanded an Act of Council to be made thereupon, and this Act to be entered in the Register of Council causes.' " [12]

This royal act did not erase the record from the memories of the members, nor diminish their conviction in its rightness.

After the dissolution several of the bolder leaders of the opposition were questioned and disciplined. Coke and Phelips were committed to the Tower, Selden, Pym, and Mallory to other prisons. Four others were "exiled" — that is, removed by being sent as commissioners to Ireland. It has been suggested that it was due to the lack of leadership and influence in the House by privy councillors that the gentler methods of earlier days now gave way to threats and punishments.

King James's Last Parliament

In James's fourth parliament the leadership and the program were similar. The parliament of 1624 (February 19 to May 29) "is in reality but the conclusion of the 1621 Parliament," say the editors of *Commons Debates;* "almost the same schedule of bills was carried through in 1624, the same grievances were reviewed and even the final chapter of the argument over foreign affairs is recorded then." Coke and Sandys were present in spite of James's desire to exclude them.

Still there were noticeable differences. The old king, failing in health and faculties, left real authority in the hands of Prince Charles and Buckingham. When in 1623 these two had returned from Spain and the English learned that their prince was home again, "alive, a Protestant and a bachelor," and that the Spanish treaties were to be abandoned, joy was universal. Affairs moved more smoothly, owing to what Gardiner calls the temporary "league which appeared to be springing up between the Prince of Wales and the English nation." This harmony was also apparent in the first weeks of the parliament. Freedom of

[12] Tanner, *Constitutional Documents of the Reign of James I,* pp. 275–276.

debate was not an issue, for James's opening speech invited counsel in foreign affairs — "I assure you ye may freely advise me." The Commons rejected Eliot's attempt to revive the Protestation by raising his voice "for those favours their ancestors had enjoyed." The king, with the prodding of Charles and Buckingham, was converted to war with Spain, but favored a land war in the Palatinate, while the Commons urged a naval war in Elizabethan style. They made a liberal grant, though less than James had asked.[13] The money was to be paid into the hands of commissioners appointed by the Commons to superintend its receipt and disbursement, though the king reserved for himself the direction of the war.

The pages of the *Lords Journals* are filled with great matters: how to advise the king on vital issues of war and diplomacy, the recovery of the Palatinate, the prince's marriage. At home the impeachment of Lionel Cranfield, Earl of Middlesex and Lord Treasurer, confirmed and re-established, now in its correct technical form, this constitutional power of parliament revived in 1621. Though the Lord Treasurer, like Bacon, was convicted of misuse of his office, the real offense to some was that he was one councillor who still advised the maintaining of friendly relations with Spain! In his trial "he maintained his innocence with much spirit, and bitterly complained of the law which denied to him the benefit of counsel's assistance." [14]

There were frequent conferences between the Lords and Commons, usually with "good correspondency" between the Houses. The diaries reveal the zeal of the Commons to put through bills left over from 1621 and even 1610 and 1614. On February 23, for instance, Sir Thomas Hoby "moveth that all those good general bills that passed the last convention, or were ready to pass, may be first read according to the order as they were prepared last convention, viz. . . ." These included the Magna Carta bill, but this was not reported back from committee before the end of the session. On April 9, when Sir Edwin Sandys reported from the Committee of Trade on "the over-burthening of trade," impositions were again debated and their legality questioned. Purvey-

---

[13] Three subsidies and three *fifteenths* (about £300,000) to be paid in one year, with a conditional pledge for more when proved necessary.

[14] He was convicted, but "his remonstrance on the harshness of the law induced the lords to make an order that in future cases of impeachment the accused should be furnished with copies of the depositions for and against him, and that on demand he should be allowed the aid of counsel." — Plucknett's edition of Taswell-Langmead, p. 398.

ance was still a grievance, descending from the major burden of "horses, carts and carriages for his Majesty's service" to such a minor annoyance as "hawk's meat."

Besides the subsidy bill, all told, thirty-two acts, public and private, became law. These included the bill on monopolies. An exception contained in the act wisely gave the Crown the right to grant letters-patent for new inventions, for a period of fourteen years or under, "to the first inventor or inventors of such manufactures."

The closing ceremony took place on the afternoon of May 29. As the Clerk records it, Sir Thomas Crewe the Speaker, "came with great Reverence, and low Obeisances unto his Majesty, and being at the Bar, in a learned Speech, he declared, 'That God (to his own great Glory) had brought this Session of Parliament, so happily begun, to so happy an End. . . . That their Time was wholly spent in Business of Parliament, which had prepared many Bills profitable for the Common-wealth, and shewed the several Natures of those Bills, some for the Service of God and Restraint of Recusants; some to redress the Enormities of the Common-wealth; others of his Majesty's Grace and Bounty to his People; . . . and others to settle Strife in particular Estates: All which do await and humbly desire his Majesty's Royal Assent.' " His parting plea was typical of the intense concern still felt for affairs abroad. " 'And making his earnest Prayers unto Almighty God, to direct his Majesty's Heart to make His own Sword His Sheriff, to put His Son-in-Law into Possession of his Palatinate, the ancient Inheritance of His Royal Grandchildren;' he ended, humbly craving Pardon for himself and his own Errors committed this Session." [15]

[15] *Lords Journals*, III, 423–424.

XIV

Charles I and His Parliaments, 1625-1629

❖❖

FOR the purpose of these studies we must be content with a brief survey of the early parliaments of Charles I (1625–1629). There were dramatic episodes, a pointing up and climaxing of the parliamentary theories and practices of the preceding reign, and effective cooperation between the Houses. One striking achievement was the securing of the Petition of Right, and incidentally the recording in the *Journals* and diaries of a formidable array of precedents. The dramatic scene which closed the 1629 session, with the Speaker being held in his chair, was literally and physically a winning of the initiative!

Charles I succeeded to the throne on the death of his father (March 1625) at the age of twenty-four. As might be expected, after the harmony between prince and parliament and the popular enthusiasm evinced in 1624, he was well received. But this was the prince who had been nurtured from childhood on the doctrine of the divine right of kings. As sovereign he was convinced that he should not, in fact could not, divest himself of his authority. Seeming concessions implied a reservation that they might be withdrawn when occasion offered. His chief councillor continued to be the friend and companion of his youth, Buckingham. It was to the duke that Sir Robert Cotton referred (in notes for a speech never delivered) when he spoke of "the young and simple counsel by which the king was led."

In the first fifteen months of the reign, two parliaments were summoned and rather abruptly dissolved, as was the third, which met in two sessions, 1628–1629. The intervals between witnessed new incompetence in the government's handling of affairs both at home and abroad. Opposition was intensified and the rift widened, until the concept of "the King in his Parliament" seemed remote indeed.

The First and Second Parliaments, 1625 and 1626: The Duke "Reigns"

In the summer of 1625 there were two brief and troubled sessions, one at plague-infested Westminster from June 18 to July 11, and a second at Oxford, August 1 to 12. The first impression made by the young king was favorable. His opening speech was well received, for it was short and to the point. But fears were soon aroused by the government's seemingly Catholic leanings. Neither king nor councillors gave adequate information on plans for the prosecution of the war: would it be the desired naval war against Spain? Through it all was the growing distrust of the favorite, Buckingham.

In the first session the Commons did not appoint their usual committee for grievances, but resolved to seek an answer to the grievances framed in James's last parliament. Tunnage and poundage were voted for one year only, instead of the customary life grant, to permit examination of the whole question of impositions. A meager two subsidies were granted as a token of good will. It was Phelips's speech in the debates on supply that is credited with keeping the House to this amount. He pointed out that the government had acted contrary to precedent in asking for supply at the beginning of the session. The amount was great in view of all that had been granted in the last parliament. It was a burden to the taxpayer, already suffering from the many violations of his rights, the liberties of the kingdom, and the privileges of the House. As to the imminence of war, no enemy was declared, no reckoning made of the recent waste in lives, money, and honor. Then followed the inevitable contrast with other days, the glories of Queen Elizabeth, "who with less supplies and aids, increased herself at home, wasted her enemies abroad, consumed Spain, raised the Low Countries, revived and strengthened France." Best then, be content with a modest grant — the two subsidies — plus a petition and remonstrance. For himself, he concluded, "he was so far from desiring to augment, that he should feel shame if any man further could be found to suggest it." [1] None was. Privy councillors abandoned further pressure.

---

[1] Based on Forster's paraphrase of the speech, I, 289–290.

As the Oxford session proceeded, members inclined more and more to innuendoes directed at the duke. It was easy to produce unpalatable precedents of "evil counsellors" of past ages, their misdeeds and fates. Particularly bitter was the debate of August 10. Seymour struck at the sale of offices and honors: "Who will bringe up his sonne in learning when money is the way to preferment? The price of a sergeant is as knowen as the price of a calfe; and they which buy deare must certain-elye sell deare." Sir Guy Palmes reminded the House that "For the disorders in Henry 7th's tyme, Empson and Dudley were hang'd in Henry the 8th's tyme." [2]

It was Phelips again who is credited with making clear to the Commons that the duke was deliberately seeking a break with the parliament, with intent to blame the Houses for any subsequent failures in foreign policy. Phelips's evidence served to unite the opposition, and resulted in prompt plans for the impeachment of Buckingham in the next parliament, even though Phelips himself was excluded.

Dissatisfied with the limited supply and alarmed at the veiled threats directed against the duke, Charles dissolved his first parliament.

The second parliament sat for about four months, February to June, 1626. In the interval had occurred the ill-fated expedition to the harbor of Cadiz, designed, Elizabethan style, to damage Spanish ports and shipping and plunder treasure ships. The duke had hoped thereby to arouse English enthusiasm and to induce the next parliament to grant subsidies for the war. But the fleet, poorly equipped and commanded, returned without treasure, prizes, or prestige.

Several of the ardent spirits of the 1625 parliament were missing from the Commons in 1626. They were "pricked for sheriffs" (that is, appointed) intentionally to disqualify them for the House, including Seymour, Phelips, and Sir Edward Coke. But with Sir John Eliot to lead, there was still a considerable group of country gentlemen and lawyers to carry on. These included such able parliamentarians as Sandys, Spencer, and Pym, and among the lawyers, Glanvile, Noy, Selden, Whitelocke, and Sir Henry Martin. London's Recorder, Sir Heneage Finch, was elected Speaker.

In the Upper House there was a distinct group of opposition Lords in sympathy with the leaders in the Commons, among them Archbishop Abbot, Lord Keeper Williams, and the earls of Pembroke, Arundel, and

[2] *Debates in the House of Commons in 1625* (Camden Society, 1873).

Bristol. The exclusion of the last two by royal command was a violation of two of the privileges of peers — freedom from arrest and right to the summons — and so constituted a grievance to the whole House.[3]

The main interest in the Lower House centers on proceedings to impeach the duke. Eliot's speech of February 10 set the program which was followed, and it was Eliot who kept the Commons to their course whenever privy councillors tried to divert them. The committee system was used most effectively. The usual committee of grievances was appointed. Subcommittees of inquiry were to report to it under special heads. In addition there was appointed a committee for secret affairs to deal with "evils, causes and remedies," to be "separately taken and reported," including the "condition of the subject in his freedom."

While engaged in preparing the charges the Commons received word from the king: "I must let you know that I will not allow any of my servants to be questioned amongst you, much less such as are of eminent place and near unto me. . . . I see you especially aim at the Duke of Buckingham." The latter, he assured them "hath not meddled or done anything concerning the public or commonwealth but by special directions and appointment, and as my servant." Nevertheless the Commons were not to be diverted. As the session wore on, from each subcommittee came from day to day its report to the grand committee. But whatever the grievance, blame was directed at one delinquent — Buckingham.[4]

The impeachment of the duke took the form of twelve articles or charges, two or three each presented by the five "managers" and their assistants, with a prologue by Digges and what proved to be a scathing epilogue by Eliot. All told, the charges amounted to gross mismanagement of public affairs. They included plurality of offices, selling titles and places of judicature, and misuse of public funds; imperfectly guarding the narrow seas so that shipping was ruined, and mercantile interests injured.

Eight of the charges were presented before the Lords on May 8 with the accused himself present, outfacing his accusers, indeed, according

[3] The Earl of Arundel was committed to the Tower during the session "for permitting his son, without the king's license (as head of the house of Stuart) to marry Elizabeth Stuart, daughter of the Duke of Lennox." The Earl of Bristol (John Digby) was refused his writ of summons to parliament. As he had been ambassador to Spain at the time of Prince Charles's and Buckingham's visit, it was feared he might make disclosures damaging to the duke.

[4] The quotations that follow, unless otherwise indicated, are from the *Lords* or *Commons Journals* or the *Diaries*.

to the newsletter-writers, even jeering and laughing. So incensed were the Commons that the next day was spent in debate for and against commitment of the duke during impeachment proceedings. In the end it was not the duke who was committed, but the orators, Digges and Eliot, whose eloquence had introduced and concluded the charges.

It was on Thursday, May 11, that the House was stunned by the news that Eliot and Digges had been taken to the Tower. They adjourned until next day and on reassembling insisted there be "no business till we are righted in our liberties." The House "sat long silent." It was Mr. Wilde who first ventured to speak, advising petition to the king for the restoration of the missing members and the preservation of their liberties. He reminded them of Magna Carta, "the Good Charter of our great inheritance, gayned with soe great cost, so often confirmed, we ought with all care to convey the same to our posterity as our Ancestors have done to us."

May 17, with the House in Committee of the Whole, the Chancellor of the Exchequer tried unsuccessfully to satisfy the Commons that it was for offenses done outside "this House" for which Eliot was committed. Wilde ventured to deal directly with the royal power of commitment. He admits that there is in the prerogative a certain authority for imprisoning subjects outside parliament, "but in parliament I find no case or precedent that there is any warrant for it."

On May 18 Eliot was examined in the Tower on questions drawn up by the Lord Keeper, but nothing was elicited to justify the charge of "extra-judicial crimes." Next day the order for his release was signed. On the 20th he returned to the House, where a councillor, Carleton, repeated the charges, and the members had the opportunity to enjoy Eliot's spirited defense, even to his justification of calling the duke "that man." Said Eliot, "That there should be offense taken that I should call him that man, truly I do yett believe he is no God." It was "resolved by question that Sir John Eliot had not exceeded his Commission which he had from his House in any thinge that he spake at the Conference with the Lords concerning the impeachment of the Duke of Bucks, *nullo negative.*"

Though Charles permitted the release of the two members, he ordered the Commons to drop other matters and turn at once to supply. On their refusal to comply, the parliament was dissolved and the favorite saved for another two years of misgovernment.

"Liberty of the Subject": The Five Knights' Case

The immediate problem for the government was how to raise the funds which parliament had not supplied. In July 1626 the justices of the peace were asked to solicit a "free gift." In September a forced loan was substituted. Collectors were to ask from each taxpayer the amount he would have been assessed had parliament voted five subsidies! Although collections were successful in some areas, opposition was voiced by high and low, including several peers, some of the local commissioners themselves, and a number of the gentry and lower classes. Some veiled their refusal under the excuse of poverty, hard times, and large families. Bolder spirits frankly refused on grounds of unconstitutionality, promising that they would gladly pay if the tax was imposed "in a parliamentary way." The judges paid their quotas, but refused to sign a document declaring the loan legal.

Several gentlemen were bound over to appear before the Privy Council. Others were imprisoned, often being sent into places of confinement far distant from their homes. Lesser folk were pressed for military service. As funds were still lacking to provide quarters and provisions for soldiers, some were billeted in private homes. Indignation was aroused by the outrages committed by these unwelcome guests. As martial law was proclaimed in districts where they were stationed, disputes between civilians and soldiers were handled by military courts. Added to these grievances at home was another failure abroad. In spite of Charles's marriage with the French princess Henrietta Maria, hostile relations with France increased. Buckingham himself led an expedition to the Isle of Rhé to relieve the French Protestants besieged in La Rochelle. It proved as ill-equipped and unsuccessful as the Cadiz expedition. The Isle of Rhé was dubbed his Isle of Rue.

Finally on January 2, 1628, the government relented. Orders were given for the release of the gentlemen who had resisted the loan. Seventy-six in all were permitted to return home. On January 30 Charles authorized the issue of writs for a parliament.

Before this occurred, however, five knights [5] had made of themselves a test case to question not merely the illegality of the loan but the authority of King and Council to exercise powers of arbitrary arrest;

[5] Sir Thomas Darnel (hence sometimes called Darnel's Case), Sir John Corbet, Sir Walter Earl, Sir John Heveningham, and Sir Edmund Hampden (cousin of John Hampden, later celebrated in the Ship Money Case). They had not been *tried and convicted* on failure to pay the loan, but merely imprisoned as a threat and warning.

that is (as was the case here), detention "without cause shown" — without formal charges. They sued out their writs of *habeas corpus* in the King's Bench.[6] The hearing was held before the judges on November 22.

The warden of the Fleet Prison returned that they were detained under a warrant from the Privy Council "by special command of the King." This led to important arguments as to the sufficiency of such a return as a legal cause of detention, as no reason was revealed for this "special command" — no specific charge made against the prisoner.

"The gentlemen's counsel for *Habeas Corpus* (Mr. Noy, Sergeant Bramston, Mr. Selden, Mr. Calthorp) pleaded yesterday with wonderful applause, even of shouting and clapping of hands which is unusual in that place." [7]

Sir Robert Heath, Attorney General, argued for the Crown, supporting the prerogative, and maintaining the necessity of silence or secrecy in matters of state or times of national danger. The judges accepted the sufficiency of the return, as a temporary measure at least, refused bail, and remanded the knights to prison.[8] Yet formidable arguments and precedents for "liberty of the subject" had been assembled and publicized.

The Third Parliament, 1628: "Liberty of the Subject" and the Petition of Right

The events of 1626–1627 at home and abroad described above were reflected in the elections to the parliament. As sheriffs had been appointed back in November, it was too late for the government to exclude unwanted members by the device employed in 1626 — "pricking for sheriffs." All the active leaders and opponents of the duke were elected: Wentworth, Eliot, and Phelips; the lawyers Selden, Noy, Littleton, and Whitby; and Sir Edward Coke, now in his seventy-sixth year. In many constituencies those who had opposed the forced loan were elected, including 27 of the 76 who had suffered imprisonment. Thus there was returned a large majority not only opposed to government policies but filled with righteous indignation.

A few days before the opening of the parliament (March 17), a meet-

---

[6] This was a writ issued by the Court of King's Bench commanding the warden of a prison to "have the body" (*habeas corpus*) of the prisoner before the judges, and to show cause for the arrest and detention. If the return (charge) was insufficient, the prisoner was released; otherwise let out on bail or remanded to prison to await trial.

[7] Father Cyprien de Gamache, *Court and Times of Charles I* (2 vols., London, 1848), I, 292.

[8] It was assumed that King and Council might presently release or "show cause."

ing of the leading members of the Commons was held at Sir Robert Cotton's. "There was a general feeling," writes Gardiner, "that the attack upon Buckingham should not be repeated, and Eliot, who was of the contrary opinion, withdrew his opposition in the face of the general sentiment, reserving his right to revert to his original position at some future time. To the others it was becoming clear . . . that the main struggle was with the King and not with Buckingham. . . . Coke and Phelips, Wentworth and Selden, concurred in the opinion that the violated rights of the subject must first be vindicated." The contest in this session, then, was to center on principles rather than persons.

King Charles failed to sense the popular temper. He opened the session with a short but ungracious, even threatening, speech: "Yet I think there is none here, but knows what common Dangers is the Cause of this Parliament, and that Supply, at this Time, is the chief End of it. . . . Every Man now must do according to his Conscience; wherefore, if you (which God forbid) should not do your Duties in contributing what this State at this Time needs, I must, in Discharge of my Conscience, use those other Means, which God hath put into my Hands, to save that which the Follies of particular Men may otherwise hazard to lose. Take not this as a Threatening (for I scorn to threaten any but My Equals) but an Admonition from Him that, both out of Nature and Duty, hath most Care of your Preservations and Prosperities."

The Commons none the less resolved themselves into a committee of grievances to consider "the liberty of the subject in his person and in his goods." Liberty had been threatened in the four respects eventually set forth in the Petition of Right: the forced loans, arbitrary arrest and imprisonment, the billeting of soldiers, and martial law. Of these the second seemed most dangerous, threatening not only individual liberty, but indeed parliament itself. The immediate practical problem, then, was how best to guarantee these liberties. The Petition of Right was the last of a series of possible solutions offered by Commons, Lords, and king in the course of the session.[9]

The arguments which carried most weight with the Lords were those which the Commons presented in conference April 7 and again on April 17. Several of the ablest lawyers in the House were chosen to

[9] These included a bill on Magna Carta offered by Sir Edward Coke early in the session; four resolutions in Commons presented to the Lords, April 7; counterresolutions of the Lords sent to the Commons, April 25; and the king's offer to confirm Magna Carta and the "six statutes" interpreting the same.

confer with the Lords "concerning certain ancient and fundamental Liberties of England." Each of the principals was assigned two assistants. In the words of the Lord President, reporting to his fellow Lords: "The subject of all was about the Liberty of the Subjects. To set this forth, they employed Four Speakers. The First was Sir Dudley Dygges, a man of Volubility and Elegancy of Speech. His part was but the Induction. The second was Mr. Littleton a Grave and Learned Lawyer, whose part was to represent the Resolution of the House, and their Grounds whereupon they went. The third was Mr. Selden, a great Antiquary and a pregnant Man; his Part was to shew the Law and Precedents in the Point. The fourth was Sir Edward Coke, that famous Reporter of the Law, whose Part was to shew the Reasons of all that the others had said; and that all which was said, was but in Affirmance of the Common Law."

All this really amounted to a rearguing of the Five Knights' Case with some amplification of evidence, a more effective division of labor, and more publicity. The conference was not only reported back to both Houses, as was usual, but the conferees were instructed by the House: "Sir Edward Coke, Sir D. Digges, Mr. Littleton, Mr. Selden, which argued the Case of the Liberty of the Persons of the Subjects from Imprisonment, to bring in, by Thursday next, their several Arguments, fair written; as also the Copies of the Records produced by them; and the Clerk to insert the Arguments into the Journal, and to have Liberty to give out Copies of them."

Littleton's effective handling of Magna Carta and its interpretation as set forth in the *Parliament Rolls* and *Statutes* was praised by John Eliot: "the understanding of the former and latter times of the scope of Magna Charta, so exquisitely retrieved out of the most hidden and obstruse corners of antiquitie by my most learned friend." Sir Edward Coke, assigned to show "that all that which was said was but in affirmance of the Common Law," naturally contributed little that was new. Still, he was in rare good form, and his pungent phrases served as exclamation points to all that had gone before.

In vain the Lords attempted a compromise in the form of a clause saving to the king his "sovereign power." [10] Charles finally accepted the document without a saving. Although it has been called from that time

---

[10] ". . . with due regard to leave entire that sovereign power wherewith your Majesty is trusted for the protection, safety, and happiness of the people."

to this the *Petition* of Right, the royal assent gave it the force of a statute, a constitutional statute, embodying a kind of fundamental law, second only to Magna Carta.

Having at last achieved redress of grievances, the Commons voted five subsidies. They were preparing a petition on tunnage and poundage and a request for the removal of Buckingham when, on June 26, the parliament was prorogued to meet again January 20, 1629.

The Third Parliament, Second Session, 1629: Eliot's Resolutions and Dissolution

Awake, sadde Britaine, and advance at last
Thy drooping heade; let all thy sorrows past
Be drownde and sunke with theire owne teares, and nowe
O'erlooke thy foes with a triumphant browe.
Thy foe, Spaine's agent, Holland's bane, Rome's friend,
By a victorious hand receivde his ende.
Live ever Felton, thou hast turned to dust
Treason, ambition, murther, pride, and lust.

WHEN on January 20, 1629, the two Houses reassembled, one grievance at least had been removed — the Duke of Buckingham! But let Trevelyan tell the story:

"Waggoners, wending through the August harvests in the dust of the Portsmouth road, gave friendly lifts to a needy and impatient pedestrian, lieutenant of the late army of Rhé, but unpromoted, unpaid and starving, and seemingly oppressed with melancholy. In this way Felton reached the city where our ships rode waiting for the wind for France, found the Duke, and stabbed him dead at a blow.

"England burst into rejoicings. Men drank the murderer's health in the London streets. Popular songs were composed and sung in his honour. To avoid outrage from the mob, the Duke's body received secret interment in the Abbey; at the false funeral next day, the city train-bands, who protected the hearse, shouldered arms and beat up their drums, as if they were marching to a Coronation."

Charles did not forget or forgive the joy of his people. After this he had more able councillors, but never one that was dear to him.

The first act of the Commons was to order that "a Committee should be appointed to examine what innovation hath been made upon the liberty of the subject against the Petition of Right since the end of the last Session of Parliament." These included tunnage and poundage and impositions. The king had continued to levy customs and raise rates. Several merchants on refusal to pay had been punished by restraint of goods and imprisonment. One of these, John Rolle, whose goods had been seized, was a member of the House. Privilege of Parliament was assumed to protect the goods as well as the persons of members.

Other grievances included arbitrary penalties imposed by Star Chamber and the strict censorship of the press controlled by the same court. It was charged that "divers printers had been pursuivanted for printing of orthodox books, and that the licensing of books is now only restrained to the Bishop of London [Laud] and his chaplains."

The religious issue had not been forgotten in the first session. Eliot had coupled the two great causes of religion and liberty, and the government's leniency towards recusants was protested by joint petition of the Houses. It was now clear that Laud was the king's chief ecclesiastical adviser. Both favored the new ritualistic anti-Calvinist movement within the Anglican Church — what the Puritans called "Popery and Arminianism." [11] These grievances evoked theological rather than legal arguments. Much space in the parliamentary diaries is devoted to the recording of scathing Puritan harangues in which Old Testament epithets served more adequately than laws to express the speaker's scorn. The following, for instance, unreasonable in its extremes, nevertheless suggests how visions of armadas and gunpowder plots remained to haunt the Puritan extremists: ". . . if you mark it well, you shall see an Arminian reaching out his hand to a Papist, a Papist to a Jesuit, a Jesuit gives one hand to the Pope and the other to the King of Spain; and these men having kindled a fire in our neighbouring country, now they have brought over some of it hither, to set on flame this Kingdom also."

King Charles, deploring these debates on religion, which in fact violated the proclamation he had issued in 1628, as well as the resistance to tunnage and poundage, decided to dissolve parliament. When on March 2 the Speaker, at his order, put to the House the question for adjournment, he was greeted with a chorus of Noes. Members were determined at least to place on record, in a statement prepared by Eliot, their position on vital issues. When the Speaker rose, he was thrust back in his chair by two of the members, Holles and Valentine. The doors were locked to exclude the king's messenger, whose entrance and removal of the mace would have ended the sitting.

[11] So called from the Dutch theologian, Arminius (d. 1609).

After quiet was restored, there were arguments for and against the right of the House to adjourn itself and on the importance of reading the declaration of grievances. Said Strode, "I desire the same, that we may not be turned off like scattered sheep, as we were at the end of the last session, and have a scorn put on us in print, but that we may leave something behind us." Said Speaker Finch: "I am not the less the King's servant for being yours. I will not say I *will* not put the reading of the paper to the question, but I must say, I *dare* not." Eliot enlarged on the grievances, even proposing the impeachment of one of the privy councillors, but finally in despair threw his paper into the fire. It was then that Holles repeated from memory the three resolutions which Eliot had drawn up, and put the question. Each was approved in turn by Aye, Aye, from hundreds of voices. The House then voted its own adjournment, the door was flung open, and out rushed the members carrying away before them in the crowd a king's officer standing at the entrance. The public ceremony of dissolving took place on March 10. The resolutions declared a capital enemy of the kingdom anyone who should introduce innovation in religion, advise the levy of tunnage and poundage, or pay the same. These, like the Protestation of 1621, were opinion, not law, but expressed the views of a large part of parliament and of the nation.

The royal proclamation, as we have anticipated above, had an ominous note in its emphasis on the calling and continuing of parliaments as something "which is always in our own power" and the hint that the future of parliaments might depend on more tractable subjects: "We shall be more inclinable to meet in Parliament again, when our people shall see more clearly into our intents and actions."

This time the interval was to be a long one, eleven years, but it *was* an interval. Even more than in Tudor reigns did it prove true that the ruler could not long carry on without a parliament. There was no standing army or adequate navy. Government, its expenses and equipment in both peace and war, were more costly. No seventeenth-century king could have "lived of his own." In times of national danger some degree of popular support was also essential.

Lest in preceding chapters attractive personalities and striking events have tended to divert the reader from an assessment of values, we may pause here to summarize what parliament had achieved in *winning the initiative.* Let us imagine what an "old parliament man" might have pointed to with pride. Perhaps a group of friends and neighbors are meeting in some country house to talk over old times, to hope and plan for the future. Such gatherings, we know, did take place on the eve of the Long Parliament.[12]

Very likely in the group would be a "man of law" — a barrister or one of the gentry who had spent at least a little time at one of the Inns of Court in order to become "a better Commonwealth's man." He might recall judgments in the courts, some for and some against the popular cause. Perhaps he was present in King's Bench in 1627 to share in the applause over arguments for the "liberty of the subject" in the Five Knights' Case. But it is the Commons, not the Courts, with which we are most concerned here.

Many a session of parliament, of course, put through useful acts, public and private, of a noncontroversial character. On major issues there was the act against monopolies and the notable Petition of Right. The revival and, in some instances, successful use of impeachment was something to boast of. Procedure in the passing of bills, the use of committees (especially the Committee of the Whole), and conferences between the Houses had been perfected. The Commons had consistently handled disputed elections as well as the enforcement of their privilege of freedom from arrest.

On other controversial issues clear-cut claims were registered and in some instances put into effect, notably the right of the House to debate all matters of public concern, even foreign affairs, as set forth in the Protestation. The *Journals* and Diaries, the *Law Reports,* and even some newsletters were loaded with precedents. Above all, there was a self-assurance and courage that no royal threats could daunt.

[12] See p. 259.

XV

The Long Parliament Comes to the Rescue

✿✿

"WE SHALL account it presumption for any to prescribe any time unto us for Parliaments . . ." On this note King Charles embarked on eleven years of personal rule. It has been suggested that he might have conciliated opinion or prepared for absolutism, but actually he did neither. There was now no favorite like Buckingham. Councillors were, on the whole, men of integrity and ability, but royalist and uncompromising. The Bench was increasingly packed, the prerogative courts active. Laud, Bishop of London and from 1633 Archbishop of Canterbury, was unselfish and conscientious, but a staunch supporter of the State Church and conformity. To him discipline and order were of the essence of religion, to be enforced by episcopal visitations and the Court of High Commission. Oddly enough, Laud has been called the founder of Anglo-Saxon supremacy in the new world, since it was during his regime that some twenty thousand Puritans and Independents fled to America. At home, because of the lax enforcement of the penal laws against the Catholics, some even believed that Laud hoped for the reunion of the Anglican Church with Rome. Secretary Windebank also inclined towards what seemed a pro-French and pro-Catholic policy.

Thomas Wentworth, Lord Strafford, had spent some years on what seemed at the time a masterful handling of the Irish problem. He returned to England in 1639 ready to support the king in a policy of "thorough," but his high-handed efficiency led to his being dubbed "Black Tom the Tyrant." He had been one of the leaders in Commons in 1628 and had supported the Petition of Right, but later inclined to more conservative views. Charles employed him first as President of the Council of the North, 1628–1632, and then as Lord Deputy of Ireland, until his return to England in the spring of 1639.

Personal Rule in Action; Grievances and Opposition

Charles's first act after the dissolution of parliament in 1629 was to arrest nine of the opposition leaders. They were charged with "notable contempts against the King and his government and the stirring up of sedition against the state." Claiming privilege, they refused to plead before any court but parliament. After a time some apologized and were released. Three refused, were heavily fined, and returned to prison. John Eliot died in the Tower on November 27, 1632, a martyr to the cause of freedom of speech and action in parliament.

As the years wore on, grievances multiplied. The government continued to levy tunnage and poundage in spite of the resistance of the whole body of London merchants for several months, 1629–1630. With no parliamentary subsidies forthcoming, attempts were made to raise revenue by devices technically legal but obsolete and unpopular. These included compulsory distraint of knighthood, forest fines,[1] and sale of monopolies. As to the last, the Act of 1624 was evaded by forming a group of purchasers into a corporation. These devices, especially the first two, fell on some of the peers and gentry, as did tunnage and poundage on the merchants — the very elements of the nation most likely and able to protest.

Most resented was the tax known as "ship money." For centuries rulers had called on port towns to supply ships. In early days the Cinque Ports had been rewarded with valuable privileges. Now, in 1634, some ports had to pay the equivalent in money, as the ships demanded were of a size to be found only in London. The next year, on the grounds that English commerce in the North Sea was in danger of attack, ship money was levied on inland districts as well as the ports. Thus it became a direct tax imposed without consent of parliament, and that in time of peace. " 'The people,' the Venetian ambassador recorded, 'are well aware that this opening for the royal authority cannot be allowed without a momentous restriction of their liberties. They exclaim aloud and

---

[1] Every person whose annual income from land was £40 or more was compelled to accept knighthood or pay a fine, a practice not used since Henry VII's reign. Large areas, once a part of the royal forest and sold long since by Charles's predecessors, were reclaimed unless the possessors paid heavy fines.

lament the violation of their privileges.' It seemed to them that they were 'spending their liberty more than their cash.' " [2]

This was the period in which the prerogative courts came to be more resented, even hated, than heretofore. Star Chamber had done its work so well that it had outlived its usefulness. A study of the court's records indicates only an occasional instance of poaching, near riot, etc. Instead the court was handling well a field of law which it had itself built up, such as libel, perjury, forgery, and frauds in commercial life. It was in its role as an administrative court that the danger lay — "a sword of political power" — since the privy councillors who constituted the court were thus judges of their political opponents.

Star Chamber also cooperated with High Commission [3] in enforcing censorship and punishing Puritan critics of the bishops. Particularly resented was censorship of the press. A decree of the Star Chamber in Elizabeth's reign had ruled that no book or pamphlet might be printed without the leave of an archbishop or of the Bishop of London. This rule affected both authors and printers, lecturers and clergymen, and even members of Puritan "conventicles." The Court of High Commission, in its trials, continued to use the oath *ex officio,* by which the accused was compelled to bear witness against himself. If he refused, he might still be detained in prison. This procedure, criticized by the Puritan lawyer Nicholas Fuller and the great judge Sir Edward Coke in James's reign, was still resented, not only by the accused but by all the lawyers trained in the Inns of Court and, in fact, by most Englishmen.

On one occasion Laud's censorship even invaded what we should call academic freedom. In the congenial atmosphere of the Inns of Court barristers and students still venerated the common law and pursued their studies with readings and moots (lectures and mock trials). But in the spring of 1639 Edward Bagshaw, Reader of the Inner Temple, at Laud's complaint, was summoned first before the Council and then before the archbishop himself at Lambeth. The charge was that the lecturer, in interpreting an old fourteenth-century statute, "read against the Bishops." Bagshaw went by barge up the river, attended by some of his distinguished fellow barristers, but Laud was no more impressed than if his "guests" had been humble country preachers.

[2] Lunt, p. 419, quoting *Cal. of State Papers, Venetian.*

[3] This court, in existence since Elizabeth's reign, was a group of clergy and laity (usually including a prominent bishop) which exercised the ecclesiastical power of the Crown, especially the enforcement of the penal laws against Catholics and Puritans.

"Mr. Reader," he demanded, "had you nothing else to do but to read against the Clergy? . . . Well, you shall answer it in the High Commission." Laud's act, said Bagshaw, "made a loud noise throughout the Cities of London and Westminster." A peer merrily told him "that he had often heard of a silenc't preacher but never of a silenc't Reader before."

For several years there was little open agitation in a land "now by custom, civil and obedient to law." Without freedom of the press, the right of public meeting, political parties or clubs, there was no avenue for criticism or protest.

In the year 1637 opposition did raise its head in three striking episodes: (1) popular anger at the treatment accorded three "libellers" by Star Chamber, (2) Hampden's Ship Money Case and the universal interest it aroused, and (3) the rising of Scotland against the attempt of Charles and Laud to force upon them the Anglican Church system with its bishops and Prayer Book.

The first involved punishment for libel by three persons who had secretly composed and put in circulation violent attacks on the bishops. There was something to be said on the side of the censors, for in that age of big vocabularies and verbal energy denunciations were violent indeed, and coming from the Puritans were apt to follow the line of the Old Testament prophets! In this instance, however, the three belonged to the liberal professions — Prynne the lawyer, Burton the clergyman, and Bastwick the doctor. They were condemned by the Star Chamber to be pilloried, to lose their ears, to be branded with the letters S. L. ("seditious libeller," but popularly equated with "scars of Laud"), and to suffer solitary confinement for life. This was not a humane age. Idle crowds rather enjoyed watching the pillorying of a "sturdy beggar" or cheating craftsman, and even turned out to see hangings, but this was a different matter.

"London," Trevelyan relates, "poured out to Palace Yard, and held round the scaffolds a monster reform meeting which Government had no soldiers to disperse. The orators, with their heads through the pillory, spoke much of their faith in Jesus, of legal precedents, and of the ancient liberties of Englishmen. In the great crowd below many wept aloud, and the rudest were ennobled by that good English mood of hoarse anger at cruelty inflicted on the brave. When the hangman sawed off Prynne's ears, a yell arose to which Charles should have listened in

Whitehall, while yet it was heard there for the first time. It was a new sound even in old riotous England, for it was not the ancient voice of faction or of plunder, but the cry of deeper mutiny from brain and heart."

In the same year a test case was made for John Hampden, one of those who had dared refuse to pay ship money. His case was argued in the Court of Exchequer Chamber (all twelve judges of the three common law courts meeting together). The judges decided seven to five for the king. Finch, one of the royalist judges, went so far as to declare: "Acts of Parliament to take away his [the king's] Royal power in the defense of his kingdom are void. They are void acts of Parliament to bind the King not to command the subjects, their goods, and I say their money too, for no acts of Parliament make any difference."

But Hampden's able counsel, St. John, with plenty of convincing precedents, upheld parliament. He argued that the king had no discretion to impose such a tax unless danger to the realm was so imminent that there was no time to call a parliament. It was St. John's arguments and the knowledge that five of the judges were on their side that encouraged the opposition and won popular applause. In fact, St. John's speech in Hampden's Case gained him an immense reputation, and though he had had little practice in Westminster Hall, according to a contemporary, "henceforward he was called into all courts and all causes where the King's prerogative was most contested." In the Long Parliament he naturally became one of the leaders and appropriately led the attack on ship money.

The Scots, in an attempt to be loyal to the king of their own Stuart line and to defend their Presbyterian "Kirk," formed a National Covenant to support the king and the "true Church." This presently led to the two brief "Bishops' Wars," [4] ending with Scottish troops occupying the northern counties. Charles, on agreeing to an armistice and an indemnity, had perforce to call Parliament.

New Leaders and Tactics: London, "the Workshop of the Revolution"

The famous Long Parliament, which met November 3, 1640, continued as a normal parliament of two full Houses until the king raised

[4] So called not because the bishops participated, but because the English *episcopacy* or system of bishops was to be imposed on the Scottish Church. James had instituted bishops, but their power was nominal. Between the two short encounters

his standard at Nottingham, August 22, 1642.[5] We shall be concerned here mainly with its first year, a period of constructive work which was to be permanent in contrast to the premature and temporary extremes of the civil wars and kingless decade.

It is important first to notice certain features, commonplace today but novel in that age: the emergence of political parties; a virtual party caucus between parliaments; an electioneering campaign; the scene of action in London as "the workshop of the Revolution"; and, with London's help, the manipulation of forces.

Historians see something akin to political parties, though not so called, in the last parliaments of Elizabeth's reign, and increasingly in the early Stuart period. In the 1620's there is something of a royalist court party and an opposition country party. We have seen above some of the opposition leaders meeting at Sir Robert Cotton's at Westminster to plan for the session of 1628. Now during the eleven years of no parliaments, there met in certain country houses groups of friends, "sometimes living together for months under one roof," a veritable political house-party. Trevelyan calls this "home conspiracy the true origin of our party system," and pictures conferences "in deer-parks and on garden terraces" to watch and discuss events. The group included several great peers — the Earl of Bedford, the Puritan Lord Saye and Sele, Lord Mandeville, heir to the Earldom of Manchester, and his wife's father, the Earl of Warwick, distinguished as a colonist and sailor. The commoners were the men to be most active in leadership in the Long Parliament — John Pym, Hampden, and his counsel, St. John, of ship-money fame.

There had been electioneering, some of a vigorous kind, since Elizabethan days, but during the elections for the Long Parliament Pym and Hampden went on an extended election tour, on horseback, of course, riding through the towns and urging electors to choose known Puritans. Later in the Commons these worked shoulder to shoulder as a party and recruited adherents from the indifferent or fearful.

(in the spring of 1639 and August 1640) Charles had summoned the Short Parliament (April 13–May 5). This was abruptly dissolved when it insisted that redress of grievances *precede* supply.

[5] At this, the outbreak of the civil war, the king followed by 80 peers and 175 of the Commons, set up a royalist capital at Oxford. Thirty peers and 300 of the Commons remained at Westminster, and it was this body that continued to be called parliament. In 1648 Colonel "Pride's purge" further reduced the Commons. This remnant in 1649 "abolished" the House of Lords and continued as the *rump*, or sitting part, of the parliament until dissolved by Cromwell in 1653.

As to London, once parliament had convened and pressure from Church and State was removed, the city ceased to fear any interference. Sermons in the many churches took on an argumentative Puritan parliamentary tone. In some churches the congregation even sang psalms to drown out the Prayer Book service; in many they carried back the communion table into the nave. Pamphlets on religion and government appeared in the bookstalls, including Hakewill's masterly speech on impositions made in the session of 1610.

The city, like Paris in 1789, became "the workshop of the Revolution," an analogy effectively played up by Trevelyan. Pym was able not only to create party unity within the House but to organize effective popular demonstrations. There was plenty of material at hand. Unlike the lean and hungry mobs of revolutionary Paris, however, Pym's mobs were well dressed, well fed, and even orderly — prosperous shopkeepers and apprentices! On December 11, 1640, for instance, " 'a world of honest citizens in their best apparel' came to the doors of the House of Commons with a petition, signed with 15,000 names, for the abolition of episcopacy 'with all its roots and branches'."

Parliament had not only the backing of popular support but, oddly enough, strength through the presence of the Scottish army encamped on English soil in the northern counties and of the Scottish commissioners in London. There was a natural community of interests between English Puritans and Scots Presbyterians. From a practical point of view no abrupt dissolution was likely, for parliament's help was essential to the king in raising funds to pay off the Scots as the Treaty of Ripon, concluded with the Scots in October 1640, prescribed.

On the other hand, fears were repeatedly aroused by reports and rumors of affairs at court. In the country at large there was no plot favored by English Catholics as a body, but there were a few intriguers who gained the ear of the Queen Henrietta Maria. Through her hands went pleas to the pope or to her home-land of France for some form of intervention. Another source of foreign aid to the royalist cause, it was hoped, might come from Holland. A treaty was actually effected (January 19, 1641) for the marriage of the Stadholder's son William and Charles's daughter Mary. Early in May the prince, a lad of fifteen, plighted his troth at Whitehall to the little princess of nine![6]

[6] These were to be the parents of the famous William III, who in 1689 was to become King of England on the basis of parliamentary sovereignty and the Bill of Rights.

To turn to the parliament itself, the Speaker of the Commons was William Lenthall, an able barrister. Gardiner credits him with being the first to realize the impartial role of Speaker even in times of political controversy: "He was content to moderate and control, and to suggest the means of reconciling differences, without attempting to influence the House in its decision."

There were, as usual, a number of other lawyer members, such as St. John and the more conservative Edward Hyde. When it came to rising to a point of order or supplying a precedent, it was not a practicing barrister but the member from a Suffolk borough, the antiquarian Sir Simonds D'Ewes, who was equal to the occasion. Sir Simonds had studied at the Middle Temple and been called to the bar in 1623, but it was his lifelong studies in England's "antiquities" that stood him in good stead. Fortunately Sir Simonds also kept an elaborate day-by-day diary or *Journal* [7] of events in the House. Like a refrain recurs the entry, "Then I stood up, and I spake and I said . . ." For instance, he tells us how he opposed a motion "that we should make an order to receive noe petitions," but "I spake against it and dashed it, shewing that, though we dispatched little and men complained of it, yet to make an order here to refuse petitions would be a just grievance. It was expresselie against Magna Charta, *Nulli negabimus iusticiam* [To no one will we deny justice]."

The Commons were also fortunate in having a scholar as Clerk, Henry Elsynge (1598–1654), whose services were highly valued. "He it was of whom it was said that for 'his abilities and prudence, more reverence was paid to his stool than to the Speaker's chair.'" [8] He was not a lawyer, but had a B.A. from Oxford and some years in foreign travel, and was a friend of such legal scholars as Whitelocke and John Selden. He was son of the Henry Elsynge who served as Clerk of the Parliament in the 1620's, and who was author of the little treatise *The Manner of Holding Parliaments in England*, completed about 1626.[9] This is interesting not only for its description of the practices of his own day,

---

[7] Wallace Notestein, ed., *The Journal of Sir Simonds D'Ewes from the beginning of the Long Parliament to the opening of the Trial of the Earl of Strafford* (New Haven, 1933).

[8] Mackenzie, p. 57.

[9] The elder Henry Elsynge was sworn in as Clerk in March 1621 and served throughout this decade. The *D.N.B.* attributes authorship to the son, but calls it "apparently derived from a manuscript in eight chapters of similar scope, written by his father, 1626." It was first published in 1660.

but for its build-up of an historical background, supported by the citing of many good precedents from the *Parliament Rolls*. Yet, like others of his contemporaries, the author is inclined to assign too ancient a lineage to parliamentary practices and privileges. For instance, he says, "That the commons have ever had their speaker, I think none will doubt." As to "his speech antiently and at this day," Elsynge concludes, "And yet they did ever enjoy these privileges in as ample manner as now, though not formerly prayed by the speaker."

For informal conferences outside the House there was no longer, as in 1628, the hospitable table and library of Sir Robert Cotton. But at Sir Richard Manly's house in a little court behind Westminster Hall (where Pym lodged) a few of the popular leaders kept common table at their joint expense, and here they transacted much business.

Within the House of Commons, sittings began at eight or nine in the morning, and sometimes lasted until after dusk, lighted only by candles placed on the clerk's table. "At noon," says Trevelyan, "the hungry members — especially as Falkland laughingly complained, the luke-warm defenders of Episcopacy — 'ran forth to their dinners' to the neighbouring taverns, leaving the Speaker to starve in the Chair, and a handful of patriots, who had swallowed some bread and cheese in the hall, to push through in an hour business that would have taken days if properly discussed."

The Impeachment of the Earl of Strafford

In order to reinstate and establish parliament as an integral and last-ing factor in the government, three lines of action were deemed neces-sary: (1) while remaining loyal to the king himself, to remove his "evil" counselors; (2) to eliminate by legislation the most dangerous of the prerogative courts and unparliamentary taxation; (3) to insure regular meetings of parliament with sessions of reasonable length. To many minds action was needed on a fourth line, even more vital, that of reli-gion. The first three were accomplished. The fourth involved problems that seemed insoluble at the time.

As to the first, among the privy councillors two had removed them-selves, as Secretary Windebank fled to France and Judge Finch to Hol-land. Archbishop Laud was confined to the Tower, to be executed four years later. The chief target, of course, was Strafford. The Commons, on a rumor that he was persuading Charles to arrest parliamentary leaders on a charge of plotting with Scottish rebels, hastily drew up an impeachment and carried it up to the Lords on November 11. The earl, just arrived from the north and learning what was under way, hurried to the Lords to take his rightful place among his fellows. What would their reaction be? But the nobles, too, had grievances against the House of Stuart and its agents. The earl was stopped before he reached his seat by the cry of his angry peers, "Withdraw, withdraw." He obeyed, and was committed to the Tower.

Formal impeachment proceedings were not begun until March 22. The earl was accused of treason, of which he was not technically guilty. Impeachment was properly formal *judicial* procedure with real proof, which was not forthcoming. To anticipate, the Lords sitting as judges proved exasperatingly fair. As we shall see, when the Commons saw that they could not prove their charges to the Lords' satisfaction, they switched to the *legislative* process of bill of attainder. Here at least a majority of the Lords were brought into line by the army plot,[10] and the king (for a bill must have the royal assent), by one of Pym's mobs.

The trial, however, deserves more than brief mention, partly because of its dramatic quality and precise procedure, of which we have an unusually detailed description, and partly for the new constitutional theories advanced by the parliamentary prosecution.

Proceedings of the first day were merely formal. Pym opened the case for the Commons on March 23. After several days spent in presenting the charges an interval was allowed for Strafford to prepare his answer. The prosecuting committee consisted of eleven members of the Commons, including Pym and Hampden, and such able lawyers as St. John and Glyn, the Recorder of London. The charges were of two kinds: (1) acts of tyranny as President of the Council of the North and more particularly as Lord Deputy of Ireland — "great matters out of Ireland" — but this was efficiency and obedience to the Crown rather than treason; (2) advice to the king tending to the overthrow of the laws and liberties of England. This last was summed up by a contemporary, Clarendon: "Some words spoken in secret council on this kingdom after the dissolution of the last [Short] Parliament, were urged and pressed against him to make good the general charge of an endeavour to overthrow the fundamental government of the kingdom and to introduce an arbitrary power."

Under Pym's ingenious handling, the concept of treason was changed.

---

[10] Some of the officers in the army up at York agreed to march on London, release Strafford, and dissolve parliament.

He tried to show that the earl had endangered the royal dignity and even the king's life, "because those lands where the ruler was 'free and absolved from all rules of government,' as Strafford had said that he wished Charles to be, were lands 'frequent in combustions, full of massacres, and the tragical end of Princes.' " But further, to destroy the customs of the land and the liberties of the subject was treason against the whole Commonwealth.

Westminster Hall was prepared for the occasion by the erection of bleachers to accommodate the spectators, including the Commons, great ladies (peeresses), foreign ambassadors, and the Scottish commissioners. Some were said to have paid large sums for admission. A throne, erected with its back against the west wall, remained vacant, for it was contrary to custom for the peers to transact any business while the king was officially present. None the less, Charles, Queen Henrietta Maria, Prince Rupert, and Princess Mary were accommodated by the device of seats arranged like a box in a theater, with a lattice in front. In the intensity of his interest in the proceedings, Charles soon tore away the lattice. As Baillie puts it: "the tirlies, that made them to be secret, the King brake doun with his own hands; so they satt in the eye of all, bot little more regarded than if they had been absent."

We are fortunate in having a description of the trial from the *Letters and Journals* of Baillie, who was one of the Scots commissioners. As an outsider to whom the scenes in London and Westminster Hall were novel, he reported to his friends in Glasgow details that an Englishman would probably have taken for granted — even, for instance, the number of bars of ermine as the distinguishing mark of the ranks of the peerage! To quote in part Baillie's fascinating account:

Westminster Hall is a roome as long as broad if not more than the outer house of the High Church of Glasgow, supponing the pillars wer removed. In the midst of it was erected a stage like to that prepared for the Assemblie of Glasgow, but much more large, taking up the breadth of the whole House from wall to wall, and of the length more than a thrid part. At the north end was set a throne for the King, and a chayre for the Prince; before it lay a large wooll-seck, covered with green, for my Lord Steward, the Earle of Arundaill; beneath it lay two other secks for my Lord Keeper and the Judges, with the rest of the Chancerie, all in their red robes. Beneath this a little table for four or fyve Clerks of the Parliament in their black gouns; round about these some formes covered with green freese, whereupon the Earles and Lords did sitt in their red robes, of that same fashion, lyned with the same whyte ermin skinnes, as yow see the robes of our Lords when they ryde in Parliament . . .

Behinde the formes where the Lords sitt, there is a barr covered with green: at the one end standeth the Committee of eight or ten gentlemen appoynted by the House of Commons to pursue; at the midst there is a little dask, where the prisoner Strafford stands and sitts as he pleaseth, together with his keeper, Sir William Balfour, the Lieutenant of the Tower. At the back of this is a dask, for Strafford's four secretars, who carries his papers and assists him in writing and reading; at their side is a voyd for witnesses to stand; and behinde them a long dask at the wall of the room for Strafford's counsell-at-law, some five or six able lawyers, who were [not] permitted to disputt in matter of fact, bot questions of right, if any should be incident.

This is the order of the House below on the floore; the same that is used dailie in the Higher House. Upon the two sides of the House, east and west, there arose a stage of elevin ranks of formes, the highest touching almost the roof; everie one of these formes went from the one end of the roome to the other, and contained about fortie men; the two highest were divided from the rest by a raill, and a raill cutted off at everie end some seatts. The gentlemen of the Lower House did sitt within the raile, others without. . . .

The House was full dailie before seven; against eight the Earle of Strafford came in his barge from the Tower, accompanied with the Lieutenant and a guard of musqueteers and halberders. The Lords, in their robes, were sett about eight; the King was usuallie halfe an howre before them: he came not into his throne, for that would have marred the action; for it is the order of England, that when the King appears, he speaks what he will, bot no other speaks in his presence. . . .

A number of ladies wes in boxes, above the railes, for which they payed much money. It was dailie the most glorious Assemblie the Isle could afford; yet the gravitie not such as I expected; oft great clamour without about the doores; in the intervalles, while Strafford was making readie for answers, the Lords gott alwayes to their feet, walked and clattered; the Lower House men too loud clattering; after ten houres, much publict eating, not onlie of confections, bot of flesh and bread, bottles of beer and wine going thick from mouth to mouth without cups, and all this in the King's eye . . .

The earl, at the bar, with his commanding presence, dignity, and obvious sincerity, won sympathy, even admiration, amongst the peers and many of the spectators. His defense was impressive. In Baillie's words again:

My Lord of Strafford was, in his answer, verie large, accurat, and eloquent; consisting of a preamble, wherein he shew, of eight or nine articles, the good service he had done to the Crowne and countrey dureing the tyme of his employment, and of particular ansuers to the twentie-eight articles of the charge. The reading of it took up large three houres. His friends was so wary that they made three clerks read by turnes, that all might hear.

It was on April 10 that the rift between Lords and Commons became apparent. Next day the bill of attainder [11] was first read in the Commons and passed by a vote of 204 to 59. Although it was a breach of privilege to publish division lists, the names of the 59 were posted and they were derided as "Straffordians." On May 5 Pym revealed his knowledge of the army plot, and on May 8 the bill received its final passage by the Lords. This, like any piece of legislation, of course, required the royal approval. Again Pym's manipulation of forces served the turn. The mob which milled about the Palace of Whitehall through that Saturday night, designed to force the king into signing the attainder, was so effective in its numbers and its roar that courtiers in the Palace "confessed themselves to the Queen's priests, and marked on stair-cases and at passage-turnings where men could make a stand." Further, when the Sunday dawn saw the siege continue, "all day long fresh congregations came up hot from Sabbath gospellings in the City churches." Under pressure from courtiers and deputations from both Houses, and fearful for the life of his queen, Charles at last gave way at nine o'clock of that Sunday evening.

Three days later on Tower Hill two hundred thousand persons are said to have witnessed the death of "Black Tom the Tyrant," traitor not to his King but to the Commonwealth!

Measures to Restore the Rule of Law and Parliamentary Government

Although the great judge and parliament man Sir Edward Coke had died in 1634 at the ripe old age of eighty-two, his spirit was present in the halls of parliament. It was only natural that popular leaders should have set as one of their early aims the recovery and publication of his treatises, the three unpublished volumes of the Institutes. His commentary on Magna Carta was a perfect justification in principle of their

[11] Impeachment is a judicial procedure. The Commons are prosecutors, supporting their charges by evidence. The Lords are sole judges. Attainder is a legislative act. It may be introduced in either House, and after passing both, requires the royal assent. No evidence is necessarily presented. The act recites in its preamble the charges (sometimes asserting that they are notorious, "of common fame," etc.), declares the guilt of the offender, and pronounces judgment.

current policies and legislation. According to the diary of Sir Simonds D'Ewes, as early as December 5, 1640, "a motion was made to recover Sir Edward Coke's written bookes or other bookes being 19 in number which were taken from him during his last sickness etc. and a Committee appointed to search for them, of which I was one." For February 13 D'Ewes records: "Sir Thomas Roe shewed that all the bookes which had been taken out of Sir Edward Cokes librarie weere now restored to his executors who would deliver them to Sir Robert Coke sonne and heir of the saied Sir Edward. Then it was moved that those three bookes of his, His Jurisdiction of Courts, The Pleas of the Crowne, and his Comment on Magna Charta might be printed." On May 12, 1641, Coke's heir was authorized to publish the commentary on Magna Carta according to the intentions of the author. It actually appeared in print in 1642.

The legislative work of this first year was largely permanent. It was to become the basis for the Restoration settlement in 1660. Could the ghosts of Coke and Eliot have returned to Westminster, with what interest and satisfaction they would have examined an up-to-date (1641–1642) volume of the statutes!

Some acts were negative. They abolished those prerogative courts which had served as props to absolutism — the Star Chamber and its branches, and High Commission. The Privy Council was to be henceforth an advisory and executive body. It was deprived of all judicial work except appellate jurisdiction over places outside England. This last is reflected today, nominally at least, in the Judicial Committee of the Privy Council. The Star Chamber Act had a preamble which, like the Petition of Right, quoted Magna Carta and other precedents. As early as November 13, the victims of the Star Chamber, including Prynne, Bastwick, and Burton, were ordered released to give them an opportunity to bring their complaints before the Commons. On March 2 the House voted that reparations be made to Bastwick, and a similar resolution was subsequently adopted for the others. Other acts prohibited the levy of unparliamentary taxes — ship money, tonnage and poundage, and the various arbitrary fines recently employed. It was not felt necessary to repeat the principles already embodied in the Petition of Right.

Recalling the hasty dissolutions of 1626 and 1629, parliament had passed an act to the effect that it could not be dissolved without its own consent. More significant for the future was the Triennial Act. This provided that parliament should meet at least once in three years, and prescribed what action was to be taken should the royal order for the issue of election writs not be forthcoming. No future parliament was to be dissolved, prorogued, or adjourned within fifty days except by its own consent.[12]

On the religious issue no agreement seemed possible in an age when the concept of toleration was still a thing of the future. The Anglicans wanted to preserve the State Church virtually unchanged in its organization and doctrine. Moderate reformers would retain the bishops with limited powers, and perhaps abolish a few "offensive" formulas or ceremonies. The radicals wanted to abolish episcopacy "root and branch," substituting a state church under *parliamentary* control; to abolish the Prayer Book and make the doctrine of the Church completely Calvinistic. There was as yet in the parliament no actual Presbyterian or Independent party. These divisions gave the king the opportunity to rally a strong Cavalier Anglican party and to divide the opposition.

When, in October 1641, news came of the revolt in Ireland, including an attempt to surprise Dublin Castle and to massacre some of the English colonists in Ulster, an army was needed to deal with the situation there. But who would command it — King or Parliament? Neither trusted the other.

The division was accentuated in the vote on the Grand Remonstrance, a detailed attack on the royal policy. This was carried November 22 by eleven votes, and ordered to be printed and published. On whichever side a member voted on this occasion, on the same side was he to fight in the civil war.

Charles retaliated by actually entering the House of Commons on January 4, 1642, with a file of soldiers to arrest five leaders who, he felt, were primarily responsible. They had been warned in time and escaped down the river to the protective refuge of London. But how times had changed within the walls of St. Stephens Chapel! When Charles entered the House he passed to the Speaker's chair between rows of silent, standing members. Receiving no help from the Speaker, he satisfied himself that his "birds were flown" and went back as he had come, with the cry of "Privilege, privilege" raised as he went. What the Speaker had said to him was: "May it please your Majesty, I have neither eyes to see nor

---

[12] If the king fails to issue the summons, the chancellor is to act; if the chancellor fails, the peers or any twelve or more them. If no summons comes from Westminster sheriffs, bailiffs and mayors are to call elections; as a last resort the electors themselves to proceed to election! For selections from the text of these acts see Stephenson and Marcham, pp. 476–486.

tongue to speak in this place, but as this House is pleased to direct me, whose servant I am."

Then came the strange interlude, the time of troubles: intermittent civil wars and futile negotiations; the execution of the king; a republic, the Commonwealth; and a military dictatorship, the Protectorate. "The absence of the King created a vacuum . . . and strange things rushed in!" But these were ahead of the times. All in all the cause of *absolute* monarchy had definitely lost, but the cause of *limited* monarchy gained.

In 1660 it was declared that "the government of England is and by rights ought to be by King, Lords and Commons." There was a return to the rule of law, including the statutes validly enacted before the outbreak of the civil war. The Crown was still the real executive, controlling administration and policy. The role of parliament was unquestioned in legislation and finance. The problem of how to make this division of power work remained to be solved. The size of the "political nation" was still limited, but nothing could quite efface the years in which parliament alone — opposed to or without a king — had conducted the business of government. It was a parliament with a rich and varied heritage of practices, privileges, and precedents. One might apply to it the statement which has been applied to Switzerland and its long lived self-government: "Perhaps the secret is age. It is like the English gardener's recipe for good turf — prepare the soil well, use good seed, then roll it for 600 years."

SELECTED BIBLIOGRAPHY AND INDEX

Selected Bibliography

✿✿

SECONDARY ACCOUNTS

(The items that are starred are recommended on special periods and topics.)

Adams, G. B. *Constitutional History of England*. New York, 1921.

* Bindoff, S. T. *Tudor England*. Pelican Books, 1950.

* Chrimes, S. B. *English Constitutional Ideas of the Fifteenth Century*. Cambridge University Press, 1936.

* Coulton, G. G. *Chaucer and His England*. New York, 1908.

Dasent, A. I. *Speakers of the House of Commons from the Earliest Times to the Present Day*. London, 1911.

Forster, John. *Sir John Eliot, a Biography, 1592–1632*. 2 vols. London, 1872.

Gardiner, S. R. *History of England from the Accession of James I to the Outbreak of the Civil War, 1603–1642*. 10 vols. London, 1883–1884.

Gray, H. L. *The Influence of the Commons on Early Legislation*. Harvard University Press, 1932.

Holdsworth, Sir William S. *A History of English Law*. 9 vols. London, 1922–1926. (Vols. I, II, IV, V.)

* Ilbert, Sir Courtenay. *Parliament, Its History, Constitution, and Practice* (Home University Library of Modern Knowledge). Revised by Sir Cecil Carr. London, 1948.

Joliffe, J. E. A. *The Constitutional History of Medieval England from the English Settlement to 1485*. London, 1937.

Lunt, W. E. *History of England*. 3rd ed. New York, 1945.

* McIlwain, C. H. *The High Court of Parliament and Its Supremacy*. Yale University Press, 1910.

Mackenzie, Kenneth. *The English Parliament*. Pelican Books, 1950.

* McKisack, May. *The Parliamentary Representation of the English Boroughs during the Middle Ages*. London, 1932.

Maitland, F. W. *The Constitutional History of England*. Cambridge University Press, 1908.

Myers, A. R. *England in the Late Middle Ages*. Pelican Books, 1952.

* Neale, J. E. *The Elizabethan House of Commons*. London, 1949.

———. *Elizabeth I and her Parliaments, 1559–1581*. London, 1953.

———. "The Commons' Privilege of Free Speech in Parliament," in *Tudor Studies Presented . . . to Albert Frederick Pollard*, pp. 257–286. London, 1924.

Notestein, Wallace. *The Winning of the Initiative by the House of Commons*. London, 1924.

Ogg, F. A. *English Government and Politics.* New York, 1930.

Pasquet, D. *An Essay on the Origins of the House of Commons,* translated by R. G. D. Laffan, with Preface and Additional Notes by Gaillard Lapsley. Cambridge University Press, 1925.

Pickthorn, K. W. M. *Early Tudor Government — Henry VII.* Cambridge University Press, 1934.

——. *Early Tudor Government — Henry VIII.* Cambridge University Press, 1934.

Pike, L. O. *A Constitutional History of the House of Lords.* London, 1894.

Plucknett, T. F. T. *A Concise History of the Common Law.* 2nd ed. Rochester, N.Y., 1936.

——. "The Lancastrian Constitution," in *Tudor Studies Presented . . . to Albert Frederick Pollard,* pp. 161–181. London, 1924.

——. "Parliament," in *The English Government at Work, 1327–1336,* ed. James F. Willard and William A. Morris, Vol. I, Chap. 2. Cambridge, 1940.

——. *Statutes and Their Interpretation in the First Half of the Fourteenth Century.* Cambridge Studies in English Legal History, 1922.

——. Revised and enlarged edition of T. P. Taswell-Langmead, *English Constitutional History from the Teutonic Conquest to the Present Time.* Boston, 1946.

* Pollard, A. F. *The Evolution of Parliament.* London, 1926.

* Richardson, H. G., and G. O. Sayles. "The Early Statutes," *Law Quarterly Review,* L (1934), 201–223, 547–571.

——. "The King's Ministers in Parliament, 1272–1377," *English Historical Review,* XLVI (1931), 529–550; XLVII (1932), 194–203.

Scott, Florence R. "Chaucer and the Parliament of 1386," *Speculum,* XVIII (1943), 80–86.

Seymour, Charles, and D. P. Frary. *How the World Votes: The Story of Democratic Development in Elections.* 2 vols. Springfield, Mass., 1918.

* Steel, Anthony B. *Richard II.* Cambridge, 1941.

Templeton, Geoffrey. "The History of Parliament to 1400 in the Light of Modern Research," in R. L. Schuyler and Herman Ausubel, *The Making of English History.* New York, 1952.

Tout, T. F. *Chapters in the Administrative History of Medieval England.* 6 vols. Manchester, 1920–1933. (Vols. III and IV.)

——. "The English Parliament and Public Opinion," in *The Collected Papers of Thomas Frederick Tout,* Vol. II, pp. 173–190. Manchester, 1934.

*——. *The Place of the Reign of Edward II in English History.* Manchester, 1914.

* Trevelyan, G. M. *England in the Age of Wycliffe.* (1st ed., 1899.) London, 1920.

*——. *England under the Stuarts* (Oman Series). London, 1916.

——. *English Social History, A Survey of Six Centuries, Chaucer to Queen Victoria.* London, 1943.

Vernon-Harcourt, L. W. *His Grace the Steward and Trial of Peers.* London, 1907.

Wedgewood, J. C. *History of Parliament, 1439–1509.* 2 vols. London, 1936–1938. (Vol. I, *Biographies of Members of the Commons House, 1439–1509.*)

White, A. B. *The Making of the English Constitution.* New York, 1925.

* Wilkinson, B. *The Constitutional History of England, 1216–1399. With Select Documents* (in translation). Vols. I and II. London, 1948, 1952. (Vol. II, *Politics and the Constitution, 1307–1399.*)

* Willson, D. H. *The Privy Councillors in the House of Commons, 1604–1629.* University of Minnesota Press, 1940.

SOURCES

The Anonimalle Chronicle of St. Mary's Abbey, York, 1333 to 1381, ed. C. H. Galbraith. Manchester, 1927.

Commons Debates, 1621, ed. W. Notestein, F. H. Relf, and H. Simpson. 7 vols. Yale University Press, 1935.

Commons Debates for 1629, ed. W. Notestein and F. H. Relf. University of Minnesota, 1921.

D'Ewes, Sir Simonds. *The Journals of All the Parliaments during the Reign of Queen Elizabeth*. London, 1682.

Elsynge, Henry. *The Manner of Holding Parliaments in England*. (First printed, 1660.) London, 1768.

Fortescue, Sir John. *De Laudibus Legum Angliae*, edited and translated with Introduction and Notes by S. B. Chrimes. Cambridge Studies in English Legal History, 1949.

――――. *The Governance of England*, ed. Charles Plummer. Oxford, 1885.

Historia . . . Mirabilis Parliamenti . . . per Thomam Favent (Description of the Marvellous Parliament of 1388 by Thomas Favent), ed. May McKisack. Camden Miscellany, Vol. XIV. London, 1926.

Journals of the House of Commons, Vol. I, 1547–1629. London, n.d.

Journals of the House of Lords, Vols. I–IV. London, n.d.

Lodge, Eleanor C., and Gladys A. Thornton, eds. *English Constitutional Documents, 1307–1485*. Cambridge University Press, 1935.

Maitland, F. W., ed. *Records of the Parliament at Westminster in 1305*, or *Memoranda de Parliamento*. (Rolls Series.) London, 1893. (Introduction, pp. ix–cxxi.)

Modus Tenendi Parliamentum (with a translation), ed. T. D. Hardy. London, 1846.

Parliament Rolls, or *Rotuli Parliamentorum, 1278–1503*. 6 vols. London, 1832.

Rotuli Parliamentorum Anglie hactenus inediti, 1279–1378, ed. H. G. Richardson and G. O. Sayles. (Camden, Third Series, Vol. LI.) London, 1935.

Statutes of the Realm, Vols. I–V. Record Commission, 1810–1828.

Stephenson, Carl S., and F. G. Marcham, eds. *Sources of English Constitutional History*. New York, 1937.

Tanner, H. R. *Constitutional Documents of the Reign of James I, A.D. 1603–1625, With an Historical Commentary*. Cambridge University Press, 1940.

――――. *Tudor Constitutional Documents, A.D. 1485–1603, With an Historical Commentary*. Cambridge University Press, 1940.

Wilkinson, B. See first list.

Index